Portugal's Other Kingdom

T H E A L G A R V E

UNIVERSITY OF TEXAS PRESS 🌟 AUSTIN

Portugal's Other Kingdom

THE ALGARVE

by Dan Stanislawski

Library of Congress Catalog Number 63-007363

ISBN 978-0-292-74182-9, paperback

To Michael and Anna
who were there also

My gratitude can be expressed here to only a small proportion of the Portuguese who treated me generously. To the hundreds of friendly fishermen who will never see this book I want to express thanks again, just for the record. Especial thanks go to the members of the staff of the Posto Agrario do Sotavento, in Tavira, and particularly to Eng. João Maria Cabral, its director (also director of a national agricultural research program with offices in Lisbon), Eng. Bento dos Santos Nascimento, and Eng. José Assunção. In visits made during several years to this excellent research center I have always been treated with great generosity. In Faro, Eng. Alberto Correia Vargues, of the Junta das Frutas has always been most helpful.

In Lisbon many people were of aid; especially I should like to mention Comandante Melo de Carvalho, of the Direcção das Pescarias, Dr. Herculano Vilela, Director of the Maritime Biological Institute, and Eng. João Cabral Marques de Beja Neves of the Instituto Nacional de Estatística.

Not enough thanks can be given to my wife, who worked with me in the field and in the writing of this book.

CONTENTS

ILLUSTRATIONS

MAPS AND GRAPHS

Portugal's Other Kingdom

THE ALGARVE

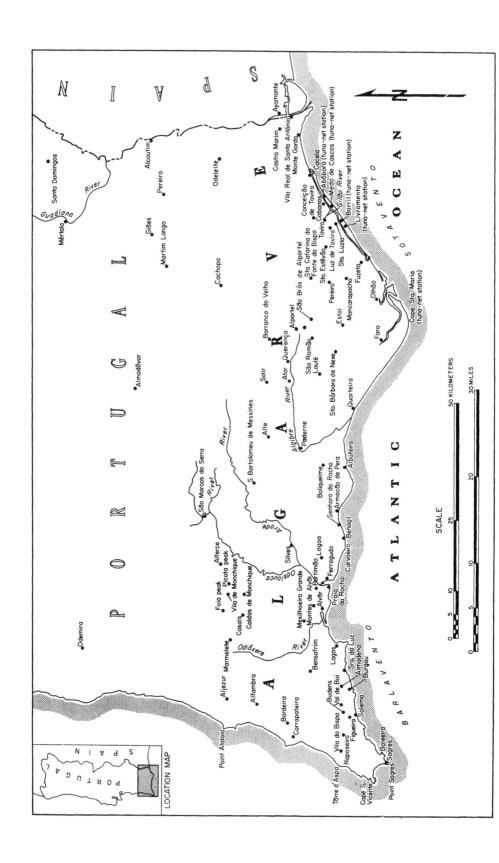

LOCATION MAP

SPAIN

PORTUGAL

SPAIN

PORTUGAL

Mértola
Santo Domingos
Guadiana River
Alcoutim
Pereiro
Odeleite
Giões
Martim Longo
Cachopo
Castro Marim
Ayamonte
Vila Real de Santo António
Monte Gordo
Cacela
Abóbora (tuna-net station)
Meio de Cascas (tuna-net station)
Conceição de Tavira
Cabanas
Gilão River
Barril (tuna-net station)
Almodôvar
Livramento (tuna-net station)
Barranco do Velho
Sta. Catarina da Fonte do Bispo
Sto. Estêvão
Tavira
Luz de Tavira
Sta. Luzia
São Brás de Alportel
Alportel
Querença
Pereiro
Estoi
Moncarapacho
Fuzeta
Olhão
Ator
São Romão
Loulé
Faro
Cape Sta. Maria (tuna-net station)
Salir
Sta. Bárbara de Nexe
Alte
Algibre River
Paderne
Quarteira
São Bartolomeu de Messines
Albufeira
Boliqueime
Senhora da Rocha
Armação de Pera
São Marcos da Serra
River
River
Arade
Silves
Odelouca
Alferce
Picota peak
Foia peak
Vila de Monchique
Caldas de Monchique
Casais
Mexilhoeira Grande
Montes de Alvôr
Alvôr
Praia da Rocha
Portimão
Lagoa
Ferragudo
Carvoeiro
Benagil
Odemira
Aljezur
Alfambra
Marmelete
Odiáxere River
Bensafrim
Lagos
Sra. da Luz
Val de Boi
Almádena
Burgau
Salema
Bordeira
Carrapateira
Point Atalaia
Torre d'Aspa
Vila do Bispo
Raposeira
Figueira
Budens
Baleeira
Point Sagres
Cape S. Vicente

PORTUGAL

ALGARVE

ALGARVE

BARLAVENTO

SOTAVENTO

ATLANTIC

ATLANTIC OCEAN

SCALE

50 KILOMETERS
0   5   10   25

30 MILES
0   5   10   20

Introduction[1]

▀▬▀

GEOGRAPHERS ONCE STUDIED islands or oases, trying to find in semi-isolated and relatively self-sufficient areas the simple, direct responses of a culture group to the land upon which it lived. In that early period of time the belief was common that in areas where modes of life had achieved stability there might be values pertinent to our problems. In this century, however, in the United States, we have reached a state of mind in which we show little interest in uses of the land other than our own, except to bring aberrants into conformity with us. This attitude stems from the tacit assumption that other places and peoples can be brought to a higher state of well-being only by duplicating our methods.

Even if we accept such a premise we must realize that hundreds of millions of people with other cultural backgrounds and in other en-

[1] This introductory statement and the material from Chapter 6 (Monchique) were originally published in *The Geographical Review*. I express here my gratitude for permission to reprint. D. S.

vironments want to live and change in their own way. We are increasingly in contact with these other peoples and we must gain, if not understanding, at least an appreciation of their attitudes and wishes. Our experiences and techniques have been based on surplus production and the habit of waste without penalty. This is not the case with most people with whom we are now associated internationally. We must know something of the necessities in their frugal economies or we will fail to communicate with them. For example, we cannot understand European olive growing by the statistics available to us or by a quick glance as we travel; one must know the economic context to understand why a Mediterranean farmer insists upon planting a grain and perhaps other things beneath his trees. He is not being shortsightedly obstinate, as many people assume him to be, because he will not eliminate one of the crops in order to increase the other; and in spite of international statistics, his method may be the best; he must have a second or even a third crop on his land as a crutch upon which to lean in case of failure of the first. Whereas we may think of specialization, trade, and surplus saved as the answer to that problem, he has no surplus and has had long experience with shabby governments, poor and frequently obstructed transport, taxation that can be confiscatory, and a long list of other conditions that lead him to the very sensible conclusion that if he doesn't create his own security he will have none.

If we do not completely accept the premise of our perfection, then a further proposition might be suggested which should not be rejected lightly in a world of quick disillusionment: can it be possible that our present self-adulation will sometime prove to be empty vanity? If so, knowledge of other ways and other values might serve us. In such case it would not be a frivolous antiquarianism, a mere cataloguing of oddments, to study and to write about small culture areas in which men exploit their land in ways different from our own. We will fail to do full justice to our field if we limit our efforts to forming generalizations and laws regarding patterns of action and attitudes toward the land on the basis of our own experiences and the values derivative from them. We have another, equally valid obligation: that of observing the land with whatever sensitivity and sharpness of observation we may possess, in

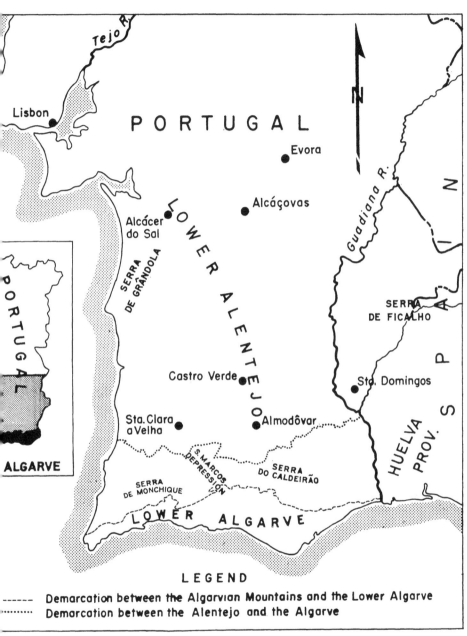

LEGEND

----- Demarcation between the Algarvian Mountains and the Lower Algarve
.... Demarcation between the Alentejo and the Algarve

Southern Portugal

order to record differences in local attitudes toward its use. We might well follow the advice of the ethnographer Franz Boaz (who was trained as a geographer) to gather material from local and disparate culture groups before it is lost. Implicit in such a course of action is the belief that although our culture is dominant and in the process of submerging others by its strength and appeal, it is not the residuary of all virtues, and that many isolated and small culture areas, now going out of existence, have discovered ways of living with their land that offer valuable suggestions to us.

In this book I try to describe what I believe to be the personality of a province of present Portugal; but one with disparate subareas, all of which have both led their own lives and contributed to the quality of the whole. It will be clear to the reader that there is no claim that anything new or old has been imposed upon anyone by the physical environment, but rather that the nature of the land has been a framework within which choices have been made. Within that framework the inhabitants of the subareas, conditioned by their cultural inheritance, have established an association with the land.

1. The Algarve: The Association of Men and Land[1]

▪▪

THE SOUTHERNMOST FRINGE of Portugal, a narrow area lying along the shore and separated from the rest of the country by mountains, faces Africa, unlike most of the rest of Portugal, which fronts the open Atlantic. In its physical nature and in some of its present ways of life, it is as African as it is European. Fittingly, it bears the Arabic name, Algarve (*al-gharb*, the west).

RELATIVE ISOLATION OF THE AREA

Historically, its contacts have been mostly with the Mediterranean, but actually, through long periods of time it has been left to itself. The

[1] Over half of this chapter is made up of material originally published as "The Livelihood of the Ordinary People of the Portuguese Algarve" in Stanley Diamond (ed.), *Culture in History,* essays in honor of Paul Radin. I am grateful to Columbia University Press for permission to reprint it. D. S.

7

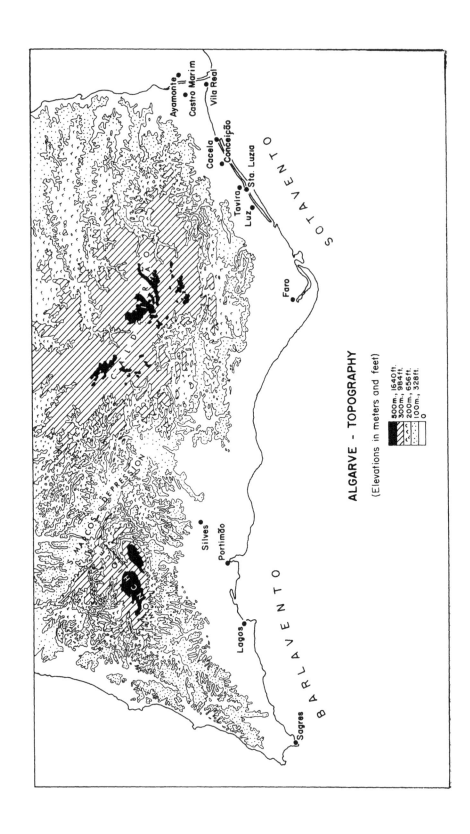

ALGARVE - TOPOGRAPHY

(Elevations in meters and feet)

500 m., 1640 ft.
300 m., 984 ft.
200 m., 656 ft.
100 m., 328 ft.
0

Cynetes, or Cónios, the earliest known inhabitants of the area, were in touch with the Tartessians of Andalusia. Later the Cynetes were probably under the influence of the Celts, but they remained self-sufficient and essentially independent. Punic peoples (Phoenicians and Carthaginians) established fishing and salting bases along these shores; the Greeks may have made landfalls.[2]

These contacts were not disruptive. Not until the advent of the Romans were conditions materially altered; then city life was introduced, and probably irrigation, along with a greater organization of agriculture. However, the area was at the extreme limit of Roman control and Roman interest could not have been great, for the Algarve was no prize to attract ambitious men, as was the area of Baetica (the lower Guadalquivir Valley). The Visigoths, successors to the Romans, were really more cattlemen than farmers and their social interests were more feudal than urban. Adding little or nothing to the area that is now southern Portugal, they fortunately had too little concern with it to create disturbance. Following them, or rather in the middle of the period of Visigothic rule in Iberia, there is a little-known period of almost four generations, after the year 550, during which time Byzantine emperors maintained some sort of control over the region. The record of this rule is almost a blank; one can only surmise that mastery of such a remote and relatively unimportant area was only incidental to larger designs. One may suppose that the Algarve then, as through most of its historical experiences, remained quiet and self-contained.

Moslem conquest, in the early eighth century, ended the Visigothic period and brought about developments as important in their way as were those of the Romans: intensive horticulture, intensified cultivation of the olive, carob, and fig, and greater use of irrigation. New plants were introduced, including the lemon and the bitter orange. Rice, cotton, and a sweet orange may also have been brought to the region by the Moslems.[3] For five hundred years after the conquest, from the early eighth to the mid-thirteenth century, the Algarve lived

[2] António García y Bellido, "Colonización Púnica," *Historia de España,* Tomo I, Vol. II, 315; and "La Colonización Griega," *ibid.,* p. 504 (map).

[3] Orlando Ribeiro, *Portugal,* p. 77.

productively under Moslem rule. The Arabs who settled in Silves, which became the capital of the region, came originally from Yemen, a country with a long history of irrigation. The plants that they knew and their techniques, especially of irrigation, were eminently suited to the land. In the twelfth century Edrisi described Silves as a lovely city surrounded by orchards and gardens;[4] but it was not only Silves, but the Algarve in general that was improved under the Moslems. It is they who are to be credited with establishing the basis of the present physiognomy, even though New World plants have altered the horticultural balance and schedule.[5]

Although the Christian reconquest changed many political and economic relations in the area, the fundamentals of its agricultural way of life were not greatly disturbed. There were no great areas of available lands, like those of the Alentejo to the north, to be granted by Portuguese kings to their supporters in the military campaigns. The settled and efficiently exploited Algarve received different treatment from that accorded some other areas of Iberia. Many Moslems remained, some accepted Christianity, and others were kept by the conquerors to labor and pay tribute. The latter arrangement was common in the great areas given to the religious-military order of Santiago. The earlier way of life went on, only partly and gradually changed under new management.[6] Continuity is implied by the title of the Portuguese kings after the event. They became "Kings of Portugal and the Algarves," a title recognizing the unique character of the region.[7] In the fifteenth century the

[4] Abu-Abd-Alla-Mohamed-al-Edrisi, *Descripción de España*, pp. 187–188.

[5] Especially important were the additions of maize and potatoes. Maize was known in Seville in 1500 and spread from that region into the Algarve in the early sixteenth century; the spread of the potato was considerably later. See Orlando Ribeiro, "Cultura do Milho, economia agraria e povoamento," *Biblos*, XVII, Tomo II, 1941, pp. 645–663.

[6] See H. V. Livermore, *A History of Portugal*, pp. 98, 135; and Orlando Ribeiro, *Portugal*, p. 82 (map).

[7] In 1189, the Portuguese king, Sancho I, conquered Silves and added "King of the Algarve" (or "King of Silves and the Algarve") to his other titles (See Alexandre Herculano, *Historia de Portugal*, Tomo III, Livro III, 216). However, the city and region were retaken by the Moslems in 1191. Only after the final conquest of the region, in 1249, could the title, King of the Algarve, be used again. After the

road leading north from Tavira was still known as the "road to Portugal,"[8] and even today it connects regions in which the inhabitants of each are conscious of their distinction from the others.

Other Portuguese are quick to say that Algarvians have personalities peculiarly their own, distinct from those to be met anywhere else in Portugal. They are known to be good sailors, men of commerce who are not averse to contacts with strangers, who talk readily, and who make friends quickly. Their long economic history is reflected in present-day fishing industries and in an intensive agriculture partly based upon exports. The latter fact is of particular interest, as the Algarve is the only Portuguese province that exports more than it imports.[9]

ADJACENT REGIONS

Neighbors on both north and east have pursued distinct ways of life, and each presents to the observer a different face from that of the Algarve. The Alentejo, to the north, is a region of great wheat fields and flocks of Alentejano sheep that feed on the stubble after the harvest, of seemingly limitless stretches of holm or cork oaks with wheat planted beneath them, and of herds of agile pigs that feed upon acorns. While a large proportion of the population is concentrated in villages or towns, small clusters of buildings at the centers of great landholdings, to which the absentee owners occasionally come from their town houses in Lisbon, are characteristic of the landscape.

Comparable to the Alentejo in many ways is the Huelva province of Spain, across the Guadiana River eastward from the Algarve, where great tracts of land are devoted to relatively few crops, each of which exclusively occupies an area. Wheat and maize cover broad acreages, vineyards reach into great distances, and flocks of Merino sheep are

conquest of Arzila and Tangier in 1471, Affonso V called himself "King of Portugal and the Algarves [plural] on this side and across the sea in Africa" (see João Baptista da Silva Lopes, "Corografia" ou memória económica estadístaca e topográfica do Reino do Algarve, p. 6.

[8] A. de Amorim Girão, Geografia de Portugal, p. 417.

[9] The list of exports is made up chiefly of canned sardines, anchovies, mackerel, tuna, fish meal, dried fruits, carobs, and salt. Pyrites from the mines of Sto. Domingos and cork from the mountains also appear on the export lists of the Algarvian ports.

The *carro* with its upper framework (next to a cork oak).

common. The population lives in compact towns or villages of almost uniformly white houses. Goods are transported in cumbersome two-wheeled carts which carry one load in the body and another slung beneath, almost touching the ground. Windmills for grinding grain, still common in the Algarve, have gone out of use in most areas of Spain. The head covering of an Algarvian woman who wears a kerchief tied over her head, topped by a man's felt hat, is not typical of adjacent Spain and it is not seen in the Alentejo, save for a small area in the interior.

Algarvian personality

The image that is evoked by the word *Algarvian*, one of vitality and color, is based upon the quality of life that has developed in the lowland areas of the province. Seeing it for the first time, one is struck by the polychrome scene; on the roads are brightly painted carts drawn by sleek mules, their harnesses decorated with metal and colored de-

12

A typical Algarvian cart.

signs. Even the rope which reaches under the mule's forequarters to hold down the shafts is of brightly dyed henequen fiber, and as if all this were not quite enough color, long red and green tassels are hung on either side of the animal's head. Forming a backdrop for this traffic, white rock and plaster walls, carefully maintained and frequently calcimined, border the roads. Behind the walls, or facing directly upon the roads, are immaculately kept houses, painted in one or more of a great variety of colors, and topped by the pride of the Algarvians—fretted, lacelike chimneys.

First coming to it, one immediately realizes that he has entered a unique culture area; it has no duplicate. The dispersal of houses throughout the countryside is in contrast to the urban concentration typical of its neighbors. In the clear air of the bright, dry climate, these scattered Algarvian homes glisten in white or colors. Their owners, who for the most part live in them and work the land around them, are proud of appearances and are frequent painters; calcimining is usually done by the woman of the house, who uses a palmleaf brush on the end of a long chestnut pole. They favor a bright color, either for the body of the house or at least for a trim; the solidly white house of Spain is not the rule here. Pride in appearance is reflected also in the care given to the walls and the garden. However, it should not be assumed that the women of the Lower Algarve are overburdened. The time that they spend on their houses and gardens is available because of a prosperity lacking in most parts of Portugal and Spain. Their position is in sharp contrast with that of the women in adjacent areas.

There is no shoelessness.[10] Most women seen on the country roads are not walking, but are riding donkeys; most men are driving mule-drawn, two-wheeled carts. Women are ordinarily not burden carriers. Burdens are carried either by the numerous donkeys or by the mule-drawn carts. However, prosperity is a relative matter, and to most Americans the life of the Algarvian as described below may seem harsh.

The individual, scattered homes give the impression of an intimate, friendly life that one does not sense in the broad areas of monoculture in the Alentejo, in the Algarvian mountains, or in the Huelva province. Adding to this feeling of friendly intimacy is a second characteristic of the Lower Algarvian landscape, the large number of small plots of cultivated land and the variety of planting in them; virtually every plot has more than one crop growing at the same time. Not recognizable at first glance are the overlapping rotation system, the efficient use of water, and the staggering of work through the year, so that no month is without its productive effort.

The vital, glistening province once was called the Kingdom of the Algarve, and implicit in the title was the recognition that it was not like other parts of Portugal. In fact, until nearly the end of the eighteenth century its boundary within the present republic was treated as if it delimited a foreign country; taxes were levied upon imports and exports as if it had no rights of membership in the Portuguese state. Even now, while it is Portuguese in sentiment, it is so only in spite of differences in

---

[10] However, shoelessness may not be a cultural matter and should not be taken as an indication of poverty. The women of Barcelos and its vicinity in north Portugal walk barefooted, but their bodies are bedecked with heavy gold jewelry.

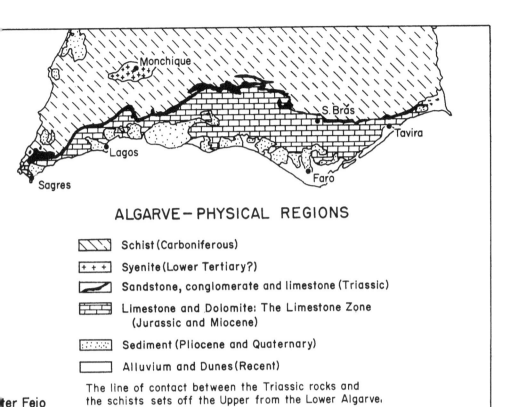

ALGARVE – PHYSICAL REGIONS

- ⟦\\\⟧ Schist (Carboniferous)
- ⟦+ + +⟧ Syenite (Lower Tertiary?)
- ⟦◢⟧ Sandstone, conglomerate and limestone (Triassic)
- ⟦▥⟧ Limestone and Dolomite: The Limestone Zone
  (Jurassic and Miocene)
- ⟦:::::⟧ Sediment (Pliocene and Quaternary)
- ⟦ ⟧ Alluvium and Dunes (Recent)

The line of contact between the Triassic rocks and
the schists sets off the Upper from the Lower Algarve.

ways of life and because of an historical accident, the discovery of the route around Africa and the part that the Algarve and Algarvians played in that accomplishment.[11]

ROCKS, VEGETATION, AND CLIMATE

Color in the landscape, however, is not all man-made. Living and working take place among the variegated rocks of several geological periods. From older to younger rocks, going from the northern border toward the south, one passes from the grey schists[12] through the narrow

[11] Dan Stanislawski, *The Individuality of Portugal*, pp. 172–174, 214.

[12] The grey schists of the Carboniferous were elevated and subsequently eroded into rounded mountain slopes. They constitute the mountain areas—the Caldeirão on the east and Monchique, with its syenite core, on the west. Although both are politically within the province of the Algarve, they are quite distinct from the rest of the province, and each will be described in a separate chapter.

15

belt of red sandstones and conglomerates, into the area of white, and in some cases orange, dolomites and limestones, and finally to the grey sediments near the south shore.

Through the year, these rock colors are seasonally embellished by the tints of both spontaneous and cultivated vegetation. The area of the grey schists, with a vegetation cover including cistus, heather, broom, and gorse,[13] is lovely in the spring, when purple, pink, yellow, and large white flowers appear, to blend with many shades of green. In the limestone area, the colors of the vegetation are those of the differing greens of the fig, carob (*Ceratonia siliqua*), almond, and olive, brightened in January and February by the pink and the white blossoms of the almonds and largely underlain by the green of planted grains. In the autumn, the drying grains make a tawny contrast to the green of the trees. The littoral of Tertiary and Quaternary materials, where most of the spontaneous vegetation has been eliminated, shows the colors of the large number of different crops, planted in small, irrigated plots.

Protected by mountains on the north, the Algarvian lowland does not suffer the winter weather of the Alentejo; facing the south, it shares the climate of the Mediterranean. Throughout the year the climate is characterized by little cloudiness, good visibility, a high degree of insolation, and little wind (exceptions must be made for the stations near Cape S. Vicente). Rainfall comes in the late fall and in the winter months when the zone of North Atlantic fronts has spread to the south; but as the Algarve is almost at the extreme reach of these storms, they appear on relatively few days of the year and ordinarily are of brief duration.

Along the coast rain falls normally on only seventy days in the year. Temperatures are mild and there is no frost in the typical year. Summer conditions, with almost a half year of drought and warmth, reflect the dominance of the Azorean high-pressure area with stable air and clear skies. However, even within this relatively small area climatic differences are of sufficient magnitude to differentiate life and economy.

[13] Several species each of the genera Cistus, Erica, Genista, and Ulex, respectively.

16

CLIMATIC STATIONS OF THE ALGARVE

Temperature (in Fahrenheit)
Precipitation (in Inches)

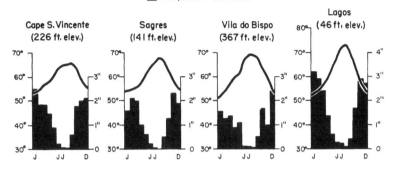

Cape S. Vincente
(226 ft. elev.)

Sagres
(141 ft. elev.)

Vila do Bispo
(367 ft. elev.)

Lagos
(46 ft. elev.)

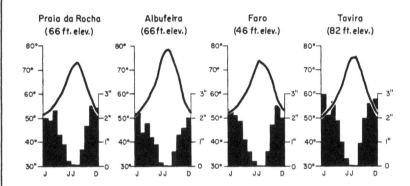

Praia da Rocha
(66 ft. elev.)

Albufeira
(66 ft. elev.)

Faro
(46 ft. elev.)

Tavira
(82 ft. elev.)

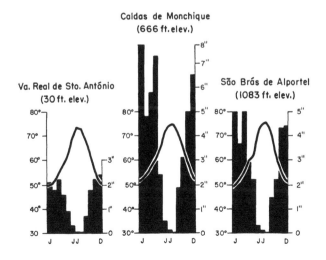

Caldas de Monchique
(666 ft. elev.)

Va. Real de Sto. António
(30 ft. elev.)

São Brás de Alportel
(1083 ft. elev.)

From equable "oceanic" conditions at the west, the range in temperature between the means of the coldest and warmest months is markedly greater at more easterly stations. For example, at Vila Real de Santo António, on the Guadiana River, it is over twice that of Cape S. Vicente (23.4° F. compared to 11.3° F.). Maximum winter temperatures under the influence of the Atlantic are substantially the same everywhere. All stations fall into the C, or "moderate" classification of Köppen;[14] however, the three Cape stations noted above are *Csb* (with mild summer temperatures), whereas the others are *Csa* (warm summers), that is, typically Mediterranean.

Rainfall differences are not great in number of inches, but they are important, because in some areas of the west the totals fall below the minimum necessary for many typical Algarvian crops.[15]

LAND SYSTEMS

The Algarve boasts no baronial estates; fifteen acres of good, irrigated land constitutes marked prosperity for an Algarvian farmer. Although absentee ownership does exist, title to land is held mostly by Algarvians whose absence from their properties would not usually be longer than a few days at a time. Typically, such owners live close by their farms. Association with the land, concern for it, and supervision of it are coincident, as well as continuous.

It is common to estimate the value of property in the Algarve in terms of either the product or the amount of labor necessary to work it. The value of a piece of property is often quoted in *alqueires* (multiples of 20 liters of grain)—that is, in terms of production. Or it may be described as of so many *geiras*, a term referring to the amount of land that can be worked in a day by a man with a yoke of oxen.[16] In the

[14] W. Köppen, "Das geographische System der Klimate, Teil C, *Allgemeine Klimalehre*, Band I, *Handbuch der Klimatologie* (W. Köppen and R. Geiger, eds.), pp. 25–27.

[15] Climatic statistics basic to the generalizations given above are from *O Clima de Portugal*, fascículo VII, *Baixo Alentejo e Algarve*.

For the period 1949–1958 the record as shown in the *Anuário Climatológico de Portugal* has been checked. Stations with a complete ten-year record are essentially in accord with the figures of *O Clima de Portugal*.

[16] This word is obviously the equivalent of "Iugum" to which Varro referred. He

Algarve this term now usually means the amount of land that can be worked in a day by a man with a mule; a term that suggests size, but more than that, implies ease or difficulty of cultivation. Both modes of estimating land values bespeak an intimate association between the men and the land that they work.

Farm labor in the Algarve falls into three categories. First is a group of landless laborers. Second is a considerable group of farm owners whose properties are insufficient to support their families and who work part time for others. The third, an also considerable group, is made up of those people whose properties supply at least a minimum for family maintenance. This group is not always clearly distinguishable from the second, for at the border line between them necessities blend into amenities.

Of the three categories, that of the self-sufficient small farm owner is the most easily described. He probably owns less than ten acres of land, and, with the aid of his family, can work it without other labor. Such a family can exist upon a farm of two and a half acres of good irrigated land or eight acres of unirrigated land.

For the farmer with insufficient land to feed his family, there are various opportunities to supplement his income. Some go into the Alentejo for the wheat harvest, when wages and the demand for labor are high. As the harvest there does not fall at the time of the peak demand for labor in the Algarve, the farm at home need not be neglected. The average "take-home pay" for such a season would normally be *a conto* (about thirty-five U.S. dollars), not an inconsiderable sum to an Algarvian. Or such a small farmer may hire himself out for limited periods of time to work on other farms in the Algarve itself, during the period of peak demand for labor. He may hire himself out in the commercial towns of the coast for one of several tasks paying daily wages.

There are several arrangements through which persons who own no land at all are employed to cultivate the land of well-to-do owners who

---

said that it was a term used in "further Spain" to describe the amount of land that could be plowed in one day by a yoke of oxen. See Lloyd Storr-Best, *M. T. Varro on Farming*, p. 36.

either have more land than they and their families can work or who have enough land so that they can live on the surplus income after the contract with labor has been fulfilled. Prosperous owners ordinarily secure labor for their farms by one of three basic arrangements: by renting the land, by hiring day labor, or by a system of sharing the crop.

Renting is not common in the Algarve, although it can be found in virtually all parts. In such an arrangement, the renter pays a predetermined figure per year for the use of the land, house, and sheds, and keeps the total usufruct. The surplus kept by the renter, although not great, is somewhat larger than that which would be received by the share farmer or the day laborer, but the renter may be badly pinched in years of poor harvests. As poor harvests in the Algarve are usually a result of poor rainfall, renting is most common in the eastern section of the Coastal Plain, where irrigation is more widespread.

In the two geographical extremes of the Algarve, the Cape region on the west and the small area near Vila Real de Santo António on the east, day labor is a typical arrangement.

Most men who work land belonging to others do so under a system of shares, which differ according to the product. In the cultivation of any of the small grains, sharing is usually half-and-half. The owner furnishes the dwelling, the animals, the seed, and elaborate tools, if they are needed. The worker furnishes simple tools, including, in most cases, the plow, the Mediterranean device with a steel point. The worker takes half of the crop, after the seed grain for the following year has been set aside. He shares equally with the owner any increment from the animals—the calves, lambs, and pigs. As cow's milk is of almost no interest (it is "not exploited," they say), it can be used by the farmer as he wishes. Extraordinary expenses, such as terracing and chemical fertilization, are the responsibility of the owner.

Except in the extreme west, where one grain may be grown exclusively on any farm, and where a system of daily wages is standard, there is more than one system of sharing on a farm, because of variety in the crops cultivated. Although all farms in other areas will plant grain, it is but one of several crops planted on the same property. Typically and almost universally, there is not only mixed planting in all seasons, usu-

An Algarvian farmer.

ally with both trees and grain or leguminous crops in the same field, but also there are at least two major crop seasons and combinations in any one year on the lowlands. In some of the favored localities and under certain systems of rotation, three crops within one year are possible.

The division of the other crops has been determined by long custom and is fairly standard, even though there may be variations from the norm by individual arrangements made between the owner and the farmer. From the fig harvest the farmer usually receives one part and the owner of the trees three to six parts, depending upon the arrangement made with regard to the division of labor and costs. The farmer usually picks the figs and lays them out to dry for fifteen days, caring for them during this process. The owner may pay for the trimming of the trees or the farmer may do it and keep the trim—a valuable economic item. Three other trees not requiring irrigation are important in the Algarve: the almond, the carob, and the olive. The harvest from them is usually divided with one part to the farmer and three to four

21

parts to the owner. In the case of olives one of several special arrangements may be made to alter the division. Picking is troublesome and the picker may demand a higher percentage of the harvest than is ordinary, if labor is in demand at the time. In some cases the picker receives one-third of the product. If the division is made in terms of olive oil, the share will depend upon the place of pressing. As much as half of the product may be taken by the press owner as his share. In all cases, the owner of the land pays for the planting, and usually for the grafting, of the trees. If irrigation is necessary during the first or second year, as in the case of almonds, for example, the owner is also responsible for this.

Characteristic crops of the Algarve

Of the many crops that the Algarvian farmer may plant, maize is of basic importance to him, and virtually all farms plant one or more of the small grains as well. Probably during any half dozen years, wheat and perhaps some rye will be raised for human consumption, as well as barley and oats for fodder. A large part of the cereal production, however, is not the result of specialized production but is a secondary crop derived from grains planted under the unirrigated trees.

A sickle is the harvesting implement. A typical summer scene in the Algarve shows a woman, or man, cutting a few stalks of grain at a time, and laying them in loose, small, neatly aligned piles of about one hundred stalks each, to be gathered later into sheaves. Even though the plots are usually too small for the use of a large machine, one wonders why, if nothing better is available, the scythe is not used. Ancient ways are sometimes unaccountably persistent. Hauling is done with mule carts in the lower country (oxcarts to the west of Lagos), and with pack frames for carrying grain on the backs of animals in the hills. Threshing is ordinarily done by driving mules, or, occasionally donkeys or cows, over the grain piled on a threshing floor. Now however, even in the mountain area, one may see threshing machines. Many farmers dislike them, saying that the straw from animal threshing is preferable for fodder and for use as beds for animals.

Also widespread are the four important unirrigated trees of the Algarve. Figs, with the greatest extension of the four, reach virtually from

Low figs near Cape S. Vicente.

the Cape to the Guadiana River. Olives are more limited in distribution, the best of them being near Tavira and Monchique. Unfortunately, the local product does not have a good reputation even among the Algarvians themselves. Carobs are of sporadic appearance almost everywhere upon the lowland, but the main concentration is upon the hilly calcareous area lying between the schist mountains to the north and the Coastal Plain to the south. They do not reach the Cape, because of fogs. The almond appears from somewhat to the west of Lagos eastward to the Guadiana. It is not as rugged and as coarse a feeder as the carob and does less well in the limestone area. It is at its best in the area to the east of Faro and stretching past Tavira, on both the coastal lowland and somewhat into the limestone area.

Interplanting of grains with almond and fig is virtually always successful. While interplanting is common with the olive and not uncommon even with the carob, in neither case is the crop notably successful, for each tree is demanding of the soil. This is especially true of the

Almonds, wheat, and an olive tree.

carob, which diminishes the amount of moisture and soil nutrients available to the associated crops. At the extremes of feasibility for olive and carob growing, interplanting is not possible.

Widespread, although not occupying the extent of land devoted to the small grains, are chick-peas. They are found on both the littoral and the hilly limestone area across almost the full width of the Algarve, usually on what the Portuguese peasants term "strong land," and wherever possible in alluvium. Here they thrive and make a good return for the land and time devoted to them.

Horse beans are planted mostly for fodder—a high protein addition to the straw which makes up the bulk of the animal food. Barley, oats, and horse beans, and at times small amounts of other legumes, are given to ailing animals or to cows just before and after calving. Horse beans are excellent for human fare in February, when they are green. Some country people toast and eat the dried beans, which also make nutritious, if unattractive, food. Horse beans may be planted separately,

Caldeirão windmills, one abandoned and one still being used.

or, like the grains, may be found interplanted with trees and even occasionally with vines.

By far the greater part of the Algarvian agricultural product comes
from irrigated fields, wells being the most important source of water.
The variety of intensively cultivated crops under irrigation and the
intricacy of their seasonal and areal arrangement has been highly developed in parts of the Coastal Plain. A chapter of description will be
devoted to the subject.

GRIST MILLS

Portuguese windmills with circular form, conical roof, and four
sail arms are not only picturesque but still functional. They are not
Quixote mills with canvas spread upon latticework. On the Portuguese
mill, sails are triangular: one side is tied along a sail arm and the point
of the triangle opposite to this side is stretched by a rope to an intermediate arm. The windmills of the Greek islands are not dissimilar, although they have more sails on each mill.

A grist mill in operation.

The windmill was apparently unknown to the Greeks and the Romans, but was known in Persia by the seventh century. In a primitive form, it was taken west along the north of Africa and into Europe by Moslems. However, it is probable that the device was altered and improved in Iberia as early as the beginning of the fourteenth century or before.[17] The millhouse is of stone and plaster; its conical roof, formerly a wooden frame covered with thatch, but now likely to be covered with sheet metal, can be turned, with its great shaft and sails, to face the wind. Virtually all working parts are made of wood: the twenty-foot sail arms that cross the great shaft projecting from the millhouse, the great horizontal shaft itself which connects within the millhouse by a cog-and-slot device with another, vertical, shaft that turns the millstone, the cogs and slots; all except the vertical shaft are made of wood. The great shaft is usually made of an especially hard wood. One such shaft, for example, was made of "brazilian wood" (the kind was not determined). It had been in service since 1856, as attested by the date carved into it at the time that the mill was built. The other working parts are usually made of wood from the holm oak (*Quercus ilex*). Only a small amount of metal is used even now. Ordinarily, aside from the small shaft turning the millstone, the only metal is a rim strapped round the slot wheel that engages the large wooden cogs. Grain fed into the center of the stone drifts out from the sides as flour. The miller takes 10 per cent of the flour as his payment.

In the Algarve, millstones are always made of limestone. A millstone is about forty inches in diameter and, when new, about sixteen inches thick. At the place of making, one is sold for three hundred and fifty escudos (about $10.50 U.S.). If it is delivered, the price depends upon distance. The cost of transport within the Algarve may amount to as much as the value of the stone, for each stone weighs about a ton and a half when new. A stone will last from three to fifteen years, depending upon the amount of work done with it. There is a busy season during and just after the wheat harvest, when a mill will probably be kept busy through most of the twenty-four–hour day for several weeks. In

---

[17] R. J. Forbes, "Power," *A History of Technology*, II, 614–619; Rex Wailes, "A Note on Windmills," *A History of Technology*, II, 625.

The cog-and-slot mechanism of a wind-driven mill.

The grindstone of a wind-driven mill.

Albufeira one miller said that he worked throughout the year whenever the wind blew. Following the maize harvest is another, but lesser, peak of activity. Ordinarily only these two grains are ground.

With long work days, the stones must be scarified about every two days (some millers prefer to do it as often as once each twenty-four hours of work). To accomplish the task of scarification, the upper stone must be lifted off by means of a crowbar and slipped onto a table or frame with rollers, where it can be incised with radial lines one-quarter to one-half inch apart at the outer edge. This is done with a heavy sledge and a four-inch-wide blade. After incising, the stone of an average mill will grind over sixty pounds of flour per hour. The amount declines progressively during the succeeding period until the stone is reworked.

The only other costly and deteriorating part of the mills is the sail. Most mills have four. The canvas for one sail now costs about $25.00 (U.S.). Because of their value, the sails are carefully tended, furled

The blades of a water-driven mill.

around the arms, and tied with ropes when temporarily out of use. When the mill is idle for a longer period of time, they are removed and carefully stored.

An interesting feature of wind-driven mills is the narrow-necked pots which are attached, sometimes in large numbers, to the great arms of the mill, "just for music" when the arms sweep through the air, the millers say. However, the sound does announce the movement of the arms—or the lack of it—and it may be an indication to the miller that the wind has shifted in direction.

The large, modern mill across the Guadiana River from Mértola is responsible for the abandonment of numerous windmills to the south and west of it. Some folk still cling to their preference for flour ground by the windmill, however. The less efficient and less "clean" grind is preferable, they say, for the particles of husks that remain in the flour are no trouble to sift out and are fine for chicken feed. At least one windmill was built in the fifties in the Caldeirão Mountains about fifteen miles north of São Brás, testifying to this traditional taste.

The stone of a water-driven mill.

In areas where water can be channelled for water mills, the windmill may not be used until about June first, when the water supply has dwindled. Water mills are more dependable than windmills until early summer; that is to say, good streams in the early part of the year are dependable and wind is capricious. However, during the last several weeks preceding summer, the water mills can work only part time, as most of the streams are not full enough to turn the wheels directly and must be fed into storage tanks about fifteen to twenty feet above the level of the wheels. When the tanks are full, the water is released into a flume or tube directed at the wheel. Algarvian tanks store enough water to run a mill for two hours on the average.

A typical water mill of the Algarve is built with a vertical shaft. The grinding stones are at the upper end of the shaft, and at the other end are horizontal blades against which the force of water is directed through a six-to-eight-inch tube. It is a simple and effective device, less complicated than the mechanism of the wind-driven mill. The great

An overshot water mill (a "modern" example, made of metal).

A tidal mill.

cog-and-slot wheels are not required, nor are the large sail arms with their costly canvases.

Only slightly more complicated are the water mills with a horizontal shaft. These mills have a large vertical wheel, with slots around its periphery that are struck by the water from a tube. The power of the horizontal shaft must be converted by forty-five–degree–angle cogs to turn another shaft fastened to the millstone. Although one step more complicated than the water mill with a vertical shaft, it is also considerably less trouble to build than the wind-driven mill. In constructing either type of water mill, no metal is ordinarily used, except for the bearing at the water-wheel end of the shaft. Hard wood must be used, and for the parts that are drenched with water it must be not only hard, but resistant to the deterioration affecting most woods under such circumstances. Millers say that the wood of the olive is incomparably the best to meet these requirements.

One other type of water mill, formerly more important than at present, but still with a few representatives left, is the tidal mill. Its shaft is turned by the force of tidal water, channelled into an artificial type of bore, and forced to strike against blades. Although this type of mill offers the advantage of use throughout the year, it requires a more elaborate structure, with channels and control gates to make use of the tides. Perhaps for this reason its use has waned even more than that of the other traditional types.

Currently used types of water mills were known to the Romans and possibly introduced into Iberia by them. The simple type with the vertical shaft, water blades below and millstone above, is certainly as old as the first century B.C., and the conversion of that type to the more efficient mill with the horizontal shaft (the "overshot mill"—that is, with the stream of water striking the upper side of the wheel—is the best of this type) was made by Roman engineers; but neither type was commonly used by them until the occurrence of a labor shortage in the fourth century A.D. The tidal mill seems to have been introduced considerably later. It is known from France of the twelfth century but it did not become common in Western Europe until the eighteenth century.[18]

GATHERING

To maintain themselves and their families, farmers in the Algarve must engage in many activities not directly concerned with farming and not even experienced by American farmers. Time, rather a good deal of it, must be spent in gathering materials for fuel, fodder, food, and—to complete the alliteration—fabrication. One cannot go far along any one of the roads without seeing a cart or a donkey laden with green or dried shrubs, trimmings, or leaves from trees.

A notable fuel is the gum cistus (*Cistus ladaniferus*), which grows in profusion upon the schists of the mountains and can be burned green (although fifteen days of drying improves its combustibility). Piled high upon mule carts, it is a common sight on the roads, being brought into the bakeries, its chief market. Occasionally it is used for home fires, but this is not common, as it is a valuable source of cash income. A large load of gum cistus sells for one hundred escudos ($3.50 U.S.). Cutting,

---

[18] R. J. Forbes, "Power," *A History of Technology*, II, pp. 589, 596, 600.

Wild growth gathered for fuel; olives on the slope behind the fence.

gathering, loading, and delivery usually involves the time of one man for three to four days. After the expense of the cart is paid, the return for labor probably comes to the almost universal Portuguese figure for unskilled labor, eighteen escudos a day (approximately $.60 U.S.).

For the homes of country people, roots, other wild growth, and the trim from cultivated trees are used for fuel. Olive trim and fig branches are preferred.

In the eastern section of the hilly limestone area, another cistus (*C. monspeliensis*), a bush oak (*Quercus coccifera*), and a species of mint (*Phlomis purpurea*) are often burned green, although they make better fuel when dried. If one can afford the root of the heather (*Calluna vulgaris*), he uses it for fires in the kitchen, forge, or fireplace, for as the forgemen say, it is a "clean fuel." The root of the heather burns steadily for a long time. It also makes a fine charcoal, although it is not used commonly for this purpose. In spite of its spontaneous growth, it is not free to the gatherer. Owners of the land from which it is gathered charge from one and a half to two escudos ($.05 to .07 U.S.) an arroba (of 32 lbs.) for it.

Various small factories or cottage industries have traditional fuel preferences. The little candy factory in Faro buys heather root from the country people to burn under the vat in which the sugar is melted for coating almonds. In the same room, charcoal made from the cork oak is used exclusively for the fires under the mixer in which the almonds are tossed with the melted sugar. The plant owner was quite positive that the fuels could not be changed without harm to the product. The pottery ovens outside of Loulé buy pine for fuel if it is available, but otherwise use branches of the *Erica australis*, or substitute a mixed load of lavender, *Cistus monspeliensis* and *C. ladaniferus*. The fuel for the little stills in the mountains that make a liquor distilled from the fruits of the strawberry trees is usually from one of the cistus or from heather, as both can be burned green. Wood of *Pterospartum tridentatum* has been used traditionally to burn the hair off the carcasses of pigs because it makes a quick, hot fire.

For uses other than fuel many things are gathered. The slender, straight rods of gum cistus are used as stalks up which peas can be trained. Only the straightest of the branches are selected and a gatherer sells them for eight escudos ($.28 U.S.) per hundred. Each branch will serve for three to four years, if carefully gathered and stored after use. For drying figs the farmer gathers fennel stalks (*Foeniculum vulgare*, Miller), which he binds together with agave fiber to make the mats upon which the figs are laid to dry in the sun. Where available, a rush (*Juncus*) is gathered from near streams for tying the sheaves of wheat. Where it is not available, as in parts of the coastal plain, the men are skilled in using the wheat itself as a binder. Two bunches of about fifteen stalks each are put end to end with the seed heads overlapping beyond each other. Just below the heads, six to ten other stalks are wound round and twisted. This gives a length almost twice that of the length of the wheat stalk. A sheaf of wheat is bound with this improvised binder and the ends of it are twisted to hold it firmly.

For fodder, not only fig leaves, but several wild plants, are gathered by the Algarvians. *Narcissus bulbocodium* and *Malva spp.* are gathered

36

Making cane baskets.

to be mixed with straw. *Dactylis cynosuroides*, a marine grass, is sometimes gathered from the shallow sea water, or the cattle are allowed to wade into the sea to graze upon it. In the latter case the animals need careful watching, for they are apt to swallow too much water and become bloated. The above are among the most important of the fodder plants that are gathered, but countless others are known to the frugal Portuguese husbandmen through long experimentation and observation.

Cane (*Arundo donax*) grows along the streams in several places in the Algarve, and craftsmen cut it to use in making baskets (for example, in Monchique and on the river near the settlement of Odeleite). Oleander (*Nerium oleander*) grows in the canyons of the dry mountains. In bloom, it is a handsome addition to the otherwise bleak landscape, and its larger branches serve for the strong framework of some types of baskets, while the smaller branches are plaited for the sides and ends. Pieces of the larger branches also serve as broom handles. Willow (*Salix viminalis*) is planted and gathered along the streams near Mon-

Making willow baskets.

chique to be made into excellent baskets and, in Faro, into tables and chairs. Agave was formerly of commercial importance, but only traces of such importance now remain. The leaves of the sparsely scattered plants may be gathered now without payment, yet only a few men do so. They remove the pulp by pounding and scraping, and then hang the fibers in the sun to dry. It is difficult to understand the present neglect of the plant and fiber, as Algarvians agree that the best ropes, bridles, and animal muzzles are made from it. Cattail (*Typha angustifolia*) is used in some places to make sleeping mats. Flax is still grown, for a small and decreasing use; esparto grass (*Stipa tenacissima*) and the leaves of the dwarf palm (*Chamaerops humilis*) are gathered occasionally in the Algarve; but the fabrication of useful articles from these plants is mostly based upon imports of fibers from Spanish North Africa.

Along the sea-edge of the Coastal Plain, with its long, warm, rainless season, salt evaporation is simple and profitable. Small salt pans are easily made along the sea front or within tidal reach on streams. Such

38

Salt pans.

pans, separated from each other by low earth barriers, are to be seen in many areas, but the largest and most ancient are those near large cities in the business of fish packing. Especially numerous and large are those of the Cape Santa Maria area and those near Tavira and Castro Marim. Collection is a simple matter of scraping up the crusts of salt after the water has evaporated.

Pottery is locally made; in Loulé, Lagoa, and Moncarapacho it is produced commercially and sold throughout the province, but it is not greatly admired and the total amount is not great. In fact, the best pottery found in a large part of the Algarve is imported from the Alentejo.

Stone working continues, in its Neolithic way, to be important. A good mason receives relatively good wages, especially in building the terraces of Monchique, a matter that will be considered at some length in a later chapter. This demand is not important in other regions of the Algarve, where terracing is minor. It is unnecessary on the Coastal Plain

Making limestone basins for pig pens. Note the quern in the foreground.

and unjustified, economically, in the schist mountains. Only a few scattered terraces are found in the Limestone Zone. However, there are products of stone working that have general importance in the province: near the settlements of Paderne, Lagos, and Silves millstones for grist mills are made from limestone. An itinerant worker makes limestone basins for water and feed for the pig pens, and also the small querns, which within this century were part of the dowry of every peasant girl of the Algarve. Some syenite "bricks" are shaped by hand to pave highways, but this work is uncommon in the Algarve; it is a north Portuguese industry, occasionally copied in the south.

Several crafts (or minor industries), presently or originally using materials that could be gathered locally, such as charcoal making, honey gathering and beehives, brandy making, basketry, weaving, and the house industries using leaves of the dwarf palm (*Chamaerops humilis*) and esparto grass (*Stipa tenacissima L.*), have a continuing, although diminishing, function. Each is areally limited and is considered in chapters concerned with the subareas.

FACTORIES

Modern methods of production are beginning to take their place beside traditional craft ways. Now appearing in the cities are phases of the transition between the old and the new systems. For example, in Portimão is a shoe shop which not only repairs old shoes, but makes new ones, with primitive methods. Its tools are few and simple—hammers, pliers, awls, and needles—but it attempts to make a product similar to that of modern factories. The little cart plant of Portimão is another example. Strips and rounds of steel and rough lumber are the basic materials from which everything for the cart is made. The bolts are made by forge, hammer, and anvil, plus threading dies. The nuts also are pieces cut from the strip, plugged, and tapped. The axles are shaped and threaded from steel rounds. The boards for the wagon sides are planed and morticed with simple tools, as is the frame of the wagon. The spokes for the wheels are shaped with a draw knife. Three men are employed in the shop, each of whom is metal worker, carpenter, and painter. It is hardly a modern shop, yet its product bears comparison well with that of modern factories.

The most important factories of the Algarve pack fish or produce an ancillary product. The activity of fishing, its centers, and the preparation of the product are so important that they warrant a separate chapter. Another group of factories process cork. They, too, will be discussed at some length below. However, there are still other plants in the province that are large enough to be called factories, even though most of them are not of the size contemplated when the word is used by inhabitants of the industrialized countries of the world. A few examples will indicate their variety. In eight of the Algarvian ports, shipbuilding, or at least boatbuilding, was registered at the end of 1959.[19] While it is true that Portimão, the port with the most tonnage built in the year, recorded only one hundred and twenty-four tons, its yards are steadily at work. Their equipment is not modern in the American sense but the result is satisfactory; these boats have long fished Atlantic coasts and the coast of North Africa. In years past, when larger fishing vessels were

[19] *Estatística das pescas marítimas,* 1959, p. 58.

A Portimão shipyard. Note the medieval pit-saw in the foreground and the fish-packing plants in the background.

being used along the southern coast, Portimão yards built them; now the approximate maximum is sixty tons. Vila Real was second in tonnage built during 1959. The smaller ports, and even Tavira, usually confine themselves to the construction and repair of small boats for sail or oar.

Portimão has a tannery for sheep and goat skins, which are used for the *albarda*, a Portuguese saddle. The tannery now uses imported chemicals and part of the cork oak. Other small factories in Portimão include a marble-and-breccia-polishing plant, a tile factory, a broom factory, and a small plant for making jute sacking. A remnant industry of Portimão, inherited from the early monasteries, is the manufacture of the candies and pastries made in a variety of designs, out of the almonds and figs of the region.

HOUSES

Algarvian distinction lies partly in its houses; in many ways they differ from those of any other region of the country, or, indeed, the

A broom factory.

peninsula. Distinction is created partly by color, partly by the use of materials, partly by design, and certainly by detail. But the combination of these elements, more than any one of them, effects the result. The Mediterranean flat roof is used elsewhere in Portugal as well as other Mediterranean countries (and it is far from standard in the Algarve), the stepped-back, upper-storied house is common in North Africa as well as in Olhão; the colors seen in the Algarve can be seen in many other parts of Europe; stone, clay, and calcimine are in common use in all Mediterranean countries; even the cleanliness can be duplicated in other areas, although seldom as strikingly. It is the combination of these traits that establishes a special quality that is recognizable as Algarvian and then, as if to crown the spectacle, there is the local chimney; this is especially Algarvian.

Typical houses of the Lower Algarve are made of unshaped, or at best roughly shaped, stones set in clay mortar and plastered over. They always look—and are—immaculate, as the women clean them fastidi-

43

The round house of the Caldeirão.

ously and calcimine them twice a year. Occasionally, the trim is painted with colors. Many mountain houses are not calcimined; the grey schist of the region has streaks of rust color through it so it does not make a completely bleak scene, but these houses have a certain grimness unknown in the Lower Algarve. In shape and interior design the mountain houses are similar to those of the lower area, with one interesting exception, that of the circular houses of the mountains of the east. These, however, are not now used as dwellings, although some are still of service for housing sheep. This ancient, perhaps Hamitic, type of house may indicate several thousand years of African influence on construction in southern Portugal.

Both in the mountains and in some areas of the lowland, another type of house is still built, the house of tamped earth, which was common in Iberia at the time of Roman domination. It is not as common as formerly and in many areas is branded as old-fashioned, but it is still common in the settlements of the hills around Monchique as well as those of

Building a tamped-earth house.

the schist mountains to the east. In the lowlands of the Barlavento such houses are still esteemed, and the people there firmly maintain that they are superior to any other type and last virtually forever. They say that it is a good house for a man of modest means, if he builds in an area with good limy soil.

Certainly there is little expenditure for construction equipment. To contain the earth to be tamped one needs boards and cords sufficient to put together a frame about fifteen inches high, twelve inches wide, and from two to five feet long. As two men usually work together, two tampers will be required, clublike pieces of wood, each with a bulbous end and a four-to-five-foot handle. These, with esparto-grass baskets to carry the earth, make up the total equipment necessary. Although the process is not difficult, some men are known to be specialists, and their judgments are respected with regard to the consistency of materials and the degree of compaction necessary to the mass.

A foundation of stone is usually made and upon this the frame is

Algarvian chimneys.

placed. A carrier brings the slightly damp mixture of clay and sandy soil, usually mixed with small stones, and dumps it into the frame. The tampers pound it down until it is firm. When the frame is full, the boards are removed and set up again on the next length of wall until the level is completed. Another level is built upon this, and so on, until the wall is of the desired height. The interior separating walls are made in the same way.

Houses may or may not have fabricated floors. In the mountains they are mostly lacking. In the lowlands more prosperous farmers may have a floor of tile or concrete. The dirt floor is always hard packed and cleanly swept. Although it may be uneven, it is seldom untidy. Rooms are clean, even with the sooty ceilings of those many houses which do not have chimneys. Most rooms have a small window and perhaps a door, although this is less generally true of the houses of the mountains, where rooms without any opening to the outside are not uncommon. In the houses of the less prosperous people, the windows are not glazed, but covered with wooden shutters. These people say that glass windows are only for the rich. The equipment of houses is meagre, usually consisting only of a simple table, a few chairs, a chest for blankets and clothes, wooden-frame beds, and a few shelves against the walls.

Chimneys, carefully made in a great number of shapes and patterns, are the special pride of the Algarvians. Particularly in the Limestone Zone are they distinctive. They are put on some houses merely for ornament, even though there is no fireplace within. An owner is proud of his chimney, spending time and thought on its special design, construction, and care. At the time of construction a builder is apt to ask "How many hours of chimney do you want?"—in other words, just how elaborate do you want it? These delicately fretted crowns are a striking feature in the landscape.

However, not all houses in the Algarve have chimneys. They are a luxury that the poorest families cannot afford. Many houses in the Lower Algarve and an even larger number in the mountains have no chimney at all. Common to the schist areas of the mountains is a bee-hive-shaped oven built outside of the house. On dry days (which means, most of the year) it can be used. On rainy days baking, if done

A houseyard oven made of schist.

at all, is done inside the kitchen, where smoke clouds the room until it filters through the tiles of the roof.

On the sand fringes of the coastal area in the center of the Algarve, fishermen still build wooden frames and cover them, walls and roof, with rushes. This is a type of house far commoner in the nineteenth century than now, when only remnant groups exist.

Fences of stone, with a cover of plaster and calcimine, parallel the Algarvian roads. Partly they represent a taste inherited from the Moors. Sometimes they serve to clear the land of excess stone; there are fences in the Limestone Zone six to eight feet high and ten to twelve feet across. Tamped-earth fences are common in parts of the west and scattered remnants appear in the eastern Algarve, attesting to a former importance greater than that of the present. People in the east say that no more of this type are now being built, whereas in the west such fences are still being constructed.

Women from the Limestone Zone going to market.

ANIMALS

For transport or food several animals are integral to Algarvian economy. Mules are the typical plow animals of the province, although donkeys and even cows may be used; and in a small area in the far west, a few red-brown Alentejano-type oxen are to be seen working in the fields. Of the mules, the best is thought to be the *eguariço*, which has been born to a mare and sired by a donkey. The *macho* of this cross is said to be preferred as being gentler than the *mula*. The *asneiro*, with a donkey mother and a horse for sire, is rejected by some people because of its ugly head, shorter stature, and coarser appearance. The poorer people prefer the *asneiro*, however, perhaps because it is cheaper, but also because it is more *rustico*, taking care of itself better and eating a wider assortment of fodder.

Both the donkey and the mule are basic to transport. A woman commonly has her donkey to carry the materials she takes to the market or brings from it. Frequently one sees several women in single file riding their donkeys along the road, each facing to the right, as it is the custom to mount from that side. Occasionally, a man can be seen riding a donkey, but almost invariably it is an old man or an ailing young one, for the vigorous, working males drive mule carts.

Each family that can afford it has a pig or two, always kept in a pen close by the house and fed with scraps from the house or from the harvest (occasionally horse beans, and, near Monchique, sweet potatoes). On a minimum diet, an Algarvian family would average the consumption of one pig a year.

Sheep are usually kept as individuals or in small flocks. An owner of the Limestone Zone or the mountains may own a hundred or more. In the first case, unless the small boy of the family is available for herding, the owner will make an agreement with neighbors owning a few sheep for common herding. (It is not unusual to see a small boy watching two, or even one, sheep grazing.) When the sheep of several families are herded in common the herder will be hired by salary (fifteen escudos a day—$.53 U.S.—would be an average figure in the Limestone Zone), or an arrangement made by which he will receive a share of the young and of the ewe's milk. A half-and-half division proves to be better than payment of ten escudos ($.35 U.S.) a day, informants agreed. They also said that a small boy might be hired to guard two or three sheep for ten escudos a month; that a larger boy could herd up to fifteen sheep. Apparently larger flocks are put in charge of full-grown men.

Although arrangements must be made with the owner of the land, usually no charge is made for grazing, as long as the sheep are moved so that the manure is spread over the land. Most landowners are more than willing to allow the sheep to graze upon the remnants of harvest in order to gain the fertilizer for their land.

A good ewe will produce about two-thirds of a pint of milk a day for two to two and a half months in the spring, when pasturage is good. All surplus above that needed for the lambs is made into cheese to be sold. Cheese is not difficult to make, and is a more desirable product for marketing than milk, because it keeps better and sells for a higher price. For example, five litres (almost nine pints) of milk worth about $.44

Long-haired sheep.

(U.S.) makes one kilo of cheese, which sells for thirty-three escudos ($1.15 U.S.).

The long-haired sheep, with its long legs, Roman nose, and black blotches on white background, is dominant in the Algarve. It came originally from the west of Africa and is far older in the peninsula than the Merino. It is found in the Algarve from Sagres to the Guadiana River. The Algarvians say that it fits into their land system and economy better than does the Merino. The latter needs more care and wider spaces in which to roam, so it does not thrive under the intimate arrangements necessary in the crowded landscape of small properties in the Algarve. The farmers say that it is not so *rustico*, that is, it doesn't adjust itself well to the general conditions and needs more attention. The long-haired sheep, less specialized, demands less care. It is a large animal, becomes fertile earlier, and produces considerably more meat than the Merino. The fibers that it yields are coarse and not of much use for textiles, but are used for mattresses and some heavy blankets. The Algarvians, of course, are not in great need of wool for clothing. In the climate of the region, a meat sheep and a milk producer offers more advantages than a wool sheep.

Although the Merinos are relatively few in the Algarve, they are not entirely absent. At the extreme east—that is, east of Tavira—one sees occasional flocks. They are there because of influence from beyond the Guadiana; many Spaniards have moved into this area in times past, when lands were cheaper in Portugal than they were in Spain.

In small numbers, there are three other types of sheep. One, called the Feltroso, is smaller and hairier than the Merino. It produces a relatively small quantity of wool of very ordinary quality. Almost all the sheep of this type are found around the city of Silves and somewhat to the west of there. In the mountains adjacent to the Alentejo, a sheep produced by the mixing of the Alentejo wool sheep and the hairy sheep of the Algarve is found. It is not valued highly, as its wool is not considered to be of good quality and the animal is small. Another mixture that is found in various parts of the Algarve, but never in great numbers, is the cross between the Algarvian long-haired sheep and the Merino. These sheep, also, are not valued highly.

Goats are to be seen frequently, but they are much fewer in number than sheep. Mostly they are to be seen in the mountains or in the uncultivated parts of the limestone area. Like sheep, one or two goats may be guarded by a small boy, or a professional herder may care for a flock of one hundred. Goats graze on virtually all shrubs, including the gum cistus and heather of the mountains. They also graze, as do the sheep, on the edges of the roads and sometimes in the stubble of the harvests. As with sheep, the herder may be hired by the day or he may take his wage as a percentage of the kids and the milk. His one tool, the sling, he makes of agave fiber. With this, he throws rocks to guide and control the flock.

VEHICLES

Packing is only part of Algarvian transport; carts of several types are commonly used. The most elegant is the *carinha*, a two-wheeled

A *carinha*.

gig, light and handsomely made. Only a prosperous landowner, or one of similar economic status, can afford one. The work cart, the *carroço*, may be open or hooded. Larger and sturdier than the *carinha*, it is designed for heavy hauling. An older type, the *carro canudo*, with heavy wheels, a heavy, low bed with upright stakes at the sides, demountable in case the load must project beyond the edges of the bed, is not commonly used now. All carts, except the *carros* for work in the fields, are brightly decorated with geometric designs or designs of flowers or fruits. The hooded *carroços* have brilliantly painted designs on the semitubular canvas top.

Water carts, and pack animals with water on their backs, are a common sight on the roads, especially between Portimão and Caldas de Monchique in the west. The water of Monchique, like so many of the mineral waters of Europe, is famous for "curing" a multitude of ills. It is not only the sick who buy it, however, for purchase of water for ordinary drinking is not uncommon. In the small towns where water is not piped to the houses, the water cart or wheelbarrow is also common. The

A water peddler.

wheelbarrow is a common device of transport in the west, for diverse small loads as well as for water.

The bicycle has taken on some importance as a transport vehicle. With a cross-pole supported on a carrying frame above the rear wheel and a large basket hung near each end of the pole, considerable tonnage, in total, is carried by it through the year.

Back-carrying and head-carrying are almost absent. Men and women, if they are carrying parcels, do so with their hands. Occasionally one sees a woman (and even a man) with a load upon his head, but the carrier is either from outside of the Algarve or has learned the technique from outside; it is strange to the Algarvian. Goods brought to market or bought there to be taken back to the country by the women are packed in the large, shapeless, palm panniers straddling the backs of their donkeys. Larger and heavier loads are hauled by men in the mule carts.

FISHING

Fishing along the south coast of present Portugal is of great antiquity; methods, except for those of large-scale commercial companies, are age-old and typically Mediterranean. Individuals or small groups using traditional techniques and devices suited to local conditions catch either pelagic or a great variety of demersal species as well as molluscs and crustaceans. In May and June, tuna (*Thunnus thynnus* L), swim eastward past the Portuguese south shore, and in July and August they again pass the shore on the return trip toward the open ocean, a habit convenient for the commercial fishing corporations. Sardines (*Sardina pilchardus*), horse mackerel (*Trachurus trachurus*), Spanish mackerel (*Scomber colias*), and anchovies (*Engraulis encrasicholus* L), are caught in greatest quantity during the summer months, when they approach the shore. But the subject of fishing is so important to the Algarve that a long chapter must be devoted to it.

SUBAREAS

Briefly outlined above are the most important activities of the Algarvians in supporting themselves. From this general description, however, a reader would not realize that there is little homogeneity throughout the province. The Lower Algarve (including both the Coastal Plain and the Limestone Zone) differs from the mountains, and one mountain area is quite distinct from the other. Although the phrase "Lower Algarve" has legitimacy for limited use, the two areas that constitute it are quite distinct in so many ways that clearly they must be treated as subareas. In all, four subareas will be considered in separate chapters: the Coastal Plain, the Limestone Zone, the Caldeirão Mountains, and Monchique.[20] Even another distinction must be made, for on the Coastal Plain there are two important economic subgroups: farmers and fishermen. A chapter must be given to each.

[20] Another subarea that is politically Algarvian is omitted from consideration, that of Aljezur, lying to the west of Monchique. Actually it is a tectonic accident in the Alentejo. Culturally it lies midway between the Algarve and the Alentejo, and economically it looks to the north, away from the Algarve.

2. Agriculture of the Coastal Plain

▰▰

THE LOWER ALGARVE as a whole is a moderately good area for farming, and parts of the Coastal Plain are premium by any definition; but this region requires careful cultivation and planning. Its present productivity can be attributed to diligence and intelligent operation; every month has its peculiar activity and product. Changes could certainly be made, for example, an increase in the number of machines used in some agricultural processes; but such alteration could hardly increase production, although it would reduce the hand labor presently involved. Now, machines are few in number and power is supplied by animals (including men). Only with difficulty could such garden culture be mechanized; present production requires infinite care of plots usually too small for the use of machines.

The long list of agricultural products is a mixture of anciently planted Mediterranean crops and others introduced in recent centuries, notably maize, white potatoes, sweet potatoes, tomatoes, peanuts, capsicum, as well as varieties of squash and beans, all brought from the New World and now fundamental items in the farming and dietary of the Algarve.

The agricultural calendar is a nicely balanced arrangement of crops and labor: the harvest begins in the summer, and most tree crops, from either irrigated or unirrigated trees, are gathered by late autumn; only the citrus harvest occurs later. Oranges and tangerines are gathered from early October through February. Irrigated garden crops, which are planted in spring and early summer, are harvested during the autumn; then field crops are planted to be harvested in the following spring or early summer.

Despite the visitor's impression of high productivity—and those who know the area are convinced that this is a fact—the statistics of agricultural production for a large number of crops indicate the opposite. This statistical misrepresentation is due to interplanting. When several crops share the same field, either at the same time or in the same year, it is obvious that the production of each will compare unfavorably with crops having no competitor.

Certain facts concerning family-land relations may be inferred from various official reports even though the reports are not always in agreement:[1] small properties are typical, but the definition of "small property" differs from the less productive west to the more intensively farmed east. For example, a small property in the extreme east of the province is officially less than ten hectares (twenty-five acres); in the west it is defined as being less than thirty hectares.[2] But ten hectares anywhere would be considered a jewel to a farmer dependent upon the property for his living. A working farmer, whose family lived on the produce of his irrigated land, told me that "to live well, a family needs

---

[1] For example, the *Inquérito às condições de habitação da família, anexo ao IX Recenseamento geral da população* (em 15 de Dezembro de 1950) differs in fundamental matters of fact from the *Inquérito às explorações agrícolas do continente, 1952, I, Províncias do Ribatejo, Alto Alentejo, Baixo Alentejo e Algarve.*

[2] Gaetano Ferro, *L'Algarve*, p. 135. The work of this author, whose other titles are given below in citations, has been very helpful to me in many respects, although the organization of the present monograph is not such that it can be frequently cited.

at least three hectares." Most farms are owned by the men who work them, and for such a man far less than ten hectares is the rule. Many farmers either do not own sufficient land for the support of their families or they own none at all, so that renting and share-working are well known. Rented lands are found mostly around the large cities and are more prevalent in the eastern Algarve than in the west. Share-working seems to exist in larger proportion in the west than in the east. The Limestone Zone appears to be transitional between the mountains and the Coastal Plain in the matter of land ownership; it has a higher percentage of owner-worked properties than the Coastal Plain but less than the mountains.

The distinction between the eastern section known in the Algarve as the Sotavento and the western section, the Barlavento, is a real one in terms of agriculture. Some agronomists in the province think that the center region might also be put apart as a third subarea. This fragmentation seems excessive to others, however, as the center region, being younger in present methods of exploitation, has merely intensified the practices of the Sotavento.

THE SOTAVENTO

The lush, prosperous appearance of the fields and trees of the Sotavento is a product of skill and care, but it would not be possible without favorable climatic conditions. The area, except on the extreme east, is protected by the mountains of the Caldeirão against the worst of the outbursts of winter cold that occasionally sweep down from the interior of the Iberian Peninsula. Winds are dominantly from the east. The *levante*, sharp and cold during the winter, and withering at times in summer, may do considerable damage, but it is not a frequent phenomenon. Summers are warm, not only during the day, but throughout the night as well. Faro records over twenty nights with minimum temperatures above 68° F.,[3] more than any other station of the province. Warmth, as well as the highest yearly mean precipitation recorded on the Coastal Plain (Tavira, 20 inches), offers advantages not accorded

[3] José António Madeira, *Características meteorológicas do Algarve no quadro geral da climatologia Portuguesa*, p. 33.

A *nora* in action.

to other Algarvian areas (unirrigated maize can be raised east of Tavira). However, in addition to rainfall, most of which falls in the winter half-year, water is available from numerous shallow wells through the use of simple water-lifting devices, chiefly the *nora*. This mechanism consists of an endless chain of pots or buckets dipping into a shallow well and pouring the water either into a storage tank or directly into a lead to the irrigation canals. The endless chain is rotated by a shaft with cogs, meshing into slots attached to a horizontal pole, which is swung round by an animal treading a path encircling the mouth of the well.

The *nora* (*noria*, in Spain) that is used in the Algarve was probably introduced by the Moslems. Another type, with a longer shaft and designed to lift water from streams, may have been used in the peninsula during the Roman period. A third and more primitive type was probably copied after that of the Carthaginians in Sardinia.[4]

[4] Jorge Dias and Fernando Galhano, *Aparelhos de elevar a água de rega*, pp. 191–204.

A *nora* being repaired.

Easily available water and warmth make this area remarkably productive. From east of Tavira westward to Faro—especially near the latter, where irrigation is used most intensively, and 90 per cent of the product comes from irrigated gardens—are luxuriant fields, with maize, white potatoes, sweet potatoes, beans, tomatoes, cabbage (of several varieties), capsicum, cucumbers, peas, broad beans, melons, squash, watermelons, and peanuts. In addition to the truck crops, orchards of oranges, lemons, tangerines, peaches, pears, plums, and apricots are common; medlars and pomegranates are frequently seen as random individuals but never planted as orchards. Occasionally maize shares the irrigation of the oranges, but interplanting with the carefully cultivated irrigated orchards is unusual. A Sotaventano tends his farm carefully and expects the maximum from it. On irrigated land two crops a year are minimum, five crops in two years are common, and three crops in one year are possible under the best conditions.

The harvest season spans the entire year. The five months from November through March are less productive than the other seven but

A "modern" *nora*.

some green vegetable is available in each month of the year, and cabbage of one variety or another is available throughout the year in addition. Not only in the Algarve, but throughout Portugal, the cabbage is ever-present and very important in the diet. At least one fresh fruit is to be had in every month also: citrus in winter, medlars in April, apricots in May, plums and pears in June, peaches, grapes, and melons in July, figs in August, and in the peak harvest month of September and through the autumn the Sotaventano is offered a great latitude of choice.

The present intensity of agriculture would not be possible without copious use of fertilizers, mostly ammonium sulphate, superphosphate, and animal manures. Lupine, rough-pea, clover, and vetch are all planted as green manures. Fish meal, available but expensive, is usually passed over in favor of the cheaper chemical fertilizers.

The agricultural calendar[5] of the Sotavento as shown on the follow-

[5] The information for the agricultural calendar and information with regard to rotations was given to me at the Posto Agrário do Sotavento, in Tavira.

ing pages includes the most important crops. The dots represent the periods of planting; the short vertical lines show the periods of harvest. It goes without saying that many other crops are grown, many more vegetables and fruits. However, they do not have the importance of those shown on the calendar and, in general, they do not appear at times different from those shown for vegetables and fruits, respectively.

In the Sotavento, especially in the area of Faro, some farms are worked by renters. The fixed cash rent is decided at the beginning of the contract period and any surplus belongs to the renter. Payment is usually made in two parts, one in midsummer and one near the end of fall. Salaried workers and share workers are in the minority. Many women work in the fields of the Sotavento, largely because of the extent of irrigation and the intensity of cultivation, which provide more tasks fitted to women's capacities.

In the intensively cultivated, irrigated plots of the Sotavento, maize is fundamental and cereals usually rotate with white potatoes. Very commonly one finds a rotation in which white potatoes are followed by maize, or one in which wheat is followed by sweet potatoes and string beans. For example, near Faro imported white seed potatoes are planted around the edge and along parallel mounds within a small rectangular plot. In March, at the time of the weeding and cultivation of the potatoes, maize is interplanted in the trenches between the potato mounds. Potatoes are harvested about mid-April. In August, when the leaves are being stripped from the maize, either cabbage or beans are put in to be harvested in December. Or there might be a slight variation from this combination in a two-year rotation: first year, potatoes, then maize with beans, followed by cabbage or potatoes again; second year, wheat followed by sweet potatoes and beans.

An intensive, small house garden near Vila Real had the following system of rotation. In three plots, tomatoes, string beans, and sweet potatoes, respectively, were planted in the winter. In spring, maize was planted in both the plot of string beans and that of sweet potatoes, before the earlier crop was harvested. On the land where tomatoes had grown, several small crops were planted including cucumbers, melons, watermelons, and capsicum. The late summer and autumn planting in-

62

AGRICULTURAL CALENDAR OF THE SOTAVENTO

(DOTS REPRESENT PLANTING; VERTICAL BARS REPRESENT HARVEST)

THE MOST IMPORTANT IRRIGATED GARDEN CROPS

Crop	Jan	Feb	Mar	Apr	May	Jun	Jul	Aug	Sep	Oct	Nov	Dec
MAIZE		•	••••	••••	••••	•••		▌▌▌	▌▌▌▌▌			
POTATO		•••	•••••••	•••	▌▌▌	▌▌▌▌▌	▌▌▌▌					
SWEET POTATO					••••••	••••••	••••••	▌▌▌▌▌	▌▌▌▌	▌▌▌▌▌	▌▌▌▌	▌▌
GREEN BEAN		•••••	••••••	••••	••••	••••	••••	•••	▌▌▌▌	▌▌▌▌	▌▌▌▌	▌▌
CABBAGE (several varieties)	▌▌▌ ••••	▌▌▌ ••••	▌▌▌ ••••	▌▌▌ ••••	▌▌▌ ••••	▌▌▌ ••••	▌▌▌ ••••	▌▌▌ ••••	▌▌▌ ••••	▌▌▌ ••••	▌▌▌ ••••	▌▌▌ ••••
TOMATO	•••••	•••••	•••••	••••	••••	•••		▌▌▌▌	▌▌▌▌	▌▌▌▌	▌▌▌	
PEA (Pisum sativum)						•••	•••••			▌▌▌	▌▌▌▌▌	▌▌
BROAD BEAN (Vicia faba)	▌▌▌▌▌	▌▌▌▌▌	▌▌▌			•••	•••••			▌▌▌	▌▌▌▌	▌▌▌▌
MELON			••	••••••		▌▌▌▌	▌▌▌▌▌	▌▌▌				
CUCUMBER		•••	••••••		▌▌▌▌▌	▌▌▌						
WATER MELON		••	••••••			▌▌▌▌	▌▌▌▌	▌▌▌				
SQUASH		•••	••••••		▌▌	▌▌▌▌	▌▌▌▌	▌▌▌▌	▌▌▌▌			
PEANUT				••••••	••••••	•••		▌▌▌▌	▌▌▌▌	▌▌▌		

THE MOST IMPORTANT IRRIGATED TREE CROPS

Crop	Jan	Feb	Mar	Apr	May	Jun	Jul	Aug	Sep	Oct	Nov	Dec
ORANGE	▌▌▌▌▌	▌▌▌▌▌								▌▌▌▌▌	▌▌▌▌▌	▌▌▌▌▌
PEACH						▌▌▌▌▌	▌▌▌▌					
PLUM						▌▌▌▌	▌▌▌▌▌	▌▌▌				
PEAR						▌▌▌▌	▌▌▌▌	▌▌▌▌	▌▌▌	▌▌▌		
APRICOT					▌▌▌	▌▌▌▌▌	▌▌▌					

AGRICULTURAL CALENDAR OF THE SOTAVENTO

(DOTS REPRESENT PLANTING; VERTICAL BARS REPRESENT HARVEST)

THE MOST IMPORTANT UNIRRIGATED FIELD CROPS

	JANUARY	FEBRUARY	MARCH	APRIL	MAY	JUNE	JULY	AUGUST	SEPTEMBER	OCTOBER	NOVEMBER	DECEMBER
CULTIVATED MEADOW	‖‖‖‖	‖‖‖‖	‖‖‖							•••• ••		
SWEET CLOVER (Melilotus segitalis)			‖‖‖					•• ••••••	•••••• •••			
FENUGREEK (Trigonella foenum graecum)			‖‖ ‖‖‖‖							••••••		
WHEAT					‖‖‖‖‖ ‖‖					••••••	••••••	
BARLEY					‖‖‖‖ ‖‖						••• •••••	
OATS					‖‖‖ ‖‖						••• •••••	
RYE				‖‖ ‖‖‖						•• •••••		
BROAD BEAN (Vicia faba)				‖‖‖‖						•• •••••		
PEA (Pisum sativum)		‖‖‖ ‖‖‖‖	‖‖‖							••• •••		
CHICK-PEA (Cicer arietinum)		•••• ••••••				‖‖ ‖‖‖						
ROUGH-PEA (Lathyrus sativus L.)	••• •••••					‖‖‖‖						
MAIZE		•••• ••••••					‖‖‖‖					

THE MOST IMPORTANT UNIRRIGATED TREE CROPS AND VINES

	JANUARY	FEBRUARY	MARCH	APRIL	MAY	JUNE	JULY	AUGUST	SEPTEMBER	OCTOBER	NOVEMBER	DECEMBER
ALMOND							‖‖‖	‖‖‖‖				
FIG							‖‖‖‖‖	‖‖‖‖‖	‖‖‖			
CAROB							‖‖‖‖	‖‖‖				
OLIVE										‖‖‖‖	‖‖‖‖‖	‖‖‖‖
VINES							‖‖‖	‖‖‖‖‖	‖‖‖			

An Algarvian hand plow.

cluded clover for forage (*Trifolium alexandrinum*), cabbage, and white potatoes in the respective plots.

In a small farm designed to supply the needs for a school near Tavira, the land is insufficient for any of it to be given to the small grains or maize, so the scheme of rotation involves only vegetables, including white and sweet potatoes. In a three-year plan twenty-five vegetables are rotated in three plots. Each of the plots, however, is also divided into four sections. The staggering of planting and gathering is such that both work and production are continuous. With adequate water for irrigation and liberally added chemical fertilizers, high production per unit is persistently maintained.

Through the Sotavento maize enters into the scheme of rotation more commonly than wheat for many reasons, the most important of which is that it makes a better seasonal component in the scheme of rotations. Wheat would eliminate some of the vegetables that fit so neatly into the rotation with maize. There is also the fact that the maize plant can be

65

totally used. The tassel is stripped first and then the leaves, both being highly favored for cattle fodder, leaving the stalk bare except for the ears. After the ears are gathered the stalk is used as bedding for cattle. Mixed with animal excretion, the stalk is ultimately worked back into the land.

Wheat, however, has its own basis of importance. Throughout the last several years, because of a state subsidy, it has yielded a return as high as that of maize, or higher. It completes the requirements of a balanced and accustomed diet. Wheat straw is fed to cattle, mixed with clover, cabbage leaves, alfalfa, or other gathered volunteer greens. As it is cultivated without irrigation, the drying-out of the soil kills many weeds that otherwise would become competitors of the irrigated plants to follow.

Near the village of Luz de Tavira, a carefully cultivated small farm used the following rotation:

	FIRST YEAR				SECOND YEAR		
Crop	% of Plot	Mo. of Plant.	Mo. of Harv.	Crop	% of Plot	Mo. of Plant.	Mo. of Harv.
Plot No. 1							
Maize	25	Mar.	July	Wheat	100	Nov.	June
Potatoes	25	Feb.	June				
String beans	50	Feb.	June				
Potatoes or Beans	25	Aug.	Nov.	Sw. pot.	50	June	Oct.
				Beans and broad	50	June	Sept.
Maize	25	July	Oct.	beans		June	Feb.
Cabbage	50	July	Nov.				
Plot No. 2							
				Maize	25	Mar.	July
Wheat	100	Nov.	June	Potatoes	25	Feb.	June
				Str. beans	50	Feb.	June
Sw. pot.	50	June	Oct.	Potatoes or beans	25	Aug.	Nov.
Beans and broad	50	June	Sept.	Maize	25	July	Oct.
beans		June	Feb.	Cabbage	50	July	Nov.

66

In this system of rotation, beans (to dry) and the vetch that we call broad bean (*Vicia faba*) are planted at the same time, but only the beans are harvested in September. The broad bean may produce a few pods in the autumn, but it is dormant during the winter and harvested generally in February.

Less spectacular than the irrigated lands, but still of importance, are the areas where the four unirrigated trees—olive, carob, almond, and fig—are important on the slightly elevated, calcareous southward projections of the Limestone Zone. Although these trees appear at their best on irrigated bottom lands, other crops are usually more profitable there and relegate them to the rocky slopes.[6] Where they are given premium locations, fine almond groves of special varieties thrive in the Sotavento, including many more varieties than is implied in the farmers' classification in terms of the hardness of the shell: the *durazia* must be cracked with a hammer, the *molar* can be cracked with the teeth, and the *coca* may be cracked between the fingers. Olive groves around Tavira have been famous for centuries and their oil is generally reputed to be the best of the Algarve—a claim disputed by the growers of Monchique. This, however, is not saying a great deal, as is indicated by the fact that the tuna-packing plants of Vila Real import oil from the Alentejo rather than use the local product. Carobs, too, are at their best in the Sotavento; large, fine-looking trees border the roads in some places or follow the field divisions. Nowhere are they dominant in numbers, but individual trees, with spreading green foliage, are a welcome sight, especially in winter when the almond and fig trees are bare.

Figs are less important in the Sotavento than in the west but are not uncommon. As winds are not a danger, they are allowed to grow to full height and become handsome trees. Underplanting is good for them in this area; without it development is precocious and damage by the Mediterranean fruit fly is greatly increased. Peas make a good companion crop, as do chick-peas and small grains.

Not to plant some crop under most trees of the unirrigated lands

---

[6] In the Limestone Zone these trees take a dominant position in the economy; they will be considered more fully in a chapter concerned specifically with that area.

Almonds blooming along a road in the Sotavento.

would be considered a waste of land. This practice is common even under the olive and carob, which are aggressive competitors and do not allow the most successful underplanting. Ordinarily, the associated crop is one of the small grains, commonly wheat, but sometimes oats or barley, and rarely, rye. Occasionally one sees maize and, on the richer soils, chick-peas. Formerly flax was planted, but now it is relegated to the remote mountain areas, where the conservative folk still cultivate it. Broad beans are planted in November, mostly alone but occasionally under trees. Used generally for animal fodder, the beans make excellent food for humans when they are tender, in February, and even after they have been dried they are edible when toasted.

Some of the more prosperous landowners may plant any one of the cultivated crops alone, believing that the total return is more satisfactory. However, such a consideration has really little importance to most Algarvians, for they are small owners interested not only in total return but in a "sheet to the windward." They do not want to hazard

Wheat and figs in the Sotavento. Note the size of the fig trees and the quality of the wheat crop.

the year's support upon the prospect of one crop. Furthermore, they are conservative people who have always planted mixed fields. But perhaps most important, although most of the farmers of the Algarve are men of humble circumstances who could readily use a larger income, to plant merely the best-paying crop would be unthinkable to them. They are permanent residents on the land who assume that their children also will be permanent. Rotation of crops for the well-being of the land is standard practice.

Small vineyards, usually a fraction of an acre each, are increasing in number, and there is a movement on foot to re-establish a wine industry of importance. During the nineteenth and the early part of the twentieth centuries the region most noted for the production of wine grapes in the Algarve was outlined by a line connecting the towns of Fuzeta, Moncarapacho, and Olhão. Fuzeta wine, a semi-sweet claret of high alcoholic content, was once considered outstanding. This opinion is no longer held, and the wine has almost disappeared. The grapes of that area have been mostly replaced by the more profitable fruit trees. Efforts of some Sotaventanos to resuscitate their wine industry have, so far, been relatively ineffectual; as the government controls planting and seems to favor other regions, their hopes at the moment can hardly be high.

On unirrigated land the rotation of small grains (wheat, oats, or barley) with broad beans or chick-peas over a two-year period is common, or, as a variant, small grains may be planted the first year with manure and chemical fertilizers, with broad beans, peas, chick-peas, or maize (in favored locations) following in the second year. Crop positions within the property are changed each year according to plan, so that all parts of the land will be benefited by the rotation system. Also on unirrigated land, legumes may be planted (usually of the genera *Melilotus, Trigonella,* and *Láthyrus*), to be used either as green manures or as fodder.

With such a heterogeneity of crops, seasonal decrease in labor demand is only relative, never complete. In November, after the peak season of autumn, the general care of the land and trees receives more attention; the excavations around the vines, to aerate the soil, may begin; if planting of young trees is planned, almonds and carobs are put out; the producing almond trees are pruned; citrus trees are treated against mildew. The work in the wineries and in the olive-pressing plants is in progress.

In December, in addition to the sowing of some crops (broad beans, peas, wheat, barley, and oats), there is planting of tomatoes and potatoes for the early market, as well as the harvesting of cabbage, potatoes, peas, olives, oranges, and tangerines. Planting of virtually all of the trees, both those that receive irrigation and those that do not, continues. Pruning of almonds is completed and that of vines, olives, peaches, plums, and apricots is commenced. Work in the wineries and olive presses continues.

In January much of the work of December is continued; the application of fertilizers to the vineyards and orchards is begun, and increased attention is given to spraying and other treatments to guard the trees against pests. The concentrated work in the wineries is finished. The earliest of the vegetables are harvested (in the east) to be sent to the large city markets. In February, intensive planting begins and the preparation and transport of early vegetables is in progress. Repair of farm walls, houses, and other structures receives more attention than in earlier months. By March, planting is in full swing, and the intensive agricultural seasons have well begun.

Domestic animals are part of the general economy, but are never more than ancillary to cultivation. Pigs (usually one or two animals) are commonly associated with the family house, and the small amount of meat eaten by an Algarvian of modest means is mostly pork. Farmers say that goats "burn the vegetation," so they are largely relegated to the mountains, where they even browse upon the gum cistus and heather, in their undiscriminating way. Cows are chiefly used for draught, but their milk may be used for cheese. Oxen are of negligible importance, except in the west. The donkey is used as a riding animal for women, for packing, and even for draught. The most valuable work animal is the mule, used commonly for plowing and for pulling carts. Sheep differ not only from those of the rest of Portugal, but somewhat from those of other areas of the Algarve as well. At the eastern edge of the Sotavento, near the Guadiana River, appear the only flocks of pure Merino sheep to be seen in the Algarve, but their number is small compared to that of the long-haired sheep. This animal is at its best in the eastern Algarve; not only does it produce more meat but its coat is considered to be of slightly better quality, and it gives more milk than does the same type of animal in the Barlavento, a situation due to the fact that the animal receives better care here (as do most animals) than in the west. The sheep are kept close to the house and are frequently fed oats, barley, carobs, maize leaves, or the leaves from the broad beans. With such treatment, the male animal may weigh as much as ninety pounds or more.

THE SPECIALIZED AREAS NEAR THE GUADIANA RIVER

Set apart from the Sotavento proper by an infertile and uninhabited area of pines, the small, sandy segment of the Coastal Plain to the west of the mouth of the Guadiana River lies between the

71

Tips of agave leaves placed over young plants to protect them from cold north winds (at Vila Real).

schists of the mountains and the ocean. Its small size (less than four square miles) and its eccentric position would seem to doom it economically, but certain qualities have been exploited to advantage: the area of pines gives protection from sea winds, the sands heat more quickly with spring warmth than do heavier soils, and there is a copious water supply just below the surface. Although this area receives cold outbursts of air from the north in winter,[7] this danger is obviated by giving special protection to the young plants; either low hedges are made by thrusting reeds into the sands, or tops of agave leaves are placed over and to the north of the young plants. The early vegetables, especially tomatoes, from this area enter the markets of Portugal a full two weeks before even those of the rest of the Sotavento. The prices during the early market period may be over ten times that which will

[7] The meteorologic station at Vila Real records the lowest January mean and the lowest mean of the minima for any Algarvian station. These temperatures are due to outbreaks of cold from the interior of the Iberian Peninsula that follow down the Guadiana River Valley.

be received at the end of the season. Such returns pay for the large amounts of commercial fertilizer that must be applied to the otherwise almost sterile sands in which the vegetables are planted.

The labor demand—a large proportion of which is hired by the day— is high here in the early months each year, but following that busy season there is a virtual collapse in the sale of their vegetables; other regions can then produce more cheaply.

Upstream from the mouth of the Guadiana River several small areas have been transformed in their economy in recent years. On lands where the river or its tributaries have deposited alluvium after having cut back the hills, pockets of fertile land, protected against the worst of the winter cold by the elevations surrounding them, and now brought into touch with markets by reason of improved transportation, have gone into specialized production, whereas they were formerly limited mostly to subsistence agriculture. Truck crops, citrus, and vines are now being expanded on the lowlands; above them, lines of fig trees follow the small valleys upslope, and almonds are newly planted. Olives are being planted in specialized groves. Whether it is a dangerous and excessively ambitious scheme, as thought by the Sotavento agronomists, or an opportunity intelligently grasped, as claimed by the farmers, is yet to be known.

THE WESTERN TRANSITION AREA

In sharp contrast to the density of population on the Coastal Plain to the north and east of Faro, there is but a thin scattering of people west of the Faro lagoons to Armação de Pera; in an area almost as long as the Sotavento, the paucity of houses and lack of cultivation is comparable to the situation in the mountains. Like the mountains in another way, this section of the coast plain, in its economy, is conditioned by geology, although different rocks are involved; it is an area of infertile Pliocene sands. In climate it is transitional between the Sotavento and the Barlavento. Occasionally reached by the *levante* from the east it is also affected by the westerlies that are common to the Barlavento. One station, Albufeira, records the greatest range between the hottest and the coldest months of any Algarvian station, a condition due to the warmth of the summer days and nights (similar to the Sotavento stations), and also to outbreaks of winter cold, apparently coming from the Alentejo through the San Marcos Depression.[8] Total rainfall in this area is as low as that at virtually any station of the Algarve—comparable to that of Sagres and Vila do Bispo in the Barlavento.

As might be expected from general infertility of the soils, cold outbreaks in winter, and low rainfall, agriculture is, on the whole, a paltry proposition. Commonly, it is limited to poor plots of maize, wheat, and barley, with an occasional carob or small grove of almonds, olives, or figs, the latter doing better than the others. In small, favored areas where irrigation water is available, citrus, pears, peaches, pomegranates, quinces, and sporadically, medlars, are grown. Near Albufeira specialty crops for export have been successful on a small scale. Early peas are raised for sale in the Limestone Zone as seed peas, or for export to England. Tomatoes are planted in the sands with large amounts of chemical fertilizer, to be picked green and loaded into boats for England, ripening sufficiently on the journey to be sold upon arrival. A part of the crop is sent to Lisbon, and occasionally some tomatoes go to the canneries of Vila Real de Santo António.

THE BARLAVENTO

After a description of the Sotavento little more need be said regarding the Barlavento (beginning east of Portimão and extending to the west coast), for it is equally Algarvian. Some distinctions must be pointed out, however, as it is in some ways, as George Orwell might have said, less equal than in others. For example, in its physical character it is distinct, by reason of its coast line of cliffs through which streams have cut their way to the ocean, building small alluvial fans over the rocky areas at their mouths. This situation is in contrast to that of the unbroken sandy beaches of the Sotavento. Also, in the Barlavento there is a greater proportion of surface made up of limestone (extensions of the limestone region to the north), unsuitable for

---

[8] This assumption, however, is without statistical verification, for there is no station to the north which gives the necessary information.

The cliff coast near Portimão.

premium garden crops, and the water table is farther from the surface. Differences are also apparent in climate as one goes from the Sotavento toward the west. The east wind, the *levante*, scarcely touches the Barlavento. Winds in winter are predominantly from the northwest and in summer from the southwest, but they are of low average velocity in all seasons, because most of the Barlavento is protected by the southern projection of the Cape against westerly winds, and by the mass of Monchique against north winds. Only in the exposed area of the Cape and to the north of it is the force of the winds an important factor.

Temperatures are mild, and fogs, except for the Cape area, are rare. Summer days are warm, but the nights are cooler than those of the Sotavento. A freezing day is almost never recorded in Lagos or Portimão (and never at the Cape). The sheltered position of most of the Barlavento has its drawbacks, however, for the rainfall is considerably less than that of the eastern area of the Coastal Plain. Praia da Rocha,

A water peddler coming from Caldas de Monchique.

near Portimão, records approximately fourteen inches per year in contrast with twenty inches at Tavira. This is a critical difference, and many crops of the Sotavento do not appear in the west.

The low rainfall of the area is indicated by the large number of gathering floors for rainwater next to the houses. Another evidence is that of the water carts that bring water from the springs at Caldas de Monchique to be sold to hotels and to prosperous households, and the carts and wheelbarrows that pick up water from wells or town faucets to distribute it, at a small charge, to ordinary folk without household supplies. Perhaps another evidence of low rainfall (or is it an evidence of lack of enterprise on the part of the population?) is the fact that there is more grazing here than in the more intensively farmed Sotavento; goats and sheep are more numerous, although the animals are not of the same quality. The Feltroso sheep of the Barlavento is relatively small, and has less wool and more hair than the ordinary sheep of the Sotavento.

76

A sheep owner is almost never a landowner. Before he can legally possess a flock, he must have guarantees of grazing rights from landowners. These rights may be based upon payments, or granted because of the improvement of the land brought about by the sheep manure. Under such a contract, it is understood that the rope folds for the animals are to be shifted each night to a new place so that there will be a wide distribution of manure.

However, none of these facts explain the difference in land use between the time of Edrisi in Silves and that of the early twentieth century. After the Moorish period up until the last two generations, agriculture in the Barlavento was somewhat neglected; now, modern engineering is changing the condition of affairs. With the completion of two new dams, one an earth dam on the Arade River above Silves in 1956 and the other of concrete, on the Odiáxere River in 1959, designed to irrigate 4,500 acres of land, a further impulse has been given to intensive farming. New lands are being planted now, creating "gardens" of even greater extent than those of the Arabs. The twentieth century has witnessed a rate of improvement not experienced since that of the Moslem period.

Modern irrigation and intensive land exploitation is due at least in part to the Portuguese desire for land and the willingness to invest in it, even though the return upon investment is negligible. With this predisposition, it is not surprising that men with profit derived in recent years from the sardine industry of Portimão should have invested it in farms and farm development in the Barlavento.

Rotations, on both irrigated and unirrigated land, are essentially the same as those of the Sotavento, with a somewhat larger number of farms limited to two crops per year or to five crops in two years—a situation that is due to the slightly slower rate of growth and maturation in the west. The earlier spring and the greater summer warmth give the Sotavento a half- to a full month's advantage.

The four unirrigated trees typical of the Algarve are all here, but the olive is of minor importance, and the carob diminishes toward the west, both in numbers and in average size of trees. Figs and almonds are well suited to most of the area, although in appearance they are

An irrigated garden, with a sweep (*picôta*) in the foreground.

not comparable to those of the Sotavento, and some of the varieties of almond, important in the east, are not successful here. The figs of the Barlavento, however, are considered to be commercially the best of the Algarve.

In an area to the west of Portimão, the almond is now being planted in increasing numbers; for a few miles to the west of Lagos it rivals the fig in importance. Neither fruit trees nor fruit (quinces, medlars, pomegranates, apricots, pears, and some citrus) have an appearance equal to those of the Sotavento, but the fruits are more flavorful, a virtue deriving from a disadvantage, the lack of irrigation development. In general, crops ripen about fifteen days later than in the Sotavento, and some irrigated vegetables and stone fruits may be tardy by as much as twenty-five days.

Grapes deserve a note, for although Algarvian wine has not had a good reputation because of excessive sweetness and too high alcoholic content to be drunk as a table wine, it is now being improved. In the area extending from Lagoa toward Silves more grapes and wine are produced than in all of the rest of the Algarve. Elsewhere, between Sagres and the Guadiana, small vineyards are scattered, but the total acreage is small. The Barlavento as a whole produces over 85 per cent of the wine made in the province.

Grapes are never irrigated and are planted on bottomlands as well as on low slopes. The lowlands produce a better crop, but the attack of mildew is more damaging. Another problem of the lowland is the fact that much of it is underlain by impermeable clays less than a yard from the surface, and the roots of the vines have inadequate room for growth.

Lagoa is the wine-making center of greatest importance in the Algarve today. Its facilities are relatively new and are being improved and expanded each year. Lagoa's co-operatives are making wines less sweet than the once famous Fuzeta wine. Also, having less alcohol and more tannin, they make satisfactory table wines. Not satisfied with present conditions, the co-operatives are conducting experiments to the end of introducing a variety of additional types. One, a wine designed to compete with or replace Spanish sherry in Portugal, has many of the qualities of an *amontillado* and is quite acceptable.

Farms are relatively small, although somewhat larger than those of the Sotavento, and are worked both by owners and by men working for absentee owners. In the latter case, the association is usually based on shares; the farmer receiving half of the grains and parts of the tree crops varying from one-third to one-sixth. Renters are rare in the Barlavento and salaried workers even more rare, except in the area of the Cape. Fewer women work in the fields in this side of the province as there is less irrigation and garden-type agriculture; proportionately greater time is spent in plowing and in other tasks that are considered to be exclusively masculine.

THE CAPE AREA

Going west from Lagos one sees a landscape that is less typical of the Algarve. Within six miles (near Almadena), the olive and carob are seldom seen, and even the almond, which until then had rivalled the fig, is poorly represented. One small addition, however, can be reported, that of rice fields in the irrigable lowlands southwest of Almadena. Of the four typical unirrigated trees, only figs remain in commercial numbers.

Calcimined white walls, remnants of the Moslem period and common along the roads elsewhere, also are rare. The typical Algarvian scene is replaced by an open landscape of rolling hills covered with wheat, occasional groves of figs and, in each of the widely separated ribbons of drainage, one or more sweeps[9] or *noras,* which mark the small oases with their irrigated maize and fruit trees. These small areas of fertility are established on Triassic marls lying in the lee of hillslopes where the water table is near the surface. The Algarvian vista of houses scattered across the countryside is left behind and Cape area population is concentrated in villages, a scene reminiscent of the Alentejo. Mules or donkeys are rarely seen; in the spring, red-brown, Alentejano oxen draw the plows, and at the time of the harvest large oxcarts are laden with wheat to be threshed.

Beyond Val do Boi there is only an occasional olive or almond, and the carob, which cannot tolerate fog, has disappeared completely. Figs are trimmed close to the ground so that they will not be damaged by the Atlantic winds. From this point westward to the Cape, the climate is noticeably different from that of the rest of the Algarve. The normal temperatures of a summer day in the "moderate-marine" cli-

---

[9] The sweep, called *picôta* or *cegonha* ("stork") in Portugal, is a standard device for lifting water from wells. A sweep pole is pinned not far from one end to an upright or between two uprights. From the longer end a bucket is suspended, while the shorter end is counterbalanced, usually with a heavy rock. The sweep is an ancient device that was used from the Far East to the Atlantic coasts of Iberia. Common in Italy during the Roman period, it was undoubtedly also known in Portugal at that time. The name, *picôta,* probably is derived from the Celtic word *pic,* which describes the fixed uprights of the device. The reason for the use of the word *cegonha* (stork) is obvious (See Jorge Dias and Fernando Galhano, *Aparelhos de elevar a água de rega,* pp. 219–220).

The Celtic basis of the word *picôta* may obviously suggest the existence of the device in the peninsula prior to Roman times, although such a conclusion would need further evidence.

Figs of the Barlavento in winter.

matic subregion of the Cape are several degrees lower than those of Lagos (and vice versa in winter). At Budens and Figueira are strips of cultivation where the last few almond trees are to be seen and the figs are trimmed even closer to the ground than at Val do Boi. The red Triassic outcrop here is near the southern shore, and just beyond it, to the north, are the mountain schists with their cover of gum cistus. Another little settlement, Raposeira, is followed by Vila do Bispo, which has grown to be the most important settlement in the Cape area because of its advantages of water, soils, and wind protection. Still beyond, after passing slopes devoid even of the sparse crop of grain, is Sagres, the settlement connected in history and by Camões with Prince Henry the Navigator. Its few houses do not make a very prepossessing scene. Around them are small plots of maize, wheat, potatoes, and occasionally other vegetables, and many inhabitants own other agricultural lands outside of the town. Here the figs are trimmed so close to the ground that they have the appearance of sprawling

81

Figs and wheat near Cape S. Vicente.

shrubs and are hardly recognizable as trees. Also trimmed close to the
surface of the land are vines, from whose grapes a type of claret is made
for local consumption, which has more tannin and less sugar than most
Algarvian wines. Cane windbreaks are stuck into the sand to protect
the most vulnerable plants against the winds.

Over a century ago it was reported that this area was poor and that
most of its inhabitants worked on land belonging to absentee owners;
this situation still obtains. One plowman reported that he tilled the land
for an owner who paid him a daily wage of eleven escudos (a little less
than $.40 U.S.) plus a very little flour, olive oil, and bacon. He also
stated that even the pitifully meagre crop of wheat now grown would
be entirely impossible without the use of commercial fertilizers. Yet
the area may once have been more productive. Leite de Vasconcellos
wrote that the vestiges of *quintas* (country houses) and the reports of
early times indicated that it was the *celeiro* (granary) of the Algarve.[10]
If it was as productive as such description would imply, destructive

[10] J. Leite de Vasconcellos, *Etnografia Portuguesa*, III, 638.

The Bay of Sagres.

exploitation, as represented by the gullying around the settlement of Sagres, has debased its quality. In a sense, it is still a granary—at least it is that rarity in the Lower Algarve, a specialized grain area—but the result of cultivation hardly justifies the ordinary implications of the term.

North of the town of Vila do Bispo, in 1959, there were areas planted to maize. The crop was approximately full grown at an average height of about three feet. Only people at the lower edge of subsistence could think of expending their effort for such a result.

Even more than the rest of the Barlavento this is an area of catchment floors for rain. Each house of any pretensions has such a floor alongside it, where the water is kept from its otherwise quick percolation through the limestones.

West of Sagres the dolomites of Point Sagres and Cape S. Vicente, standing nearly 250 feet above the ocean at the southwesternmost point of Europe, break off in vertical cliffs along fault lines. Aside from occasional fields of wheat, the only evidence of economic activities is the fishermen, who beach their small boats in the sheltered coves where erosion has worn away the marls and marly limestones between spurs of dolomite.

The westward diminution of cultivation along the coast is due partly to the nature of the soils, for the alluvial materials common to the coastal area of the rest of the Algarve are replaced by calcareous rocks or schists. Of equal importance in the situation are climatic factors. This small area is the only part of the Algarve that can be called "moderate-marine" and to which the Köppen symbol of *Csb* can be properly applied. In virtually all respects, the stations of the Cape area are moderate.[11] Total rainfall, however, is not high (Cape S. Vicente, sixteen inches; Sagres, fourteen inches; and Vila do Bispo, fourteen inches), but it comes as drizzle throughout a large number of hours. Winds, dominantly from the north, are persistent in summer and calms are rare during any part of the year. The effect of the Coriolis force upon the surface waters is such that they move offshore and are replaced by colder waters from below.[12] The effect of this cold water upon the air drifting over it toward the shore is to chill the lower surface and produce summer fogs, notable in the region of Cape S. Vicente.

The geologic and climatic characteristics are reflected in the natural vegetation. Long ago Willkomm recognized the distinction of the area when he said that all of the Algarve was Andalusian except the Cape, which was unique in its large number of endemics and also of Ibero-Mauritanian species. Furthermore, even those species that are typical of the area, but also found elsewhere, appear on the Cape in unique

[11] This is due to their oceanic position but also to the fact that a branch of the Gulf Stream affects temperatures, especially in winter, so that sea temperatures at Sagres are 6° F. higher than air temperatures. Records of the three stations show: the highest daily mean temperatures for January, the highest mean minimum, the lowest mean for the hottest month, the lowest mean maximum, never a full day below freezing at the Cape. Only in three qualities could they be said to be other than moderate: in the persistence of rain in winter, winds through much of the year, and seasonal fog.

[12] *World Atlas of Sea Surface Temperatures*, H.O. No. 225, published by the Hydrographic Office of the United States Navy. Sea temperature charts for July, August, and September; Gerhard Schott, *Geographie des Atlantischen Ozeans*, Tafel XVIII, Surface Temperatures for August.

Wheat and trees in the western area of persistent winds north of Cape S. Vicente.

forms, in adaptations to the dry soils and strong winds: dwarfed stature, resinous leaves, tubercles, and red pigmentation.[13]

North of Sagres and Vila do Bispo, near the west coast, three Algarvian settlements are semi-isolated from the remainder of the Algarve. In appearance, they seem to be transitional between the Algarve and the Alentejo. The lands that are cultivated by their inhabitants are but modestly endowed. Fogs, particularly in the summer months, are dense and frequent. Wind, strong in summer, blows almost incessantly and has slanted the trees so that some have the appearance of banners flying in the wind. Small crops of grains growing in areas cleared of gum cistus

[13] For example, *Stauracanthus spectabilis*, var. Vicentinus, and *Cistus landaniferus*, var. latifolius. These two dominant species are accompanied by *Ulex erinaceus* and *Thymus algarbiensis* and, at the extremity of the Cape, by *Astragalus massiliensis*.

M. Willkomm, *Grundzüge der Pflanzenverbreitung auf der Iberischen Halbinsel* (*Die Vegetation der Erde*, ed. A. Engler and O. Drude). Trans. for the *Boletim da Sociedade Broteriana* of Coimbra as "As Regiões botánicas de Portugual," p. 118.

Mariano Feio, *Le bas Alentejo et L'Algarve*, p. 164.

Wheat harvested near Sagres.

(*Cistus ladaniferus*) can be grown for only brief periods of years, following long periods of fallow. The most southern of the three settlements, Carrapateira, a dejected village, is perched on a spur of schist above coastal sands where the water table near the surface allows irrigation through the use of the sweep and the *nora*. Dunes and artificial windbreaks to the seaward give necessary protection against the persistent winds. With copious additions of chemical fertilizers these sands yield grains, fruits, and vegetables. Bordeira, a village to the north of Carrapateira, lives on the produce of intensively cultivated garden plots in the irrigable lower reaches of its stream. To the north of Bordeira is the area of Alfambra, where recent exploitation has led to the dispersal of houses on small farms on a southward extension of the Aljezur graben, where the sweep and *nora* supply irrigation water from shallow wells.

Before history was written, the Phoenicians chose the Cape as the site of a shrine to their God, Melkart; to Portugal of the time of Prince Henry the Navigator it became an area of major interest; and, later, presumably as an afterglow from the period of discoveries, it was deemed a granary. But politics and routes have changed again; the area is now bypassed by new highways important to national affairs. In any of the struggling settlements which cling to a precarious existence—those most remote places in the most westerly part of a province that the Arabs called "The West"—one has the feeling that this is Ultima Thule. What a contrast exists between this area of stark struggle and the Barlavento, where improvements in land use are now being made and where one recognizes the promise of even more efficient exploitation. When one tries to draw comparisons between the Cape and the Sotavento he is completely at a loss: comparison is no longer possible. The lush productivity and high efficiency of the latter area calls for terms that have no application in the most western West.

3. Fishermen and Fishing Towns

▼▲▼▲▼▲▼▲▼▲▼▲▼▲▼▲▼▲▼▲▼▲▼▲▼▲▼▲▼▲▼▲▼▲▼▲▼▲▼

Fishing as a way of life is strong upon Portuguese fishermen; near the bottom of the economic scale, they cling to their profession in spite of hazards and meagre returns. When there is no fishing, many of them beg rather than try another method of making a living. Such an attitude is perhaps not surprising when one realizes the antiquity of this way of life. Fishing and the evaporation of salt for the preservation of the catch may be the oldest commercial enterprises of Portugal; and the region of greatest antiquity in these activities is that of the south coast, the Algarve. It was along this stretch of coast that Phoenicians established their fishing and salt-evaporating bases, perhaps as long ago as one thousand years before the Christian era. Their successors and relatives, the Carthaginians, continued and expanded the enterprise,[1] and

[1] António García y Bellido, "Colonización Púnica," *Historia de España*, Tomo I, Vol. II, Part 3, map p. 315. This map shows nine Punic bases on the Algarvian coast from about Sagres to Cacela. See also pp. 380, 385.

Two tunas were the emblem on money of the ancient Phoenician settlement of

88

the activity has probably continued much in the same way and in many of the same places ever since that time.

Some of the gear presently used seems to be in direct descent from that ancient period. In fact, the most elaborate apparatus now used for fishing on this coast, the fixed net for tuna (*Thunnus thynnus*), probably harks back in its essential design to that of the Carthaginians,[2] who also caught these accommodating fish which swim so regularly by the same stretch of shallow water in their yearly migration. That the same sort of apparatus was used during Moslem times is obvious from the fact that early Portuguese used the name *almadrava*, derived from Arabic, for it—and the word in its Spanish form, *almadraba*, is still used in Spain.

After the reconquest of the south of Portugal from the Moslems, the Portuguese kings recognized the value of the enterprise. In the fifteenth century Prince Henry the Navigator received rights to the fishing of tuna in the Algarve.[3] Except for some small improvements introduced by Sicilian and Genovese fishermen in the nineteenth century,[4] the modern Algarvian fixed nets are probably much like those used by the Punic peoples. In the early twentieth century nineteen nets were operating on the Algarvian coast, distributed from almost as far west as Cape S. Vicente to nearly the mouth of the Guadiana River on the east.[5] Now there are only five, and if the trend in catch over the last half-dozen

---

Cádiz in Spain. See Mario Lyster Franco, "A pesca do atum na costa do Algarve," *Correio do Sul,* p. 6.

[2] Oppian, a Greek poet of the end of the second century A.D., in his *Halieutica,* described nets "set forth in the waves like a city, and the net has its gate-warders and gates withal and inner courts. And swiftly the tunnies sweep on . . . and rich and excellent is the spoil." See *Oppian Colluthus Tryphiodorus,* p. 401.

Phoenician fishermen sacrificed the first tuna caught each year to the God of the Sea to seek his protection. At the present time, the company owning the tuna net off Cape Santa Maria sends the money received for the first two tuna caught each year to two religious orders in the Algarve. To gain further auspices, the great net is never taken to sea without first being blessed by the priest. See António Miguel Galvão, *Um século de história de pescarias do Algarve,* 2nd ed., pp. 92, 135.

[3] Henrique da Gama Barros, *História da administração pública em Portugal nos seculos XII a XV,* 2nd ed., IX, 275.

[4] António Miguel Galvão, *Um Século de História,* p. 29.

[5] *Ibid.,* p. 112.

years is continued they will soon all be permanently dismantled. The most westerly net now is that fixed off Cape Santa Maria.

Tuna fishing along the Algarve

Tuna come from the Atlantic toward the Mediterranean Sea to spawn during May and June; then, during July and August, they reverse direction and swim back toward the ocean. Passing near the south coasts of Europe in approximately the same locations on each lap of the journey, they can be guided into the great fixed traps from which they are taken out into boats for delivery to the packing plants on shore.

By governmental regulation, the net at Cape Santa Maria is allowed to fish only the eastward passage of the tuna (unless under extraordinary conditions special permission is given to fish the return journey). Four other nets are regularly set out each year: one at Livramento, halfway between the Cape and Tavira, one at Luz, another at Medo de Cascas, near Tavira, and the most easterly at Abóbora, near Conceição de Tavira, almost midway between Tavira and Vila Real de Santo António. These four nets to the east of the Cape are used for both directions of the tuna. They are set opening toward the Atlantic in April and remain in this position through May and June up until about St. John's day, on June 24 (traditionally said to be the last day of the eastward catch). In July and August, the position of the nets is changed to catch the fish on their return from spawning when they are headed toward the open ocean. As the tuna swim closer to the eastern shore of the Algarve on their outward journey than they do on their inward passage, these four nets make their largest catch in the late summer. Unfortunately, after the ardors of a long journey along the Mediterranean and spawning, the fish are reduced in weight, and particularly in fat, so that the catch is not valued as greatly as that of the earlier months (usually not much over half the value).

One of these elaborate apparatuses for taking tuna consists of more than six miles of net occupying over fifteen hundred acres of water surface and using over forty miles of steel cable. Hundreds of great bower anchors fix it to the ocean bottom about four to five miles off shore, while thousands of cork floats maintain the upper edge near the

90

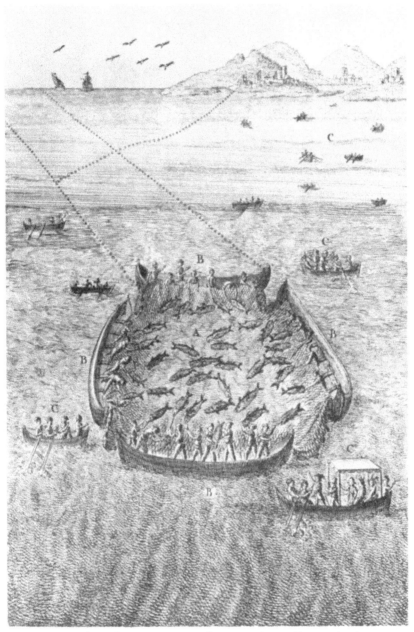

The last chamber of a tuna net as shown in Sañez Reguart's *Diccionario histórico de las artes de la pesca nacional*, published in Madrid, 1791–1795.

surface. The expense of such an apparatus is not only great at the outset but its depreciation is nearly 50 per cent each year.[6] Luckily, until recent years, these fish have been not only accommodating in their habits but large in size—commonly individuals weigh over one hundred and twenty-five pounds and may weigh over three hundred. Furthermore, their value per pound is relatively high.[7]

The great fixed net has two arms, which arch away from each other, one toward the open sea and the other toward the shore; each is from three thousand to ten thousand feet in length and reaches for about one hundred feet down into the water. Swimming between them, the tuna enter a chamber divided into three compartments. Two men are stationed in a small boat outside the first compartment to close it with a net after a school of tuna has entered. Another pair of men in a small boat are stationed within the second compartment to close the opening there and drive the fish toward the last compartment. After the fish have entered, the end compartment is sealed with a double net: the outer one blocking egress, and the inner one, which is beneath the fish, being lifted to bring them to the surface. Then, crowded together, yet swimming rapidly round in circles in their terror, the fish are gaffed by men standing on a platform just above water level. A short hook, attached to the man's arm by a loop over his wrist, is sufficient to guide the fish, as it jumps out of the water in its agony, over the edge of the platform and into a small boat stationed beyond. The scene is a graceful although sanguinary ballet.

VILA REAL DE SANTO ANTÓNIO

The product of Portugal's most ancient industry is handled by Portugal's least typical city. In a country where a city of less than five hundred years of age is an upstart, Vila Real de Santo António is an infant less than two centuries old, and in a country where straight streets are uncommon, it has a perfect grid pattern. Its present vigor and economic strength may be more a matter of fortuitous circumstances than

---

[6] *Ibid.*, p. 149.

[7] Twice the average value per pound of all fish caught by Portuguese fishermen through the decade 1949–1958.

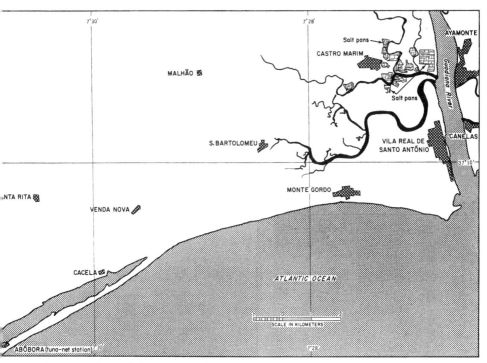

Coast at Vila Real de Santo António.

good judgment, for the Marquis of Pombal, who ordered the city built on a stretch of unoccupied sands in the latter part of the eighteenth century, could not foresee the advent of large, steam vessels, the discovery of the pyrites mine at Santo Domingos, the development of fish canning, and that of modern transportation, the latter making possible the delivery of early vegetables to the Lisbon market.

In 1773 the construction of the new city was started, by orders of the Marquis, on the right bank of the Guadiana River, in spite of the opposition of the towns already long settled in the area: Castro Marim, Cacela, and Monte Gordo.[8] These older settlements feared that their im-

[8] Francisco Xavier d'Athaide Oliveira, *Monografia do concelho de Villa Real de Santo António*, p. 76. The Marquis was a powerful and determined minister who reorganized the Portuguese state. It was he who took charge of the chaotic situation in Lisbon when the earthquake of 1755 destroyed a large part of the city, and who ordered the rebuilding of the present business section according to the grid pattern.

portance would be diminished by Pombal's new city, as subsequent events have demonstrated to be true. However, their protests were unavailing, for Pombal was powerful and ruthless and his city was completed by 1776. The reasons for his establishment of the city were varied and perhaps not all known. The situation, however, as it existed prior to the foundation was dangerous for Portugal politically and disadvantageous economically. Fishermen, largely non-Portuguese, were living in this remote corner of the country formerly claimed by Spain, exploiting a valuable resource but avoiding the payment of taxes to the Portuguese government.[9] Their catch was delivered to Ayamonte, on the Spanish side of the stream, where it was processed and sold. Pombal gave the inhabitants of the nearby settlement of Monte Gordo the opportunity of moving to the new city but they refused almost to a man, most of the foreigners and some of the Portuguese moving into Spain. Its huts were burned by order of the government and for some generations Monte Gordo was virtually out of existence.

The Pombal government expended a good deal of energy encouraging settlement in the newly founded city of Vila Real; to give it a sound economic base, several more or less official fishing companies were established and, in addition, three private concerns. The fishing companies did well, averaging 25 per cent of the gross income as profit to the shareholders during the first forty years of existence. Pombal established a paying enterprise. He brought order out of the confused and conflicting taxes and reduced their total to a maximum of 20 per cent. He also brought order to salt production so that adequate supplies were available to the fishing companies. Of greatest importance, probably, was the fact that profits which formerly had been taken out of the country, now remained in Portugal.[10]

The city itself, however, did not succeed. Conservative, simple people do not give up their old homes and their native towns casually; the arbitrarily founded settlement, of design strange to the region, and with

---

[9] *Ibid.*, p. 74. The word villa is sometimes spelled with one *l* and sometimes with two. One *l* is used on modern maps for the name of this city. In subsequent references to the city it will be called by its short name, Vila Real.

[10] See António Miguel Galvão, *Um século de História*, p. 40.

some imported settlers, antagonized the dwellers in the anciently rooted towns nearby. Their competition, to some extent, counterpoised the weight of the minister. However, although Vila Real was not the bright success that Pombal had hoped it would be, it did not go out of existence; early in the nineteenth century it was described as a gloomy, silent, seemingly deserted city, in the midst of a sandy desert.[11] Nevertheless, it was one of the major fishing centers of the Algarve,[12] even though it was then, and continued to be, a dull and seemingly unpromising place.[13]

In addition to its original difficulties, other troublesome events—a French invasion, a plague, and an earthquake—added to its distress. Only in the latter half of the nineteenth century did it finally achieve the success that Pombal intended for it; this was first brought about by the discovery of the pyrites mine at Santo Domingos to the north, the product of which is shipped through Vila Real. Steamships found the deep scoured side of the Guadiana River at Vila Real suitable for dockage, whereas the harbor of Tavira, formerly the most important of the eastern Algarve, was not. In 1865, an Italian, wanting to export tuna to Italy, established the first canning plant, using Italian olive oil.[14] With the further development of the canning and salting of tuna, the importance of the city grew until now it is the first port of the Algarve in terms of tonnage handled; although the bulk of that tonnage is made up of pyrites from Santo Domingos, the packing and sale of tuna is of fundamental importance to the life of the city. Its factories include those which pack fish in oil, others for the preparation of fish in salt,

[11] H. F. Link, *Voyage en Portugal*, II, 155–156.

[12] Adrien Balbi, *Essai statistique sur le royaume de Portugal et d'Algarve*, I, 138.

[13] In 1850, another author described the city as being a sad place, with grass growing in the streets and with poorly cultivated environs. See Charles Bonnet, *Algarve (Portugal) Description géographique et géologique de cette province*, p. 105.

[14] António Miguel Galvão, *Um século da história*, p. 81; Vicente M. M. C. Almeida d'Eca, "As pescas em Portugal," *Notas sobre Portugal*, I, 280.

And the interest of the Italians has continued. Three of the tuna-packing plants of the city are now owned by them, and Italy buys an important part of the product. See Gaetano Ferro, "Ricerche di geografia urbana nell'Algarve (Portogallo): Faro e Vila Real de Santo António," *Annali di ricerche e studi di geografia*, Anno X, N. 2 (Aprile–Giugno) 1954, p. 66.

and still others which furnish accessories to the fish-packing plants. These industries normally handle about two-thirds of the tuna caught along the Algarvian coast—which is the tuna area of Portugal—and export a major part of it to Italy. Handling such a large proportion of the tuna makes the city the natural center for the control of the industry, and all fish caught in the fixed nets must pass through its auction rooms, no matter where they may later be taken for packing.

Sale and packing of tuna

The arrival of the carrier boats bringing in the loads of tuna from the net is announced by whistles, and the buyers' agents come to the dock to survey the loads. Judging the size and fatness of the fish by eye alone, a skilled tuna buyer, it is said, can estimate its weight up to three hundred pounds, with a maximum of four-to-five-pounds error. After all possible buyers have had an opportunity to estimate the value of each boatload, the auction is announced by a second blast of the whistles. The system of auction has not changed in its fundamentals in recent generations, although the prices are now shown on an electrically controlled board in the front of the room instead of being called by the auctioneer. The price shown is for one dozen tuna and, as originally posted by the auctioneer, is presumably well above any conceivable bid, for it is reduced quickly by small amounts until a buyer signifies his purchase of the entire boatload by pressing a button on his desk. After a boatload of fish has been bought the whistle is blown at the factory whose representative has made the purchase, and its employees, men and women, recognizing the note peculiar to the factory, come from their homes to begin work.

The income of tuna fishermen depends upon the catch and the prices received at public auction, as they receive a percentage of the value. This percentage is high for the tuna fishermen (compared to that paid to sardine fishermen, for example) as their season is comparatively short, but the figure varies from company to company and may change during the season. In general, the average tuna fisherman, prior to the late years of bad catch, made from two thousand to twenty-five hundred escudos ($70 to $87.50 U.S.) each month of the season; but after the tuna season only a small number of these men were used on purse seiners and there was little for them to do during much of the year.

From the fisherman's allotment (and that of the companies) various subtractions are made, e.g., 7 per cent for the national government, about the same percentage for the national Fisherman's Foundation (Casa dos Pescadores), the principal function of which is to provide limited medical insurance to the fishermen, and lesser percentages for the fishermen's mutual (disaster insurance), and the local chamber of commerce. The figures are not the same for all ports and all years. The total may reach 25 per cent but usually it does not amount to more than 18 or 19 per cent of the value of the catch. This figure seems cruelly high but compare it to a statement made in the year 1790:

Little remains of his catch to the fisherman. For example, having arrived at shore—he pays at least one-fifth of the value of the catch in taxes; of the remaining four parts, two are paid to the owners of the nets; of the two remaining, one is divided between the religious brotherhoods (confrarias) and the religious orders of N. Senhora do Carmo, N. Senhora de S. Francisco, and Santo António. So finally the fisherman has one fifth remaining for himself. But as it is necessary for him to sell the product fresh to the buyers, mule trains buy it at low prices (they must pay low prices because they must pay for the maintenance of the mule trains and also taxes to the town where they make their purchase as well as to the town where they sell their load).[15]

Vila Real is the most specialized settlement on the Algarvian coast. Its factories and its fishermen have been occupied almost exclusively with three pelagic fish:[16] tuna (Thunnus thynnus), sardine (Sardina pilchardus), and anchovy (Engraulis encrasicholus), all fish that can be handled by the town's relatively modern packing plants. The city takes first place each year in the landings of blue-fin tuna and anchovies

[15] See Constantino Botelho de Lacerda Lobo, "Memoria sobre a decadencia das pescarias de Portugal," Memorias economicas de academia real das sciencias de Lisboa, Tomo IV, p. 358.

[16] That is, fish that spend a large part of their lives swimming in the upper layers of the water, as opposed to demersal, or bottom-living fish.

(the lion's share), and, in 1959, it took second place in number of purse-seiners and in the value of their catch.[17] It is the tuna-packing center of the country; formerly supplied entirely by its own catch, several bad years at the end of the fifties have led to recent import of fish caught off the Moroccan coasts to supply its factories.[18] In late years, particularly since the catch of tuna has diminished, Vila Real has packed increasing amounts of sardines. This interest harks back to its activity at the beginning of the twentieth century[19] and by 1960 this eastern industrial region was packing almost a quarter of the annual Algarvian total. Because of the decrease in catch of tuna, toward the end of the fifties Vila Real showed a surprising interest also in demersal fish; in 1959 it took an important position in the catch of red mullet (*Mullus barbatus*), sole (*Solea solea*), dogfish (*Mustelus mustelus*), and rays (*Raia spp*). Apparently the fishermen of the city are trying to diversify their industry.[20]

[17] Sardines and anchovies are mostly caught in purse-seines. The most important center for them is Portimão. The ships and the nets will be described in connection with that port.

Landings do not necessarily mean processing, although the figures are generally indicative. Truckers come to Vila Real from other packing centers, especially from Olhão, to buy fish for their home plants.

[18] In 1960, the catch of blue-fin tuna was 22 per cent higher than the previous year but, because of a small catch of other types of tuna, the total was only slightly better than that of the earlier year.

For this information, and for much other information and advice, I am grateful to Captain Melo de Carvalho, Director of the Office of Fisheries of the Ministry of Marine, Lisbon.

[19] In the early years of this century sardines were three times as important as tuna by value, and the chief support of the city. See Francisco Xavier d'Athaide Oliveira, *Villa Real*, pp. 171–172.

[20] The interest in anything more than tuna, anchovies, and sardines has been late in coming. In 1959, when I asked a fisherman at Vila Real about a fishing boat then at work on the Guadiana River, just off the city, he answered without looking at the boat, "They are Spaniards." Such a state of affairs is a continuation of that reported in 1790, but at that early date even Portuguese coast tuna of this area were being handled by Spaniards. See Constantino Botelho de Lacerda Lobo, "Memoria sobre o estado das pescarias da costa do Algarve no anno de 1790," *Memorias ecónomicas da Academia Real das Sciencias de Lisboa*, V, 137.

Rather than make numerous citations with regard to the statistics used in this

PORTIMÃO

Perhaps there was a settlement on or near the site of the present city of Portimão in ancient times. Its protected position, over a mile upstream from the cliffs that stand on either side of the mouth of the Arade-Odelouca waterway and at the lowest place on the stream where a crossing could be conveniently made, is one of obvious advantage. Even though there are no known records of settlement in this exact location, the scholars who claim that there must have been one are not arguing without reason.

Nevertheless, settlement on the site may have been originally made during the fifteenth century. In 1466 Affonso V gave a license for a passenger ferry to be operated across the river at the "place of Portimão" (*logar de* Portimão).[21] The same king, ten years later, referred to the

chapter, it is simpler to say that the *Estatística das pescas marítimas* from 1947 through 1959 have been used for fish landings at the various ports (pp. 12–13), for gear (pp. 18–41, 44–48), for boats in use (pp. 52–53), for registered fishermen according to the gear used (pp. 56–57), and for local boat building (p. 58). The pages cited may differ slightly from year to year; those used above are taken from the 1959 volume (the volumes are published by the Ministério da Marinha at the Imprensa Nacional in Lisbon).

For industries in general, their employees, fixed capital, and remuneration, the *Estatística Industrial of 1958* (pp. xix, 58–66) has been used. This volume gives statistics for the four major regions of the Algarve: Lagos, Portimão, Olhão, and Vila Real de Santo António. Such generalization omits certain facts as to fish packing in less important fish-packing cities such as Faro and Tavira, but the fundamental conditions are given. For this information, however, another source is helpful, the *Inquérito Industrial, Distrito de Faro, 1957*. This volume gives statistics by counties (concelhos), but again, the information relates in almost all cases to the one important industrialized city of the area.

The last two volumes mentioned are published by the Instituto Nacional de Estatística (Bertrand [Irmãos], Lda.), Lisbon.

In the case of all of these volumes, the date of release is usually more than a year after the finish of the year considered.

[21] João Baptista da Silva Lopes, *"Corográfia" ou memoria económica, estadística e topográfica do Reino do Algarve*, p. 267.

For the historical geography of the Algarve, this author is very useful. For his time, he had gathered a large part of the material available. He is, of course, especially valuable for the period of time just prior to the mid-nineteenth century. Rather than multiply the citations from this work, it is probably better to list here

New Villa of Portimão (Vila Nova de Portimão) and furthered settlement by giving it feudatory rights of haven for fugitives threatened by the law elsewhere in the country. That advantage was taken of such rights is obvious from the complaints registered by the city of Silves, to the effect that the Villa was populated by robbers, murderers, and loose women. Perhaps more important to the settlement at that time was the fact that the donatory had also received privileges from the king that allowed Portimão to take over some of the maritime commerce formerly handled by Silves.[22]

Portimão quelled the early disorders brought about by its boisterous settlers and continued the commerce that it had gained from the decline of Silves, although Lagos became the chief heir to the commercial and maritime position of the former Moslem capital. Portimão subsequently settled into a relatively quiet existence, supported by farming and a modest commerce. During the eighteenth century harbor improvements were a matter of public discussion, and during the same century the settlement was sufficiently important to be elevated to the category of city and designated to be the seat of a bishop. Although the bishop's seat was never established and the confirmation of its rights as a city were delayed until recently, as were the hydrologic improvements, the potential of the harbor and the city were recognized even then.[23]

In the last years of the eighteenth century it was described as being a small, charming, agricultural center.[24] However, it was more than

the pages in approximate order of use from which material has been taken:
For Portimão: pp. 267, 269, Map 11.
For Faro: pp. 329, 326.
For Olhão: p. 341.
For Fuzeta: pp. 370, Map 11, pp. 226, 228, Map 1, pp. 230, 88, 232, 238–241.
For Tavira: pp. 232, 261–266, 351, 367, 369.
For Quarteira: pp. 306–307.
For Albufeira: pp. 300–302, Map 1 and Map 11.
For Alvôr: pp. 272, 297, Map 11.
For Castro Marim: pp. 388–391.
For Lagos: pp. 88, 93, 130, 226, 228, Map 1, pp. 230, 232, 238–241.

[22] A. de Sousa Silva Costa Lobo, *Historia da sociedade em Portugal no seculo XV*, p. 143.

[23] J. Leite de Vasconcellos, *Etnografia Portuguesa*, II, 437–438.

[24] H. F. Link, *Voyage en Portugal*, II, 138.

Interest in fishing was so slight that in 1790 there were only thirty fishermen in the

merely an agricultural center; some of the commerce that it had taken over from Silves continued to be part of its life. In 1835, the taxes on its fishing boats were half of those levied at either Lagos or Tavira; and in 1841 it was described as being "very commercial," to the extent that it neglected its fishing. This interesting comment implies that the sale of agricultural produce is commerce whereas the sale of fish would be a different matter, perhaps representing a more fundamental way of life. Another report, made within a decade of the last-mentioned, refers to Portimão as "a little city (*ville*) amidst widespread fruit trees."[25] Here again it is the agriculture of the area that first calls the author's attention; but he also said that Portimão was the "principal harbor" of the Algarve, obviously referring to its natural qualities, as trade did not so qualify it.

In retrospect, one can see that Portimão had settled into a comfortable, somewhat bucolic, conservative existence, but always present was the potential to change rapidly once the desire came; such desire was evinced in the twentieth century, when it transformed the formerly "charming little city amidst fruit trees" into the most bustling commercial port of the western Algarve, with a newly created class of "sardine millionaires" living in homes overlooking the sea in the nearby suburb of Praia da Rocha.

Transformation into a busy industrial and commercial center came about through harbor improvement, changes in the size of vessels, new methods of packing and shipping fish, and aggressive action on the part of its inhabitants, with the aid, perhaps, of immigrants.[26] Its future as the most important fishing harbor of the western Algarve and the most important center for sardine seiners of the province was assured—and with it the relative decline of Lagos—when the most important fish-

---

settlement, compared to six hundred in Lagos and eighty in Alvôr. The fishermen of Alvôr were "better and more intelligent." See Constantino Botelho de Lacerda Lobo, "Memoria sobre o estado das pescarias da costa do Algarve no anno de 1790," *Memorias económicas*, V, 104, 107.

[25] Charles Bonnet, *Algarve (Portugal) Description*, p. 104.

[26] Including one wealthy Spaniard who invested in a sardine plant. See Raquel Soeiro de Brito, "Um pequeno porto de pesca do Algarve: Albufeira," *Comptes Rendus du Congrès International de Géographie*, III, 242–243.

packing plants were established there and most of the large fishing ships were transferred to it in the twenties of the present century.[27]

Citizens of Lagos, whose city is now eclipsed by Portimão, claim that the latter was chosen for expensive dredging operations to make it fit for the reception of large fishing ships through devious politics, and that Lagos, by a similar attention, could have been maintained as the primary port of the Barlavento. Balanced judgment as to this contention is difficult to get but the fact remains that Portimão has the better natural harbor (next to Vila Real the best of the Algarve) and is presently the best port for handling the purse-seiners of the Barlavento. It has become a commercial and industrial center based chiefly upon sardines even though most of these fish are caught either in the waters off the Lagos shore or, even farther from Portimão, beyond Lagos toward the west. There is a busy air of activity in Portimão. Its energetic men do not waste time on idle and unprofitable conversation. There is little of the garrulous friendliness here for which the Algarve is famous.

The catch of sardines in Portimão is the most important of the Algarve, both in value and tonnage. Although sardines are caught in any one of a number of simpler and earlier-type devices, most of the catch is now made by purse-seiners off the western part of the Algarvian coast. The largest and earliest type of ship using the purse-seine was the *galião*, an early type of Portuguese sailing vessel, which was converted to steam and to transport of the large purse-seines. The first of these ships appeared on the south coast in 1910 and was called a *cerco*, after the "encircling net" which it used. This net was up to three thousand feet in length and nearly three hundred feet in depth and had a mesh of apertures less than one-half inch each (one cm.). The upper edge was floated with corks and the lower edge weighted with lead. The net was shot as the ship encircled a school of fish. When the circle was complete the bottom was closed and the net hauled so that the

---

[27] In 1920, Lagos parish still had a greater population than that of Portimão; but during the following decade the parish of Portimão grew 40 per cent, while that of Lagos increased only 4.4 per cent. See Aristides de Amorim Girão and Fernanda de Oliveira Lopes Velho, *Estudos da População Portuguesa, I, Evolução demográfica e ocupação do solo continental (1890–1940)*, I, last page of statistics.

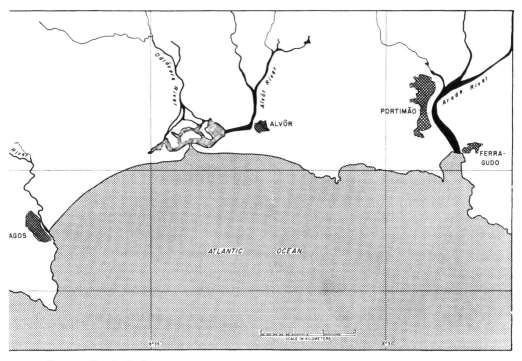

Coast at Portimão-Lagos.

catch could be brailed out with hand dip-nets and transferred to the *enviada*, a carrier vessel that accompanied the *cerco*. This seiner carried a crew of sixty to seventy men and made two shots of the net in a night of fishing. No more could be made because the fine mesh is in the center of the net, requiring it to be brought in at both ends. This necessitated its rearrangement—a considerable and time-consuming chore— before another shot could be made.

The past tense has been used in describing the *cerco* (the ship) because it has been eliminated from Algarvian waters since 1957. Its place has been taken by a smaller, motor-driven vessel, the *traineira*, which carries a net with the same-size mesh but which is one-third shorter and somewhat less deep than that carried by the *cerco*. Although this smaller net is not as useful for big schools of fish as that used by the larger vessel, it has great advantages in other ways. Its fine mesh is near one end and this means that it can be shot again without rearrangement. Instead of two shots during a night of fishing, four or five are normal.

103

Part of the sardine fleet at Portimão.

The *traineira* is more maneuverable and can take catches of small schools of fish unavailable to the larger vessel. For example, with such fast-swimming fish as the Spanish mackerel (*Scomber colias*) it can speed its action by letting out only part of the net.[28] Also it is more economical, as it carries an average crew of but eighteen to twenty men.

In the late afternoon, these ships can be seen heading toward the open ocean, where ordinarily they fish through the night, to return in the early hours of the morning following. If, however, the catch is poor, they may stay out for two or three days without returning to shore. Virtually all such ships are now equipped both with sounding devices for locating the schools of fish and with intercommunication apparatus. Summer and autumn are the best months for fishing, when the fish appear close to shore, although some fish are caught in all months except during the three-month period from January 15 to April 15,

[28] Gaetano Ferro, "La Pesca nel mare dell'Algarve," *Annali di ricerche e studi di geografia,* (Settembre-Dicembre) 1954, Genova, Vol. X, No. 4, p. 147.

when the Portuguese government forbids the use of purse-seiners because of spawning.

All fish caught off these coasts must be sold in public auction.[29] When the carrier ships arrive off the docks at Portimão, the auctioneer and the ever-present customs guards and policemen go aboard. The auctioneer calls prices per case of sardines, beginning with a figure clearly higher than might be bid, and rapidly reduces it until a buyer signifies his willingness to buy the boatload by saying "chui," a term without exact definition but one that can be emitted quickly and with a penetrating sound easily heard by the auctioneer.

Part of the price received goes to the fishermen, who are paid in percentages of the catch. Such a percentage varies from port to port and from season to season. However, in Portimão an average payment of one-quarter of one per cent goes to each man, that is, about 5 per cent of the value of the catch to the entire crew. On the average, this percentage will yield an income to each fisherman of about one thousand to fifteen hundred escudos ($35.00 to $52.50 U.S.) per month, during seven to eight fishing months to approximately six hundred men employed on *traineiras*.

After the auction, the carrier ship (*enviada*), which usually carries about two tons of fish, is unloaded by filling small baskets with about ten pounds of fish each and throwing them to a man on the dock. In case the carrier boat is not against the dock but anchored beyond another ship or two, the small baskets must be thrown first from the carrier to an intermediate ship lying against the dock and a second time to reach the dock. It is a deft performance, but slow, and possible only with labor at low wages.

When the sardine catch is below normal, or special opportunity is

---

[29] This statement is officially true and largely the fact. Nevertheless a good deal of clandestine activity escapes official eyes. It is impossible for guards to prevent all illegal sale, and there is some tacit connivance. Fishermen's lives are so near the edge of subsistence and the unpredictability and dangers so great, that the state and the commercial companies wink at some contraband and some pilfering, without which many of the employees could not live. Theoretically, if any fish is sold except at official auction, the seller will be put in jail and his boat sold at public auction, with the money being taken by the state.

Unloading sardines at Portimão.

offered, Portimão purse-seiners take other pelagic fish: horse mackerel (*Trachurus trachurus*), Spanish mackerel, or, on rare occasions, anchovies.

Using 184 smaller craft, either motor-driven or propelled by oars or sail, and a great variety of gear, nearly five hundred men fish for a miscellany of sea life.

In the twenty-three factories of Portimão over twenty-eight hundred employees (82 per cent women) pack the fish for export. However, part of the catch is bought by individuals or small commercial companies for local sale, or for salting and delivery into the Alentejo, to Lisbon, and even to North Portugal. Some small buyers (women) take the lots that they have bought and, sitting on the wharf, trim off the head and split the body before salting. For their time, the price is made higher.

Modern transport has made it possible to ship much larger amounts of fish than formerly from the Algarve, either salted or fresh. Indeed,

Packing sardines in salt at Portimão.

the consumption of fish in the Algarve itself is being reduced (although it is still fundamental to the diet of the littoral and partly through the Limestone Zone), as prices have risen because of the demand from the large Portuguese cities of the north. Trucks go to all of the fishing areas of the Algarve to buy fish directly from the boats; the fish are taken without any preparation, or with very little, to Lisbon and beyond. This activity has been especially notable in the last ten years.

Portimão is a specialized sardine-packing center. It leads the Algarve in the canning of sardines in olive oil (almost half of the total). It is in second place with regard to the other types of sardine packing, and is usually second in the pack of mackerel.

FARO

The greatest advantage of Faro, the capital and the largest city of the Algarve, is that of position; it is not only central to the province as a whole, but it is the most serviceable port for the broadest section of the Coastal Plain as well as for the most populous section of the adjacent Limestone Zone. It serves an area where numerous and important settlements have had goods for export for longer than its written history. While its harbor is not the best on the south coast, it has been useful for small boats; once they make their way through its narrow and shallow channels, which are continually being changed by new deposits of sand, their protection is almost complete. As long as small boats are important to the Algarve (and they still are) the port of Faro serves well. Its disadvantages for large ships are probably insurmountable. Actually, the largest ships coming to the Algarve at the end of the eighteenth century could not enter.[30] However, other and better harbors of the Algarve are offside; inland from Vila Real, Tavira, Portimão, and Lagos the Coastal Plain is either greatly reduced in size or nonexistent and the Limestone Zone behind is narrow, with comparatively sparse population.

The region of Faro has had a checkered history, with periods of prosperity followed by declines; but for two thousand years or more a settlement has been maintained on or approximately at the site of the present city. Originally, it may have been inhabited exclusively by fishermen; its tuna fishing probably harks back to Punic times.[31] The important Roman settlement of Ossónoba was probably on the site of the oldest section of the present city of Faro.[32] Early in the fourth century it was of sufficient importance to be made the seat of a bishop.[33]

Paralleling the history of other coastal cities, Ossónoba may have declined under Visigothic administration, as did most Roman coastal cities, but it retained its identity and continued to have an episcopal see; various of its bishops attended conciliums in Toledo, the capital of the Goths, during the sixth and seventh centuries.[34]

Under the subsequent Arab regime its name, even with a Christian identification, was not relinquished; of this fact there is tenth-century

[30] H. F. Link, *Voyage en Portugal*, p. 144.
[31] António García y Bellido, *Historia de España*, Tomo I, Vol. II, 314 map.
[32] Abel Viana, "Ossónoba, o problema da sua localização," *Revista de Guimarães*, 1952, LVII, 10.
[33] Leite de Vasconcellos, *Etnografia Portuguesa*, III, 316.
[34] Francisco X. d'Athaide Oliveira, A *Monografia de Alvôr*, p. 58.

testimony: about the year 920 a small principality was established around fortified Santa Maria de Ossónoba. About a century later this little political unit came under the control of one Ibne Harune and the name of the settlement was changed to Santa Maria de Harun. Prior to the time of Portuguese conquest (mid-thirteenth century), this name had been corrupted to Santa Maria de Faron (or Faaron or Faraon; spellings varied but always the *F* had replaced the *H*).[35] Under this name it received its town charter in 1269.[36]

As might be expected, the Portuguese conquest created difficulties for Algarvian coastal settlements; trade had been the basis of their life and locally grown food was insufficient for their maintenance. With the disruption of their accustomed channels of trade, special economic measures were necessary. In 1282 King Diniz exempted Faro from the 10 per cent import tax upon any grains necessary for local consumption.[37] It seems that the problem persisted, however, and the Faro area continued to lag in agriculture. Nearly two centuries later, in 1451, its citizens complained to the King that the stifling of the fishing industry by Prince Henry's taxes had discouraged the mule trains from bringing in the grain necessary for the people.[38]

However, Faro's trade must have been brisk, for within another century it was sufficiently important to be named a city.[39] Shortly thereafter the see of the bishop was transferred to it from Silves, where it had been since immediately after the Portuguese conquest.[40] Still, however, Faro was not the leading city of the Algarve; both Lagos and Tavira had larger populations.

[35] *Ibid.*, p. 17.

[36] Academia das Sciencias de Lisboa. *Portvgaliae monvmenta historica a saecvlo octavo post Christvm vsqve ad qvintvmdecimvm ivssv Academiae scientiarvm olisiponensis edita.* Inqvisitiones. Volvmen I, Olisipone, Typis academicis, 1888–1917, p. 715.

[37] Henrique da Gama Barros, *Historia da Administração Pública em Portugal nos seculos XII a XV,* IX, 60.

[38] *Ibid.*, p. 283.

[39] In 1540. See M. Lyster Franco *O Algarve: Exposição Portuguesa em Sevilha,* p. 34.

[40] The transfer took place in 1577. See João Baptista da Silva Lopes, *Memorias para a história ecclesiastica do Bispado do Algarve,* p. 355.

Two great calamities changed the appearance of Faro drastically: the first was the destructive bombardment by the British fleet in 1596, which obliterated most of the buildings of the city and permitted rebuilding according to an entirely different urban pattern.[41] A century after that event, the city again had grown to approximately the size of Lagos and Tavira, but remained under the local administration of the latter and the general administration of the former.[42] The second calamity was the earthquake of 1755, which destroyed most of the buildings of the city and killed 250 people. Even after two such devastating events, however, remnants of the feudal city still remain.[43] Again the city was rebuilt—the geographical position demands a city. By the end of the eighteenth century Faro had overcome the shattering effects of the earthquake and had advanced its trade to the point that it was the most important commercial center of the south coast; this development took place in spite of the fact that the largest ships of that time could not come into its harbor and that Tavira remained its administrative superior.[44] Continuing a tradition centuries old, figs remained the most important product for export. Almonds, wine, cork, oranges, and sumac (*Rhus coriaria* L.) also were on the export lists of the period.[45]

During the nineteenth century Faro gained clear predominance in Algarvian affairs; before the middle of the century it was made the political capital, and in the last half, the introduction of chemical fertilizers transformed almost sterile, sandy lands around it into farms of high productivity. The area is now the most intensively cultivated of any part of the Algarve, more so even than the lands around Tavira, which until recent generations have claimed all of the encomiums of travellers.[46]

[41] Gaetano Ferro, "Ricerche di geografia urbana nell'Algarve," *Annali di ricerche e studi di geografia*, X, N. 2 (Aprile–Giugno), 1954, p. 53.

[42] John Stevens, *The Ancient and Present State of Portugal*, p. 205.

[43] See Gaetano Ferro, *Ricerche di geografia urbana*, p. 55.

[44] H. F. Link, *Voyage en Portugal*, II, 144–147.

[45] *Ibid.*; Arthur William Costigan, *Sketches of Society and Manners in Portugal*, I, 14.

[46] Link, at the end of the eighteenth century, described the lands around Tavira in glowing terms, and his enthusiasm was shared by all other travellers. However,

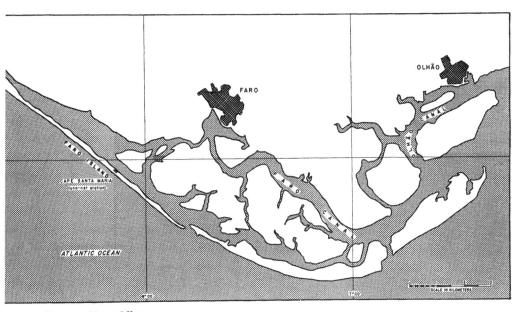

Coast at Faro-Olhão.

For some centuries, Faro's oldest business has not been its best business; nineteenth-century, and even twentieth-century, reports have little to say about its fishing. This omission is due to the fact that the catch, especially in the nineteenth century, was consumed locally and little if any appeared on export lists. Nevertheless, from the time of the Punic peoples until now, Cape Santa Maria, just south of Faro, has been host to fishermen. The fixed net, put out in the earliest times to catch tuna, is ancestral in type and place to that being used now. The Santa Maria net, because of its advantageous position, is allowed to fish only the eastward passage of the tuna. This half season is normally sufficient to yield a catch comparable to the full season of each of the other four nets.[47]

In the mid-nineteenth century over 600 men were employed in fish-

he described Faro as being amidst much sandy, uncultivable land. See H. F. Link, *Voyage en Portugal*, II, 143–149.

[47] In 1960, however, this was not the case; only 14.5 per cent of the total were caught at Santa Maria. For this information I am grateful to Captain Melo de Carvalho.

111

Fishermen's boats on the sands south of Faro.

ing, out of a total population in the city of between eight and nine thousand.[48] The number has not increased, although the total city population has grown considerably; at the end of 1959 registered fishermen numbered 599.

Faro is now base for two purse-seiners, some line fishermen of the open ocean, and various smaller boats and equipment, landing horse mackerel, anchovies, and a variety of other species. The only unique characteristic of its fishing, however, is that accomplished with typical Algarvian gear by men no longer able to go to sea and boys who are too young to do so. Cape Santa Maria, bulging out into the ocean in a complex series of lagoons, bars, and spits, is an impediment to the harbor of Faro, but it offers a large, protected area where older men and youngsters can gather molluscs, crustaceans, and fish of various species. These men and boys use sardine nets, trammels, *alcatruzes*,[49] fish spears,

[48] João Baptista da Silva Lopes, *Memorias para a história ecclesiastica*, p. 353.

[49] For a description of this device see the section, near the end of this chapter, concerned with the minor center of Santa Luzia.

112

Thatched houses of the fishermen south of Faro.

and, when allowed, channel nets (*tapadas*), as well as a variety of lines. Of 218 boats registered in the city, 204 are driven by sail or oars; only 14 have motors.

Because of its sandy, shallow-water Cape area and the fishermen there, Faro is the provincial leader in the catch of shrimps, cockles, and clams.

On the sands, toward the outer edge of the lagoons, are small groups of thatched houses, where a few families of able-bodied fishermen live. Using small boats of either sail or oars, they fish with shore seines, stick dip nets, and lines. A few deep-sea fishermen from Faro put the city in a respectable position in the yearly catch of sea breams (*Pagellus acarne* and *Pagrus pagrus*).

Although Faro rivals Portimão for second place in the number of industrial personnel, it takes almost no part in the leading export of the province, fish products. Its chief industry is that of cork processing, in which it leads the province in number of employees (1,006 in 1957);

its second most important industry is that of general construction, which thrives because of Faro's political position. For the rest, its industries are related mostly to services and to the processing and distribution of agricultural products.

OLHÃO

Character and history. In appearance, Olhão is an African city sprung up surprisingly in the middle of the Algarvian coast. The design of its older houses gives it unique character, for their type is seldom seen elsewhere in the region. These white, cubistic structures are of two or three stories in height; the roofs are flat and each upper story is smaller than the one beneath it so that the impression is that of set-back floors, comparable, on a small scale, to those of some modern New York office buildings. The second story is reached in most cases by a stairway on the outside of the house, but in others it rises from the interior through a covered stair cabin on the roof, similar to that of a ship. The terrace area of the second story is used for drying fruits, for clothes lines, for miscellaneous chores of the household, and sometimes for the pens or cages of domestic animals. The third story, which is small and of little utility except for its view, is always reached by an exterior stairway.

Olhão is not an ancient settlement. There is no record of a town charter for it in the early generations after the reconquest, as there is for many of the Algarvian settlements; and in 1698, when the parish was established, the sailors occupying the site were living in poor straw-covered huts.[50] Such was the description as recorded in the church. The adjective "poor" was obviously not applicable to the occupants, because in 1712 another priest said that the settlement was made up of three hundred families living in thatched houses, who were prosperous by reason of the fishing.[51] There is no doubt about the increased prosperity of the settlement at the end of the same century; the huts had become houses, and the community was made a villa in 1808. By that time, however, new ideas had been introduced, ideas that

[50] Mariano Feio, *Le Bas Alentejo et L'Algarve*, p. 106.
[51] Leite de Vasconcellos, *Etnografia Portuguesa*, III, 622.

114

were not common to the Algarve regarding house construction; these were brought to the area by its sailors who fished off the northern coasts of Africa.[52] Like most towns of Portugal, the early-settled area of Olhão has streets and houses distributed without formal pattern; its present areas of grid-pattern streets encircling the early nucleus are a product of the last hundred years.

But Olhão is more than quaint. It is a busy city with the most diverse activities of any of the Algarvian fishing centers. The energy of its seventeenth- and eighteenth-century sailors has continued.[53] Today its purse-seiners make it one of the three most important centers of the province for the landing of sardines, anchovies, Spanish mackerel, and horse mackerel. However, the quality of Olhão industry, differing from that of Vila Real and of Portimão, has never been based upon a concentration upon one fish. Variety of effort is the pronounced characteristic of its industrial life. Only occasionally does it take first place in the catch of any important species of those listed for the Algarvian ports, but it is usually among the three leaders in the catch of over half of them; an important second or third position is typical for it.

Line fishing out of Olhão. Nor is Olhão restricted in the techniques and types of gear used for fishing. Although its purse-seiners catch the important pelagic species which yield the greatest total profit for the city, that which gives quite another quality to the life is the intensive line fishing from the open ocean for demersal species of high value for fresh consumption. This fishing is done from open, twenty-five–foot boats, each with a small compartment in the middle; formerly sailed, they now are motor-driven, without change in fundamental design or size and may even be equipped with freezing compartments so that men may stay out for several days without returning to port to unload their catch. Ordinarily such a boat carries ten to twelve men and works

[52] Mariano Feio, *Le Bas Alentejo et L'Algarve,* p. 106. It should be mentioned that houses with horizontal roofs were certainly not unknown in the Algarve prior to the foundation of Olhão; a few scholars believe that the form is a descendant of Moslem houses in ancient Algarvian settlements, continued in Olhão only by chance.

[53] In 1790 its sailors were reputed to be the best of the Algarve. See Constantino Botelho de Lacerda Lobo, "Memoria sobre a decadencia das pescarias de Portugal," *Memorias económicas,* IV, 353.

at about fifteen miles from shore. Summer is the most profitable season; from July to September trips are made to the area facing Cape S. Vicente and up the west coast to Sines and occasionally to the mouth of the Tejo River. As the crews of these boats sell their catch at the most convenient market place (or where the price promises to be high), the figures do not always enter into the Algarvian statistics, even though the boats are based at Algarvian ports. Although this type of boat is known elsewhere along the Algarvian coast, nowhere else does it appear in such numbers and with such importance as at Olhão.

Depending upon the fish sought—which is a function of area and season—the lines used by such boats vary in length, weight, number of hooks, bait used, and somewhat in design. These trotlines are simply called *aparelho de anzol* "apparatus with hooks" in the Algarve, although locally any one may be given a name to identify its special characteristics. The line may be of cotton, silk, sisal, or manila hemp (which until lately has been considered the best as it did not rot in salt water), and now, nylon. The length may be anything from thirty to over eight hundred yards. From the main line there are short, usually yard-long, branch lines about one yard apart, each with a baited hook at the end.

Baiting the hooks of a long trotline is a considerable task in itself. I watched an experienced fisherman in Lagos baiting a relatively short line of only 170 hooks. He used mostly horse mackerel of an inferior variety known in the Algarve as *carapau azul*. Eliminating the head and the tail of the fish, he then cut the remainder into two or three pieces. These pieces were then put on the hooks. About each ten or fifteen hooks he would bait one with a piece of sardine or squid, or, other days, he told me, he might use an occasional piece of *ligueirão*, a sand clam (*Solen marginatus*), or a worm. Baiting the 170 hooks took him about an hour. As lines are often many times as long as the one upon which he worked, the time consumed in this single task may be considerable.

Commonly, the trotline will be held clear of the bottom by having perpendicular lines, each with a float at the top, fastened at forty yard intervals. There may be another line at the same location leading to a weight (usually a five-pound stone) to hold it at the proper depth,[54] or the lines with the weights may be distributed approximately equidistantly between the buoy-lines so that the trotline takes the form of a series of right angles. One boat may put out a dozen or more trotlines; they usually remain in the water several hours before being retrieved, but if the fish are numerous they may be lifted frequently. This work is ordinarily done by three to five men in a small boat. The value of the catch is distributed, after subtracting expenses for bait and after paying the official taxes, on the basis of one part each for the men, one part for the boat, and one part for each thousand hooks (that is, the owner of the line receives a part of the value proportionate to the length of his line).

Under various names—*caçada, espinhel, varestilha, meia varestilha, gorazeira, palangre, linhavão, barqueta*, and many others of local use —essentially the same type of line is used, varying in length, weight, and number of hooks, depending upon the fish sought. For example, the *gorazeira* is so named because it is used to catch the *goraz*, a sea bream (*Pagellus centrodontus* Delaroche), over rocky bottoms. Several lines put together are called a *caçada*, which may be used baited with sardines, squid (*Loligo vulgaris*), cuttlefish (*Sepia officinalis*), horse mackerel, or other fish to catch a variety of demersals, including breams, sole, gilthead (*Sparus aurata*), John Dory (*Zeus japonicus*), dogfish (*Mustelus spp.* and *Scyliorinhus spp.*), sargo (*Diplodus vulgaris*), as well as the conger eel (*Conger conger*), and the moray (*Muraena helena*).[55] The *caçada* is used particularly along the western section of the south coast and, in good weather, on the west coast north of the Cape. The *barqueta* or *meia varestilha* is a short variant of the *caçada*. It is used especially for one of the species of sea bream (*Pagellus acarne*), sargo, and sole.

A longer line, the *varestilha*, is used especially for the frogfish (*Betrachus didactylus*). A variant of it, the *rabadela*, is a heavy line —now commonly of nylon—but not of great length (usually about

[54] *Jornal do Pescador*, July, 1948.

[55] Eels are frequently caught also on especially heavy lines equipped with only two hooks. See *Jornal do Pescador*, July, 1948.

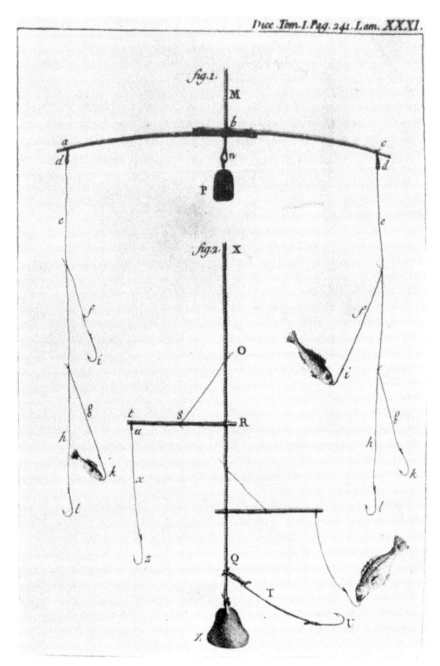

A variant of the *barqueira* as shown in Sañez Reguart's *Diccionario histórico de las artes de la pesca nacional*, published in Madrid, 1791–1795.

three hundred feet), with short lines leading out from it at about twelve-inch intervals. It is used to catch the large croaker (*Johnius regia*) and many of the demersals mentioned above, including sargo, breams, and gilthead.

These names are applied to lines with multiple hooks, but there are also other lines equipped with a limited number of hooks, for example the *barqueira*, a line from which hangs a transverse piece of wood or wire. From the transverse piece, either two or four meter-long lines, each with a hook at its end, extend downward. The whole apparatus is held down by a weight attached to the middle of the transverse piece. Now, frequently, the *barqueira* does not have the transverse piece; instead it has a nylon extension with two to five short lines leading from it. Baited with pieces of squid, cuttlefish, or mackerel, the *barqueira* is commonly used by two or three men in a small boat in water of twenty-five to forty fathoms to catch forkbeard (*Phycis blennoides*), a sea bream (*Pagrus pagrus*), and sargo, but incidentally catching a variety of other demersals.

Net fishing out of Olhão. A rectangular stick dip net, called the *sacada,* is the most productive of the nets used along the Algarvian coast by simple fishermen; and the men of Olhão lead in its use. As it is used under varied conditions by different-sized boats with crews varying in number, sizes of the nets differ greatly. Average proportions are twenty-five by forty-five yards. The mesh is the same as that of the sardine nets (and actually the *sacada* is usually made by using a part of a sardine net). Such a net is handled by two craft: one, an open boat of twenty to twenty-five feet in length; the second, a smaller boat twelve to fifteen feet long. The two boats require a minimum of eight men. The net is dropped between the two boats with attached weights to pull it down, so that it ordinarily rests partly on a sandy bottom under thirty-five to seventy-five feet of water. Poles, projecting out from the prow and stern respectively of the small boat, stretch out the side of the net where the "sack" is located. Fastened to the other end are ropes leading to the larger boat. After dark a lantern with a large reflector turned toward the surface of the water (or two or even more lanterns, depending upon the size of the net) is lighted and moved

119

across the net to the small boat so that the fish are attracted over the net. Then bait, usually minced sardines or mackerel, is cast into the water. The man in charge of operations watches until he sees a sufficient catch is available and then directs the lifting of the net in such fashion that the fish are diverted into the "sack." The process is repeated throughout the night.

For this operation with eight men the division of the catch is in twelve parts: one each to the eight men, one to the large boat, one to the small boat, and two parts to the net.[56] That is to say, the owner of each boat receives one part and the net owner receives two parts because of his ownership. Each owner may be also a member of the crew and receive his part for that service as well.

This type of net does not have a long history of use along the Algarvian coast; probably first introduced in the twentieth century,[57] it has become in three generations the most important of the nets used by small fishermen of the region. The most important part of the catch is made up of the four pelagic species: horse mackerel, Spanish mackerel, sardines, and, in summer, anchovies. However, like purse-seines, a *sacada* may take many other species, as the mesh is small and virtually any fish can be caught unless it is large enough to break the net. Unfortunately, the catch may be less valuable than that taken by other nets, as the bait often affects the flavor of the fish.

For little fishermen, the next most important net is the trammel. Sizes vary, and in the central Algarvian coast the length may be from two hundred to eight hundred yards and the width from two to six yards. The trammel is a compound net of three panels some distance apart and parallel to each other; the center panel has a fine mesh of slightly over one inch, whereas the two outer panels have a mesh of

[56] Raquel Soeiro de Brito, "Um pequeno porto," *Comptes Rendus du Congrès,* III, pp. 235–237.

[57] None was mentioned for any port of the Algarve in the *Inquérito Industrial das Pescas, 1890.* This report was used in the Office of Fisheries in Lisbon. It had no place or date of publication, but in a prefatory note two men were credited with authorship: José Bento Ferreira de Almeida and Victorio Miguel Maria das Chagas Roquette.

nearly six inches.[58] A fish swimming against the fine inner mesh pushes it through one of the interstices of the outer net, thus closing itself in a sack. Anchored against the bottom with weights, the net is held upright by corks along the top. Put out at a depth of about fifteen to twenty feet of water, it catches red mullet, gilthead, rockfish (*Scorpaena scrofa*), striped wrasse (*Labrus mixtus*), bass (*Morone labrex*), and some crustaceans.[59] This net usually involves the service of one small boat and five men, the value of the catch being divided equally between each man, the net, and the boat.

The shore seine has less use, generally, than the nets previously described, but for older men, sometimes aided by small boys and sometimes even by women (who are seldom involved in the fishing process although they often take charge of the sale), it has considerable importance still. In the Algarve the great shore seine, which requires the use of oxen (and now tractors in some northern beaches), to draw it up on shore, is not used. A typical Algarvian seine is two hundred yards in length and two yards wide at the ends, while the center is four to six yards wide in the region of the "sack." One end is fixed on shore and the net is taken out to sea by a small boat with four men. Making a horseshoe curve in their course, one man shooting the net as the others row, they bring the other end back to land at a point downshore. Then the ends are pulled in until the "sack" is drawn up on the beach. It brings in the small pelagic species, sardines and horse mackerel, in greater quantities than other fish, but virtually all fish landed on the Algarvian shores may be caught.

When the law permits it the channel net is used—a net fixed across the entry to a channel or stream. In the Algarve, as used at Olhão, it is usually two yards wide by two hundred yards long, with small mesh; fixed at the ends and weighted at the bottom, the top is raised as the

[58] *Jornal do Pescador,* July, 1948.

[59] Gaetano Ferro, "La Pesca nel mare dell'Algarve," *Annali di ricerche e studi di geografia,* X, 4 (Settembre–Dicembre), 1954, pp. 152–154. This article contains a great deal of information about the subject of fishing along the Algarvian coast. It has been of much use to me, although its arrangement is such that its citation is seldom possible in my chapter.

tide comes in. The fish, caught in the lower part, are collected by the fishermen at low tide (mullet, sole, plaice [*Pleuronectes flessus*]; sometimes conger eel and other species).

Development of other fishing industries. As Olhão is on the lagoon area of the central coast of the Algarve, its clam nurseries are extensive (72 per cent of the Algarvian total), and there is opportunity for a considerable group of men to be permanently employed, caring for and gathering clams (Tapes of four species, *T. desussatus,* the commonest).

The figures for fishermen (1211) and fishing boats (258, of which 107 are with motor) are at the head of the provincial list. Olhão fishermen lead in the value of catch by *sacadas* and in clam gathering; but it is not first place in the catch of various fish that establishes the character of the city, but rather the versatility and energy of its men. For example, after years in which the Algarve coast hardly appeared on the lists for the catch of pipers (*Trigla lyra*), Olhão suddenly appeared in 1956. Then and in subsequent years it has reported a far higher catch than the provincial total reported in any year of the previous decade. Finding a new opportunity, these fishermen grasped it.

One of the first two sardine-canning plants of the Algarve was established in Olhão in 1882 (the same year that the other was established in Lagos).[60] At the end of 1958 there were fifty-four industrial plants processing fish and fish products, and employing thirty-five hundred workers (of which 86 per cent were women). The present city is a product of energy and alertness to opportunity in industrial life as well as in fishing. For example, during several years of the early fifties it was the only port of the Algarve which packed Portuguese oysters (*Crassostrea angulata*). That the industry did not succeed and that the packing plants closed in 1957, should not diminish credit to Olhão for the attempt. If the catch of Olhão fishermen is insufficient, factory owners send their agents to buy fish from Vila Real or from Portimão to maintain the primacy of their production in the packing of anchovies, horse mackerel, and the total of all classes of sardines.

With its energy, skills, imagination, and commercial acumen, this

[60] Mariano Feio, *Le Bas Alentejo et l'Algarve,* p. 135.

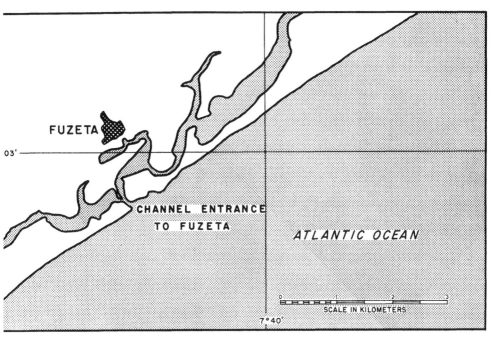

Coast at Fuzeta.

area easily stands in first place in the province in fishing, fish-packing establishments, and their products.

Fuzeta

The little town of Fuzeta, not far from Olhão, is similar to the latter in its history but very different in its present activities; it is a town of specialists. For some time after the Portuguese conquest of this coast there was no settlement, but only a fort, in this location. But in the eighteenth century fishermen settled on the beach, and before the end of the century the village was recognized as an independent parish. In 1790, ninety fishermen with six fishing boats were recorded as living in Fuzeta. Within another half century it had not only grown but had established its present fishing characteristics. In 1841 it was the home port of thirteen high-seas fishing craft, as well as twice that many smaller boats for fishing closer to shore. Its houses, obviously showing the effects of prosperity, were being changed from straw huts to masonry structures, and the extent of the town was increasing.

The techniques of Fuzeta fishermen are similar to those of Olhão in the catch of deep-swimming fish of the open ocean, but they usually limit themselves to the more valuable species. Nearly three hundred men from the town go to Lisbon each year to set out with the cod fleet in April for the Newfoundland banks; on the average, these men are the best paid of any of the Portuguese fishermen. Such a large proportion of the able-bodied young men is absent from the town during the six-month cod-fishing season that life in the town is altered; the streets seem deserted. The seasonal widows put away their best linens and save other good equipment of the house for the time when the man is home. Before his return they clean and furbish; the linens are brought out again, the houses are calcimined. A gala appearance is arranged for the return of the pater familias.

Like the men of Olhão, many Fuzeta fishermen go out to the open sea with motor boats to fish; but Fuzetans concentrate on the catch of the hake (*Merluccius merluccius*), a highly esteemed and high-priced fish that can be caught throughout the year. Normally, Fuzeta lands from two-thirds to four-fifths of the Algarvian total of these fish, catching them on the *linhavão*, one of the variants of the trotline, using sardines and cuttlefish for bait.[61] As the hake is worth twice or three times as much as the average demersal fish of the Algarve (in virtually all years it is the highest priced of all of the fish caught) the catch has yielded the town the highest income from demersal fish of any of the Algarvian settlements for most of the last fifteen years.

Occasionally, when they have time or the opportunity, these fishermen seek other species. During 1954 and 1955, for example, they caught between one-third and one-half of the scabbard fish (*Lepidopus caudatus*) landed at the Algarve; but in the three succeeding years they averaged less than one-tenth of the catch. Usually they take a mid-position for the coast in the catch of red mullet and sole (two other high-priced fish), and dogfish.

Some of the fishermen (mostly older men and youngsters) work closer to shore, using types of gear common to many other ports of

[61] *Inquérito Industrial, 1890,* p. 348; Gaetano Ferro, "La pesca nel mare dell'Algarve," *Annali di ricerche,* p. 158.

the province; normally Fuzeta stands in second or third place in the catch of octopus (*Octopus vulgaris*), using the *alcatruz* (described on p. 160). Trammels and *sacadas* are commonly used, the latter mostly for horse mackerel. Clam nurseries cover more than one hundred and fifty acres and produce ten million molluscs each year. Over seven hundred men are occupied in all types of fishing.

Lagos and Tavira

Two charming, somnolent cities, plaintive in their nostalgia, are Lagos in the Barlavento and Tavira in the Sotavento. In many ways they have had similar experiences; both were dominant in their respective regions in an earlier period of time and now both are lagging in the fishing industry, while parvenu cities, Vila Real de Santo António on the east and Portimão on the west, overshadow them; both had harbors sufficient to their periods of importance until silting and artificial changes in harbors and ports gave the other cities the advantage; at the present time each of these formerly leading cities serves as a local center for its agricultural region and as a minor competitor of the more prosperous commercial and industrial city near it; each has a small fishing fleet, remnants of the time—as late as 1835—when they were the Algarvian leaders; each has small factories to pack the fish that are landed on its docks; each has seen the silting of its harbor to the point that it is not suited to large ships.

Lagos. Neolithic remains have been found[62] near the bay of Lagos, and presumably the Punic fishing and salting base founded in this area was on or near one of the earlier Neolithic settlements. One may further conclude that the Roman Lacobriga, with its Celtic name, continued a settlement begun before the advent of the Romans. If all of these probabilities are put together, it seems that on the Bay of Lagos, and perhaps on the site of the present city, settlement has roots going through Roman, Celtic, and Punic times into the Neolithic.

This settlement in a remote land, of sufficient importance to receive notice under the Romans, dropped from the record under the Visigothic administration, but it did not go out of existence; in the twelfth cen-

[62] Athaide de Oliveira, *A monografia de Alvôr*, p. 114.

tury Edrisi mentions the port of Halc-ac-Zâwia, approximately equidistant from Silves and Sagres.[63] The position that he describes is that of Lagos. From the brevity of his notice and the dominating importance of Silves as a port, it seems certain that the coastal settlement was modest. That such was the fact is borne out by the description of it as a village under the authority of the Bishop of Silves in the middle of the following century, after the Algarve had been conquered by the Portuguese king.[64] Few are the notices regarding it in the early days of the Portuguese monarchy; however, in the mid-fourteenth century some of its inhabitants were engaged in whale fishing,[65] and in 1361 it was made a villa. The development of the town was picking up speed, and in the fifteenth century from five to six thousand people were living in the urban center and approximately two thousand more in its suburbs. To it came traders from foreign countries,[66] and in the same century it became world famous because Prince Henry the Navigator made the city headquarters for his exploring fleet and for his "school of navigation." Commercial activities greatly increased, following Henry's African discoveries; the slave market was busy; fishermen were numerous and productive. Great fixed nets were out to catch tuna, the large croaker, and sardines. The latter fish were taken also with seines; the croaker, presumably, was taken by both seines and lines, as at present. The ancillary salt industry was of sufficient importance to have attracted the notice of the king; he "still held" the monopoly.[67] Typical of the Algarve of the period, commerce flourished, while farming furnished insufficient grain for the maintenance of the population. In 1488 Lagos was relieved of the tithe on the import of grains from other parts of Portugal or from abroad.[68]

Contributing to the growing importance of Lagos was the decline of

[63] Abu-Abd-Alla-Mohamed-al-Edrisi, *Descripción de España*, p. 188.

[64] A. de Sousa Silva Costa Lobo, *História de sociedade em Portugal*, p. 146.

[65] Henrique da Gama Barros, *História da administração pública em Portugal*, p. 275.

[66] A. de Sousa Silva Costa Lobo, *História da sociedade em Portugal*, p. 146.

[67] Nearly eight and one-half million liters were used annually to salt the catch at Lagos. See Henrique da Gama Barros, *História da administração pública*, pp. 296, 298.

[68] Henrique da Gama Barros, *História da administração pública*, p. 76.

Lagos, with part of the city wall in the foreground.

Silves, the former capital of the area, which had served well for the Moslems but offered fewer advantages to the Portuguese. Silves' former commerce was taken over by the coastal settlements, especially by Lagos, which had a position of greater convenience for traffic toward the north with Lisbon, the national capital, and also toward the east, with the Mediterranean. Lagos lacked the protection that the upstream position gave to Silves, but both for African trade and as a base of attack against Moslem North Africa it served well. While it is true that it was relatively free from attack by the Moslems, another adversary came into being; King João III, in the sixteenth century, had to fortify the city because of continuing attacks by corsairs, especially the French, who frequented the coast.[69]

Before the end of the century, the seat of government was moved from Silves to Lagos,[70] and the latter settlement was officially given the

[69] Leite de Vasconcellos, *Etnografia Portuguesa*, II, 433.
[70] Gaetano Ferro, "I centri dell'Algarve occidentale," *Annali di ricerche e studi di geografia*, XI, 3 (Luglio–Settembre, 1955), p. 116.

title of city.[71] Nevertheless, and in spite of official recognition, Lagos had seen the apogee of its fame, for in the early sixteenth century, Lisbon took over the function of sheltering and supplying the fleets of discovery and commerce plying out of Portugal. Lagos' importance was increasingly based upon fishing. In 1586 there were six great fixed tuna nets anchored in the waters offshore, and almost a century later, just before the beginning of the so-called Spanish Captivity (1680–1740), Lagos was reported to have *"abundantissima"* fish, especially tuna.[72] With the Spanish Captivity the commerce of Lagos was badly diminished; such was the fate of all Portuguese maritime trading cities. Adding to its misfortunes, the earthquake and seismic wave of 1755 levelled most of the buildings in the city, killed over two hundred people, and choked the harbor with sand. The captain general of the Algarve, discouraged by the ruin, moved the seat of administration to less-damaged Tavira.

Since that time the record of Lagos as a trading center and port has been unexceptional. By the mid-nineteenth century it had reached a comfortable balance of economy. Its fishing industry, based chiefly on sardines, produced considerable wealth in spite of the sand-choked harbor that restricted entry to relatively small boats. The fish were consumed locally or sent fresh to nearby places along the coast; some were picked up by packtrains to be taken to the Alentejo. Yet with all this abundance of fish, there were periods of shortage. The simple process of salting would have been sufficient to preserve an ample supply for such periods, but the local folk were unconcerned. During times of scarcity, they imported cod. Payment for such import was no great problem, it seems, for fishing was not the only basis of well-being; agriculture also produced a surplus for export. Nature was so generous, it was said, that no one was in need of food.

In the last quarter of the nineteenth century and the first ten years of the twentieth century the city had a brief resurgence, while Portimão, the present regional leader, was languidly pursuing its quiet existence. In 1882, Lagos was chosen to be the site of the first sardine-

[71] Leite de Vasconcellos, *Etnografia Portuguesa*, II, 433.
[72] *Ibid.*, III, 704.

128

packing plant of the Barlavento.[73] At about the same time, the value of its fishing was five times that of its neighbor, Portimão; and as the number of boats and men listed for the two ports was approximately the same, it is clear that Lagos was the base of commercial fishing ships, while Portimão was the base for small boats for subsistence fishing. Lagos had, by then, five fish-packing plants (mostly for sardines), whereas none were listed for Portimão.[74] In 1890 there were seven fixed nets for sardines in the area of the city, compared to three for the area of Portimão. There was one fixed net for tuna in the Lagos area, but this fact should be noted as the handwriting on the wall: there were three in the Portimão area.[75]

The city continued to grow during the early years of the twentieth century and its eclipse by Portimão did not take place until the twenties, when the harbor of Portimão was dredged and improved. This change altered the urban balance in the Barlavento; many plants of Lagos moved to Portimão and other plants became newly established there. Most of the large purse-seiners followed, and established their bases convenient to the factories. During that decade, Portimão grew 40 per cent in population while Lagos grew only 4.4 per cent. That the disparity between the cities has increased through most of the decades since that time is shown by the figures of 11.2-per-cent growth for Portimão and a 1.7-per-cent loss for Lagos in the ten-year period between 1940 and 1950.

As a remnant of past supremacy, at the end of the fifties purse-seiners based on Lagos, using the labor of three hundred men, made the port third in value of catch of sardines, horse mackerel, Spanish mackerel, and—in good years but always in small amounts—anchovies. The ancient tradition of fishing from small sailboats or rowboats is not entirely obliterated; this western area is first in the use of shore seines and one of the leaders in the use of *sacadas* and other less important nets, as well as lines and special devices. The catch of "diverse" fish,

[73] Mariano Feio, *Le Bas Alentejo et l'Algarve*, p. 135. In the same year another such plant was established at Olhão.

[74] A. A. Baldaque da Silva, *Estado actual das pescas em Portugal*, pp. 147, 149.

[75] *Inquérito Industrial*, 1890, pp. 418, 434.

Conger eels at Lagos.

The river at Lagos at low tide.

that is, those not caught in sufficient amounts to be separately listed, is greatest in the Barlavento, and Lagos usually stands in first place in this industry.

The product of the purse-seiners is bought almost entirely by the fish-packing plants. In the Lagos zone there were ten such plants at the end of 1958, employing twelve hundred people (of these, 80 per cent were women) for an average of two hundred and fifty days in a year. For this work the average yearly total compensation is 5,670 escudos (approximately $160.90 U.S.). In comparison with Portimão the figures show Lagos to have less than half the number of factories and value of production (12 per cent of the Algarvian total, at Lagos), but an even greater disparity in mechanization is shown; Lagos uses only slightly over a quarter of the amount of combustibles consumed at Portimão and uses less than a quarter of the horsepower in electric motors.

So now this city of ancient foundation and fame has been pushed into a secondary position. The Lacobrigans (as they call themselves, after the ancient Celtic name) think and speak sadly of their former, greater days and of the political connivance that brought about the dredging of the harbor of Portimão rather than that of the preferable site (as they say) at the Bay of Lagos. A nonparticipant in the emotion-burdened discussion as to the respective rights and virtues of the rival cities wonders if the despondency of Lacobrigans over the greater commercial success of Portimão is sensible, for although Lagos still wears its nineteenth-century clothes, plus a few new patches on the garments, there is a friendly, leisured, albeit somewhat melancholy atmosphere in the city. Conversation is considered to be profitable if it is enjoyable, even though it has nothing to do with business. Certainly the brisk and commercially successful efficiency of Portimão is missing but so also is the un-Portuguese rudeness of that busy port.

One wonders also what changes in attitudes will take place if present activities bring about a commercial and industrial growth in the city. Harbor works are now going on. The bay and channel are being dredged, and the harbor area furbished as an attraction to tourists. Perhaps these activities will gain back for the city some of its former pre-eminence, but it seems doubtful that it will again take precedence over Portimão.

Tavira. Information relating to the city of Tavira is relatively sparse. Just why there should be such a paucity is not clear, for the city has a long history, reaching back, perhaps, through Roman times, and whenever reference is made to the area, "productive" and "prosperous" seem to be frequently used descriptive terms. More information can be obtained regarding the foundation or development of cities that certainly have had no greater, and many with far less, importance than Tavira. Perhaps the answer is to be found in Tavira's conservatism—its affairs have been handled without drama. Never has it experienced a period like that of Lagos under Prince Henry the Navigator. It never has had a unique position in the province, as did Silves under Moslem rule. Now, as formerly, it has a conservatism of farmers whose values are mostly shaped by agriculture but who have also traded or accepted the benefits of trade.

At the beginning of the Christian era a Roman city named Balsa had been built either on the site of present Tavira or near it;[76] probably the city itself was some miles away, but the land of the site of present Tavira was farmed as part of its supporting region.[77] It may be reasonably supposed that the region was farmed long before the arrival of the Romans, for it has obvious advantages in soils, temperatures, and rainfall; the latter is sufficient for production without irrigation. Whether or not irrigation was then used is not known, but if not, certainly the Romans introduced it to increase variety and total production.

Later, under Moslem administration, production and variety were further increased, for the Arabs introduced new plants, and where the water table is near the surface, as in the Sotavento, the Arab water-lifting device, the *nora*, serves wonderfully to lift irrigation water for the fields.

If the present site of the city of Tavira was not occupied by town dwellers prior to the Moslem dominance, it was selected by the Moslems, for the record shows it to have been one of the tenth-century settlements under the Caliphate of Córdoba,[78] and later, in 1189, it was mentioned as one of the Moslem towns conquered when the Christians temporarily held the Algarve.[79] As late as 1442, two centuries after the final Christian conquest of the area, there was still an important Moorish quarter in the settlement.[80]

In 1242 the Moslem town was finally conquered by the Christian forces and two years later it was put under the control of the religious-military order of Santiago, in reward for their share in its conquest. Soon after (1266) the Portuguese king accorded it the first title of villa in the Algarve. However, its status and associations were not made

[76] Claudius Ptolemy, *Geography of Claudius Ptolemy*, trans. by Edward Luther Stevenson, map "Secunda Europe."

[77] S. P. M. Estacio da Veiga, *Povos Balsenses*, pp. 11, 18, 29.

[78] E. Lévi-Provençal, *Histoire de l'Espagne Musulmane: Le Siècle du Califat de Cordoue*, III, 341.

[79] João Baptista da Silva Lopes, *Relação da derrota naval, façanhas, e successos dos cruzados que parti rão do Escalda para a Terra Santa no anno de 1189*, p. 44.

[80] A. de Sousa Silva Costa Lobo, *História da sociedade em Portugal*, p. 38.

clear until 1267, when the king of Castile relinquished the claim that he had asserted until then.[81]

Following the Christian reconquest, the economy of Tavira was maintained without great disruption, largely because of the intelligent conduct of the Knights of Santiago, who retained the Moslem population as laborers.[82] The Moslems were good farmers, whereas most of the Christians involved in the conquest knew little about such matters and cared less. Not only were the Moslems skilled in cultivation of the land, but they had had a long experience in trade with their agricultural products; this trade was basic to the prosperity of Tavira. Within a century after the conquest the city was chosen to be the location of the office of weights and measures for the southern area, apparently because of its commercial importance. Early in the following century reports show that it had commercial connections with Bruges,[83] and later in the same century, a traveller from Central Europe saw Flemish merchants buying grapes and figs in the market of Tavira. He reported that the fig orchards in the neighborhood of the city were as thick as forests.[84] During this same period of time official statements made before the royal legislative body, the Cortes, both in Lisbon and in Evora, maintained that Tavira's economy was based on fruit and the vine.[85] However, this last contention was a matter of special pleading on the part of men who were trying to bring about reduction of taxes on such agricultural products. Although agriculture was without doubt the most important activity of the region and its products were basic to trade,

[81] Damião Augusto de Brito Vasconcelos, *Notícias históricas de Tavira, 1242–1840*, pp. 17–18, 21.

[82] H. V. Livermore, *A History of Portugal*, p. 135.

[83] A. de Sousa Silva Costa Lobo, *História da sociedade em Portugal*, p. 145.

[84] Nicolas de Popielovo, "Viaje de Nicolas de Popielovo," *Viajes de Extranjeros por España y Portugal en los siglos XV, XVI, XVII, Colección de Javier Liske*, p. 40.

[85] Henrique da Gama Barros, *História da administração pública em Portugal*, p. 110. Figs were primary, twenty to one in comparison with raisins in some shipments of the period.

In 1455, King Affonso V guaranteed security to all ships, including British, French, German, Biscayan, Galegan, "and others," that came to Tavira to take on fruits, wines, and other merchandise. King Manoel, in 1599, gave privileges to Tavirans to sell their fruits, wines, and other products in African ports. See Damião Augusto de Brito Vasconcelos, *Notícias históricas de Tavira*, p. 122.

fishing also profitably occupied the attention of an important segment of the population, as it had for long centuries in the past. Its importance immediately after the conquest may be inferred from the fact that the Portuguese king arrogated to himself the salt monopoly and the products of whaling in the town charter of 1266[86] A century later, in 1352, an official letter refers to traders from the north who were bringing wheat to trade for the products of whaling;[87] and a document of another century later, in 1453, established by royal decree certain privileges for Algarvian fishermen with regard to the sale of their catch.[88]

At the end of the fifteenth century—while Lagos was at the height of its importance and had far more fame than ever came to Tavira—the latter paid almost the same amount in taxes to the government as did the spectacular city where Prince Henry the Navigator had established his base.[89] Nevertheless, in spite of its quiet conservatism, its importance to the region and to the nation because of its contribution to Portuguese international affairs was obvious and the villa was promoted to the category of city in the early sixteenth century.[90]

From that time on, changes in the economy of the Tavira area have involved only degrees of difference with the conditions that have long obtained. In the early years of the eighteenth century a Portuguese writer referred to the vicinity in terms that could have been taken from statements made centuries before, referring to the delightful area of the noble city.[91] An Englishman of the same period of time referred to the abundance of wine, oil, and several fruits; but then he added, "there is little grain."[92] It seems that the problem of grain shortage that was

[86] Damião Augusto de Brito Vasconcelos, *Notícias históricas de Tavira,* pp. 21–22.

[87] Constantino Botelho de Lacerda Lobo, "Memoria sobre a decadencia das pescarias de Portugal," *Memorias económicas,* p. 330.

[88] Damião Augusto de Brito Vasconcelos, *Notícias históricas de Tavira,* p. 122.

[89] A. de Sousa Silva Costa Lobo, *História da sociedade em Portugal,* p. 57.

[90] The exact date is in doubt. A. de Sousa Silva Costa Lobo (*História da Sociedade,* p. 56) says it was in the later fifteenth century. João Baptista da Silva Lopes (*Corográfia,* p. 352) says 1520. J. Leite de Vasconcellos (*Etnografia Portuguesa,* III, 431) says between 1513 and 1521.

[91] J. Leite de Vasconcellos, *Etnografia Portuguesa,* III, 705 (citing P^e Carvalho).

[92] John Stevens, *The Ancient and Present State of Portugal,* p. 208.

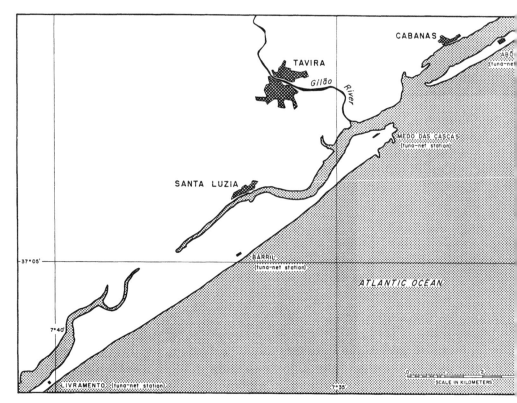

Coast at Tavira

reported in the period immediately after the reconquest continued to plague the region.

If it had not been for the conservatism of Tavira, the calamity that befell most of the other cities of the Algarve in 1755 might have been used to further its development and leadership. The earthquake and seismic wave of that year caused tremendous damage in Lagos and Faro, the other important cities of the coast, but left Tavira in far better condition. The captain general of the Algarve at that time, his home and buildings destroyed in Lagos, moved the seat of authority to Tavira. Apparently Tavira took this matter casually, and without breaking stride kept on at its accustomed pace. Toward the end of the century another Englishman and a German describe the area in terms really no different from those always used before. By their description it was located in the most beautiful area of the Algarve, with fine fields of grain, beans, and flax, with almonds, carobs, figs, olives, and pomegranates.[93] A third Englishman of the period was so enthusiastic that, after having been to Lisbon and Coimbra, he described Tavira as being "clean and opulent" and the best city he had seen in Portugal.[94]

Continuing its earlier balance of economic affairs, Tavira kept fishing subsidiary to agriculture, and the farming landscape was that which struck the eye of travellers. In fact, fishing may have suffered some decline, for in 1790 there were fewer sardine nets than had been used previously;[95] notwithstanding this decline, one informant stated that fishing was important, especially for sardines and tuna, but for other species as well.[96] Whatever the importance may have been, however, there was clearly some neglect of fishing in order to pursue other, and presumably more profitable activities. Before the middle of the nineteenth century there is criticism of the inhabitants of Tavira because of their concentration upon the export of agricultural produce to the detriment of the fishing industry. The boats based upon the harbor were used to take such produce to Gibraltar, to Cádiz, and to Lisbon, where foreign ships—especially Catalonian and Sardinian—came to buy it. So few boats were left to use in fishing that a part of the fish necessary for local consumption was supplied by Fuzeta. The condition of the river was such that only small boats could come into the harbor, yet nothing was done about the matter except occasionally to discuss it.[97] Yet the city continued to prosper on the basis of its agricultural export; an author of 1850, in terms to which any reader of the history of Tavira has become

[93] Arthur William Costigan, *Sketches of Society and Manners in Portugal*, I, 42; H. F. Link, *Voyage en Portugal*, II, 149.

[94] Robert Southey, *Journals of a residence in Portugal, 1800–1801, and a visit to France*, p. 43.

[95] Constantino Botelho de Lacerda Lobo, "Memoria sobre a decadencia das pescarias de Portugal," *Memorias económicas*, pp. 350–351.

[96] H. F. Link, *Voyage en Portugal*, II, 151.

[97] The problem of the choked river was not a new one; all of the Sotavento is continually receiving the product of erosion from the cliffs of the Barlavento. In 1441, an official complaint made it clear that the entry was dangerous when the tide was out. See Henrique da Gama Barros, *História da administração pública*, p. 107.

accustomed, spoke of "beautiful streets . . . well cultivated lands all around the city . . . but it lacks grain."[98]

Many citizens of the city now speak of the shortsightedness of earlier inhabitants who failed to take advantage of the opportunities for commercial fishing that have been grasped by both Vila Real and Olhão.[99] They say that the silting of the Gilão River at Tavira could have been corrected by dredging so that the city could have taken its place among the canning and fish-export leaders of the province. They ask why it is that with the great fixed nets for tuna all set out in waters near Tavira that the product is mostly processed in Vila Real.

Since 1890, when the first real population census was taken in Portugal, statistics show that the Tavira area has run a poor third to Vila Real and Olhão in rate of increase. In the sixty-year period between 1890 and 1950 Tavira parishes gained only 28.4 per cent, whereas the parish of Olhão gained 53.9 per cent and that of Vila Real 69.2 per cent.[100] Such statistics make a strong argument for those who assess progress in terms of industrial advancement and size of population. There is another attitude which is strongly held in Tavira, however. Its adherents maintain that they find the slightly drowsy air of the city to their taste. They say that while the concentration upon agriculture has perhaps produced the drowsiness, certainly Tavira has one of the most handsomely kept agricultural landscapes to be found anywhere; that Tavira does well what it best can do, exploit an agricultural resource intensively and successfully. It has none of the social problems of *latifundismo*, because the land is mostly worked by small farmers with generations of experience behind them. There are few of the problems of poverty here that confront both Vila Real and Olhão. In fact, the problems of poverty in Tavira are mostly confined to the families dependent upon fish-

[98] Charles Bonnet, *Algarve (Portugal) Description,* p. 101.

[99] The first tuna-packing plant of the Algarve was established in Vila Real and the first sardine-packing plant of the Sotavento in Olhão.

[100] Aristides de Amorim Girão and Fernanda de Oliveira Lopes Velho, "Estudos da população portuguesa I. Evolução demográfica e ocupação do solo continental (1890–1940)," quadro estatística (statistical chart), *Recenseamento Geral da População,* IX, 15 de Dezembro de 1950, I, 126–128.

Tavira roofs.

ing industries: with those of the fishermen who use *sacadas*, shore seines, trammels, *sardinhais, alcatruzes*, and miscellaneous gear; with those of the crew of the one small purse-seiner based on the city; and with those of the workers in two small factories (employing 154 women and 12 men) that pack horse mackerel, Spanish mackerel, sardines, and tuna.

One hears much less complaint in Tavira than in Lagos about nearby rival cities that have prospered and grown by reason of fishing. Tavira remains conservative, somewhat aristocratic and self-satisfied. With its many churches and its characteristic houses with four-slope roofs (probably imported from the Orient during the period of Portuguese worldwide expansion, and rare in other cities of the Algarve), it continues its stable way, based upon a thriving agriculture with fishing as a second string to its bow.

QUARTEIRA, ALBUFEIRA, AND ARMAÇÃO DE PERA

Near the center of the Algarve is a stretch of coast, including the above settlements, that has been used for fishing bases since time beyond record. Quarteira and Armação de Pera have been identified as Punic fishing and salting bases[101] and although Albufeira is not so identified, it is hard to believe that its excellent hill-girt beach, situated between the other two towns, would not have been used. However, it must be noted that the name is certainly Arabic and that the earliest notice now known (or at least, the earliest notice that I have found) is one relating to its existence at the time of the conquest of the Algarve by the Christians.[102] So it is possible that, in spite of its qualities of location, the site was first used for settlement by Moslems.

From the wide beach at Quarteira, one can see the last of the rocks and cliffs of the Barlavento, or western Algarve, from which the ocean is wearing away the sands now being deposited on the beaches of the eastern Algarve, the Sotavento. Albufeira's beach lies in an opening between the rocks where a small stream reaches the ocean. Armação de Pera has a situation partly similar to that of Albufeira but with a wide beach on its Sotavento side and high cliffs close by on the west.

Even though the livelihood of the fishermen living in these towns is being cut from under them by modern techniques concentrated in a few large settlements, they go about their profession with age-old methods. In fact, it is so difficult for these fishermen to adjust themselves to any other type of life that, like fishermen in many places elsewhere in the Algarve and in Portugal, they beg in nearby villages when in need and do not try to find work in agriculture. They form a group quite distinct from farmers and have a distaste for the life of the agriculturist. However, the reverse is not true; in summer, when farm work may be slack, or wages high for fishermen, many farmers take work with the fishing fleets of the larger cities.[103]

[101] António García y Bellido, "Colonización Púnica," *Historia de España*, Tomo I, Vol. II, map p. 315.

[102] Scriptores, *Cronica da Conquesta do Algarve*, cited in Leite de Vasconcellos, *Etnografia Portuguesa*, III, 680.

[103] Raquel Soeiro de Brito, "Um pequeno porto de pesca do Algarve: Albufeira," *Comptes Rendus du Congrès International de Géographie*, III, 233.

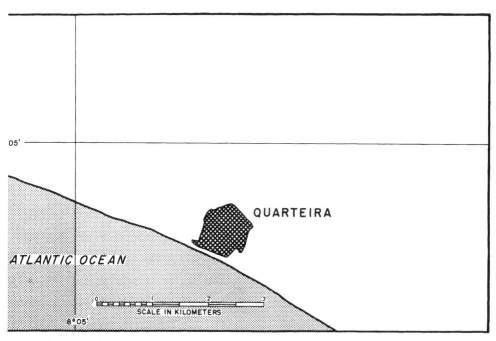

Coast at Quarteira

Quarteira. Today, the most specialized of the settlements is Quarteira. Located south of a large area of largely sterile sands that yield small agricultural returns even when large amounts of chemical fertilizers are applied to them, there is good reason for the inhabitants of the town to turn their attention away from the land and toward the sea. Although settlement on the site was made in ancient times, it may not have been maintained continuously. Probably no Moslem settlement existed, even though the location of a tuna net there in the sixteenth century suggests a continuation of earlier, similar use. In that century, the support of the Portuguese kings gave the settlement some importance as a fishing and commercial center, but most of its activity was ended abruptly by the earthquake of 1755, when because of the shock and the seismic wave that followed it there was great destruction of buildings and life. The secular damage, however, came from the obstruction of drainage which created malarial swamps, making the area notorious as one of intermittent fevers. In the mid-nineteenth century the remnants of its

141

pre-catastrophe industry and prosperity were represented by a few poor fishermen living in straw huts.

Recent improvements in drainage and in health conditions, as a consequence, have once again given Quarteira an opportunity of development; it is now the leading fishing center between Portimão and Faro. Its fishermen (329 at the end of 1959) catch a varied assortment of fish, mostly those that can be caught in relatively shallow waters; there are no motor-driven boats based on Quarteira and its 169 oar- and sail-propelled boats can no longer compete with motor-driven craft in fishing far from shore.

Quarteira is a museum for types of gear that have become unimportant or have been abandoned elsewhere; such variety of gear can be explained only by the stubborn conservatism of its fishermen who use only gear that is the same as the types to which they are accustomed (and which do not require great capital) or similar to them. The only striking addition to their equipment within recent generations is that of the *sacada*.

Of the ancient types of gear, they use the ordinary shore seine and also a relatively small edition of it called the *chinchorro*, ordinarily about one hundred yards long and up to fifteen yards wide at the center, where the "sack" of finer mesh holds the catch. The *chinchorro* is also used in some of the small fishing centers to the west of Quarteira, but is hardly known to the east.[104] Commonly used also are the trammel, here called *caçanal*, the *alcatruz* for octopus, the lobster pot for crayfish (*Palinurus vulgaris*), and various types of trotlines and devices similar to those described above.

The net called the *sardinheira* is still important here, while it is almost unknown elsewhere in the Algarve except in a few small fishing settlements of the Sotavento that, like Quarteira, have clung to ancient types of gear. This drift net, from ten to twenty yards wide and up to eight hundred yards long, is commonly used in January and February, when

[104] Other variants of the shore seine are the *levada* and the *bugiganga* (or *mugiganga*). The latter is considerably smaller than the others, usually not over two to three yards high and forty yards long. It is used at stream mouths, a practice usually discouraged by the government.

On the beach at Quarteira.

the large schools of sardines are spawning near shore. The nets are put out by a small boat with a "master" and five men, across the current or wind, usually a little after sunrise and again a short while after dark. As the nets suffer considerable damage, three-eighths of the value of the catch is allotted to them and one-eighth to the master. The other half of the value is divided into seven equal parts, one going to each of the six men and one to the boat. This net, named when its primary function was to take sardines, is now more frequently used to catch schools of horse mackerel.

Another drift net of importance in this region is the *seberta* (or *descoberta* or *amalhadeira*), a net of two meters in depth that may be almost a mile in length. It is put out either just before sunrise or just after sunset over water of at least fifty feet in depth. Placed across the current by a master and four men, so that one side rests upon the ocean bottom, it catches the highly valued red mullet, sea bream (*Pagellus*

143

acarne), sole, and bogue (Box boops). In winter, when the water is not clear, it may be put out at any time of day to catch the bogue.

At most beaches of the Algarve the sand smelt (*Atherina presbyter*) is caught in channel nets. At Quarteira, however, the net used is one peculiar to the site; similar to the *seberta* but much smaller, it is handled by two men in a small boat. Fixed in shallow water in the early morning with the lower edge weighted against the bottom, the fish are driven into it by the men beating the water with their oars. The division of the catch is in four parts: one each to the men, the net, and the boat.

This is the area of greatest importance in the catch of cuttle-fish, which are caught mostly with the *toneira*, a three-inch tubular body of lead with a half-inch diameter; it has a crown of twenty to thirty barbs of about half an inch each, turned back at about a forty-five–degree angle toward the body. Around the body is wrapped a piece of white cloth, which attracts the molluscs when it is dropped into the water and agitated by raising and lowering the line. Usually it is used at night with a lantern, over water of thirty-five to forty feet in depth, two or three kilometers from shore. Fishing with it is a monotonous but productive chore. Sometimes, using live squid for bait (when the fishing for the squid itself is not productive), the *toneira* is used to catch one of the sea breams (*Pagrus pagrus*) or the croaker. In Albufeira it is the most important fishing device after the *sacada* net,[105] and although it is not in the same status at Quarteira, it holds a respectable position.

Many other devices may be used on a small scale by individual fishermen, as, for example, the fish spear, which may be used openly when the law allows, or clandestinely at other times.

Quarteira in spite of its ancient-type gear, is one of the Algarvian leaders in the catch of the short-finned tunny, the croaker, the pargo (a seabream, *Pagrus pagrus*), the red mullet, and squid. It is usually in first place in the catch of sole and cuttlefish.

Albufeira. With an Arabic name and having had sufficient importance at the time of the Christian reconquest to be awarded to the re-

---

[105] Raquel Soeiro de Brito, "Um pequeno porto," *Comptes Rendus du Congrès,* III, 234. Oppian, in the second century A.D., described this device. See *Oppian Colluthus Tryphiodorus,* p. 437.

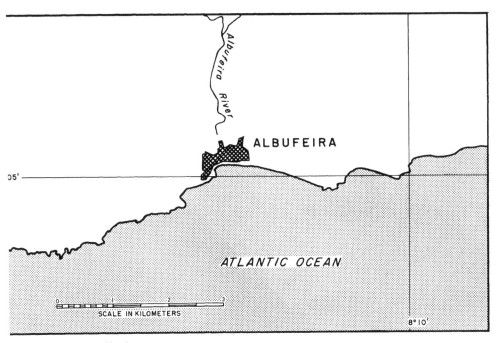

Coast at Albufeira

ligous-military order of Avis, Albufeira is no newcomer among the cities of the Algarve, even though it perhaps may not claim the antiquity of either Quarteira or Armação de Pera. That its thirteenth-century importance continued after the Christian reconquest is shown by the facts that it received a town charter in the early sixteenth century and that its fishing was of sufficient importance in the year 1505 for the taxes upon it to be given to the Duke of Coimbra. Specifically, his rights were to the taxes levied upon the fixed tuna nets of the area.

The earthquake of 1755 virtually destroyed the town, shaking down all but twenty-seven structures and leaving those badly damaged; 227 people were killed by the quake and by seismic waves. Nevertheless, the settlement re-established itself as a fishing center, for in the first half of the following century it was fifth in order of the Algarvian towns in taxes paid upon its fishing boats (paying more than Portimão). At that time, its fishermen used lines and fished close to shore for the most part and in summer took employment in the fixed tuna nets off the Lagos shore. Later in that century three fish-processing plants were operating,

145

Albufeira.

and its fishermen not only supplied their own needs but exported to other parts of the Algarve and even to the Alentejo. Fishing continues to be an important part of its economic life. Its fishermen use the traditional gear used in Quarteira (but not all of the types). The trammel called the *solheira* is used here more widely than in the nearby towns; it differs from the ordinary trammel in being less high, longer, and with larger mesh. Used particularly for sole, it is shot early in the morning in clear water over sandy bottoms and hauled during the early afternoon.

Of the thirty-two fixed nets for sardines that were licensed in 1890 to operate on the Algarvian coast,[106] the only two still operating are off-shore from Albufeira. Sometimes called the *valenciana*, this net is much like the fixed net for tuna, but smaller. It is only about fifty feet deep and its one lead arm is about one thousand feet long. The compartments, on a smaller scale, are similar to those of the tuna net. Designed to catch

[106] *Inquérito Industrial, 1890*, p. 321.

Boatloads of horse mackerel.

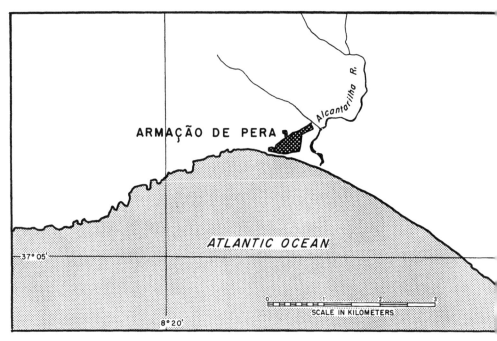

Coast at Armação de Pera

sardines primarily, it also takes horse mackerel, Spanish mackerel, the short-finned tuna (*Sarda sarda*), the croaker, and occasional demersal species. Although such nets are poor competitors with purse seines, the conservative fishermen of this coast have maintained these two. Surely, however, like their earlier companions, they will be gone before long.

In Albufeira at the end of 1959, 110 boats were registered, of which only 2 (totalling thirteen tons) had motors. There were 191 registered fishermen, including 62 at the fixed sardine nets.

However, in spite of the continuance of fishing, attention has been turned also to other activities; with the copious use of chemical fertilizers, early vegetables are grown to be shipped to other parts of Portugal and, to some extent, even to foreign markets. By reason of its late nineteenth- and twentieth-century energy, the town has increased its population rapidly. Of the coastal settlements, only Portimão has grown more quickly in the last half century. It must be remembered, however, that the population of Albufeira was relatively low at the beginning of the century and its total population now is not large. The whole parish, in 1950, had only 8,500 inhabitants.

Armação de Pera. Armação de Pera is the least important of the three settlements in all regards except that of a growing tourist industry. Not long ago one of the fixed nets for catching sardines was anchored offshore in its territory; this has now been dismantled permanently. Its remaining fishermen catch mullet, sole, gilthead, octopus, squid, cuttlefish, and some sardines and horse mackerel with traditional gear of the type used by the fishermen of Quarteira and Albufeira.

MINOR CENTERS

Of three dozen small fishing beaches or settlements on the Algarvian coast, over half do not land enough fish to be put on the records. Most of their catch is consumed by the fishermen and their families or, escaping the guards, is sold without auction and taxes. Some of these small beaches deserve mention by reason of their unique catch.

Minor centers of the west coast and the Cape. Three of them are on the strip of Algarvian coast that faces westward, where conditions are not favorable to fishing of any sort; the winds are persistent, the surf high, the fogs of summer frequent, and along most of the coast the ocean breaks against cliffs standing vertical to it. Only in a few places are there openings in the cliffs where a dozen small oar- or sail-propelled fishing boats are beached. The men who take off from these beaches are farmers who leave the land to be worked by their wives and children during the periods of the year when it is profitable to fish. It is no wonder that there are no specialized fishermen here; the wonder is that men risk themselves for such a small return. The total catch has little importance economically (that is, to the country as a whole; it certainly has to the men involved). This is the only area of the Algarve where a great delicacy, goose barnacles (*Pollicipes cornucopia*), is gathered. During autumn men go in their small boats to the headlands near Torre d'Aspa to take them from the rocks or sometimes even have themselves lowered over the cliffs to pry the barnacles from the rocks with knives. The goose barnacle is gathered also by men at the beach of Atalaia. Here, and also at a small strand where the men of Carrapateira beach their boats, the

149

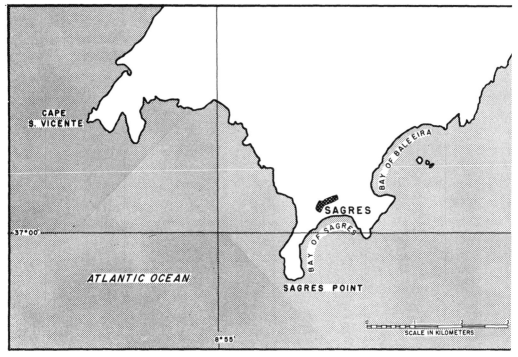

Coast at Sagres

crayfish takes second place in value of catch. At Carrapateira it is not the goose barnacle that is the specialty but rather the spider crab (*Maia squinado*), and in this species Carrapateira is, in some years, the Algarvian leader.

Cape S. Vicente, the *Promontorium Sacrum* of the Greeks, was known to the Phoenicians before the beginning of the first millennium B.C., if the opinion of Strabo is to be accepted; and it is probable that on the coastal zone out to the Cape, Phoenicians were living and trading, dedicated chiefly to the catching and salting of fish.[107] If Phoenicians were living there, it would not be surprising if a temple had been built, as the legend stated, to honor the Tyrian god Melkart, some of whose characteristics were incorporated into the Greek legendary hero, Hercules.

[107] According to Strabo the Phoenicians "possessed the best of Libia and Iberia" before the time of Homer, and just after the Trojan War went beyond the Pillars of Hercules (Gibraltar) and founded cities there. See António García y Bellido, "Colonización Púnica," *Historia de España*, Tomo I, Vol. II, 315–316, 328, 331.

150

The Greek historian Ephorus, of the fourth century B.C., stated flatly that a temple to Hercules existed. However, as reported by Strabo, at the end of the first century B.C. Artemidorus went to the spot and saw no temple, but only stones arranged according to patterns; he also reported that at night men were not allowed on the Cape, as it was then inhabited by the gods.[108] Whose gods these may ever have been, it is obvious that the site was well known and presumably had had sufficient importance long enough for myths to grow about it.

It is probable that the Phoenicians and Carthaginians beached their craft and put out their fixed nets for tuna in the Bay of Sagres or around the point in the little Bay of Baleeira, where today the fishermen of the town of Sagres come in with their boats. That the area was used by the Romans may be implicit in the name, Sagres; Edrisi, in the twelfth century, spoke of a small Moslem settlement there. The Christians, in turn, probably took over this settlement, and between 1448 and 1451 Prince Henry the Navigator established his Villa do Infante in the same region, perhaps merely taking over the ancient settlement.[109] Whether or not Sagres is a lineal descendant of a Phoenician settlement, its economy harks back to that period of time; only in this century was its fixed net for catching tuna dismantled. One claim to fame that has been attributed to it, however, should be corrected—that which states that the ships of Prince Henry sailed from the little Bay of Sagres on their voyages of discovery. Lagos was the port for the ships of Prince Henry; Sagres served only occasionally as a temporary stop in case of need.

Furthermore, if a harbor near the Cape had been used, it would have been Baleeira, a snug little re-entry into the plateau sheltered from the westerly and northwesterly winds that plague the Bay of Sagres. It is one of several little harbors on the south coast between the Cape and Lagos that have been used since time out of mind by fishermen using various nets and devices. However, the Baleeira fishermen are best known for their specialty catch; more crayfish are landed there than in any other port of the Algarve. Here, between May and October, the

---

[108] *The Geography of Strabo,* trans. by Horace Leonard Jones, p. 7 (3.1.3–4).

[109] At some unknown date before 1486 Sagres had been made a villa. J. Leite de Vasconcellos, *Etnografia Portuguesa,* II, 446–448.

At Baleeira.

crayfish are stored for several days at a time in great concrete tanks built into a recess in the rocks of the cliff, large enough to hold several thousand. When the time is propitious (when prices are high) they are auctioned and trucked off to Lisbon and other cities of Portugal.

Lobster pots, usually made of chestnut staves, with wire mesh at the ends, are put out in groups of a dozen to twenty on a line, each separated from those adjacent by about fifteen yards; they are baited with one of several types of fish, but commonly with squid, and dropped to rest upon the bottom in water from about 120 to 240 feet deep. The line between each of the pots is held away from the bottom by spherical glass floats so that it does not become entangled in the rocks. A surface float, above the end of the line of pots, marks its location.

Crayfish are the specialty and the greatest single source of profit to Sagres fishermen, but a great variety of fish in small amount are also caught with nets, lines, and other devices. All are supposed to be brought

152

Lobster pots.

Before the auction at Baleeira.

in to be auctioned under the eye of the local police and customs offi-
cials; the catch is laid out on the beach in small groups, according to
species of fish and according to size within each species, where buyers
can appraise them before the professional auctioneer begins the sale.
In one auction—a small one—local women, buying for their homes, and
a professional buyer, acting for two large restaurants in Lisbon, were
the only customers.[110] The auctioneer began his quotations at almost
double the price at which the fish were finally bought. Quoting rapidly,
his figures fell until finally "chui" made the contract. Some of each of
the following marine fauna were sold at that auction: bass, whiting,
moray, octopus, forkbeard, comber (two varieties), spider crab, scabbard fish, croaker, two varieties of sargo, rockfish, striped wrasse, sole,
crayfish, squid, horse mackerel, pout, electric ray, flounder, red mullet,

[110] The cheapest fish were bought by the local people. When sardines, horse
mackerel, and Spanish mackerel are being caught in *sacadas*, buyers representing
the factories of Portimão are there also.

and sea bream.[111] That is to say, in a small auction on a small beach on an unexceptional day, nineteen species of eighteen genera of fish, plus two crustaceans and one mollusc were brought in by the local fishermen to be sold. Of the prices received in the auction, a minimum of 18 per cent was taken by the official institutions, aside from charges for licenses for the use of various types of gear, and various charges for each fisherman which, on the average, amount to about sixty to seventy-five escudos per year (roughly $2.00 U.S. to $2.50). This sum may not seem large, but when the chief earner of a family has a yearly income of less than the equivalent of two hundred dollars a year, it is important.

Minor centers of the Barlavento. A few miles northeast of Sagres is the beach of Salema, lying just inside the most important fishing grounds for sardines by purse-seiners; but here the local fishermen are not so much concerned with sardines as they are with the great miscellany of sea fauna that they catch with primitive gear. Here, as at the little harbor of Baleeira, the specialty during the late summer and autumn months is squid, caught with the *toneira*. When the catch of the squid itself is not going well the fishermen often use the live squid, pierced through the soft underpart, as bait to fish for the large croaker. The fisherman is even saved the trouble of watching his line, for the squid signals, by its struggles, the approach of the croaker. Fishermen from both beaches use both lines and weels—willow or wire traps similar to the lobster pots, but not as large and somewhat elongated—to catch morays. Both places specialize in the catch of the scabbard fish, a long, flat, silver-grey fish, usually about one yard long and three to four inches wide, and about one inch through at its thickest part. This fish appears in large numbers in the middle months of the year. During May, June, and July, by far the greater part of the total catch is landed along the strip of coast to the west of Lagos. Occasionally the season is early and the catch may begin here in April, or a late season for this area may extend into August. Usually, however, any scabbard fish

---

[111] The following species have not been previously identified: whiting (*Gadus merlangus*), comber (*Epinephelus aeneus*), rockfish (*Scorpaena scrofa*), pout (*Gadus luscus*), electric ray (*Torpedo torpedo*), flounder (*Platichys flesus*).

caught later than July are landed by Olhão fishermen. Also, in occasional years, some are caught in January, February, and March. When this is the case it is the fishermen of Fuzeta who land them.[112] The scabbard fish is usually caught with a line and two hooks. Behind the hooks is either a white cloth or a tubular sheath of aluminum, and a ring. When the line is drawn through the water, the ring makes it turn; this movement—and the sheen of the metal or brightness of the cloth—attracts the fish. When hooked, they are not hard to land, but for a novice their first emergence from the water can be a frightening experience; the ferocity of their appearance, with glaring eyes and bared teeth, is enough to make the fisherman recoil—as indeed he should do, for if he is not adept in handling the fish he can receive a nasty bite, which is apt to become infected. These fish come near the surface for about a half hour at sunup and especially about sundown. At these times they will strike at virtually anything offered. Two skilled men in a boat may catch as many as 150 in one brief session. H. Muir Evans makes an interesting comment on the *Lepidopus caudata*:

It is a gregarious and roving fish and is found from Norway to the Cape of Good Hope and extends as far as New Zealand and the Atlantic coast of America. It is found near the surface and also at a depth of 300 metres and is a very fast swimmer. A curious habit of this fish has given it the name of "frost fish" in New Zealand; on cold nights it has been known in vast numbers to swim towards the shore, and there is heaped up a ridge of corpses. This is said to be due to the effect of cold, but this is unlikely because it has not been known to behave thus in Norwegian waters. Further, the effect of cold on fish is usually to make them seek deeper waters, as is well known from the sole's habits. I think a more reasonable explanation is that we have here an example of the mass migratory immolation that has been described in lemmings and springbuck.[113]

Two other small beaches between Salema and Lagos should be mentioned, Burgau and Luz. Their catch is not large and it is miscellaneous, with some small specialization in squid and octopus.

[112] This information has been taken from the official records of the decade of the 1950's.
[113] H. Muir Evans, *Sting-fish and Seafarer*, p. 62.

Across the bay from Lagos is a settlement of ancient foundation, Alvôr, although the present site is not precisely that of earlier times. It has been suggested that on this location or near it was the Roman Portus Annibalis, which name implies an even earlier history for the settlement under the Carthaginians. However, even though Portus Annibalis has not been convincingly located, there is some evidence upon which to base the belief that the Romans found fish-salting establishments near the site of present Alvôr when they first came to the region and that they maintained them in operation. There is also some evidence that Roman construction was made upon foundations of an earlier period of time.

Whether or not a settlement existed there under Gothic rule and even early Moslem rule is not now known; there is no doubt, however, that in the late period of Moslem control it was an important town, for when the Christian crusaders conquered it in 1189, they killed 5,600 people "sparing neither sex nor age."[114] This conquest was not permanent; Alvôr fell again into Moslem hands two years later and was made by them one of the strongest centers of defense on the Algarvian coast.[115] They held it until permanent Christian reconquest of all of the Algarve was accomplished in the middle of the thirteenth century.

That it continued to have some importance to the Portuguese kings is indicated by the fact that a royal document of 1314 referred to its ancient salt beds. Its importance was sufficient in the year 1495 that King João II, fatally ill, left the small settlement of Monchique to go there, presumably because of its better facilities for his care.[116] By the end of the fifteenth century it was clearly one of the most important settlements of the Algarve, with approximately 5,000 inhabitants in the area.[117] Such importance was not without reason, for its harbor was commercially useful and its fortifications strong, but its usefulness decreased as the troubled postconquest generations receded and populations partly supported for martial purposes decreased. In 1706 a report

[114] Francisco Xavier d'Athaide Oliveira, *A monografia de Alvôr*, pp. 53, 62–63, 103, 109.

[115] A. Herculano, *História de Portugal,* Vol. III, Liv. 3, 166.

[116] Garcia de Resende, *Chronica de El-Rei D. João* II, III, 67.

[117] A. de Sousa Silva Costa Lobo, *História da sociedade em Portugal,* p. 140.

Netmaker at Alvôr.

mentioned 350 persons as inhabitants of the town, most of whom were dependent upon fishing and maritime pursuits.[118]

The earthquake of 1755 greatly damaged the buildings of the settlement and, in addition, the seismic wave that followed deposited enormous quantities of sand, choking the bay. Previous to the catastrophe, the harbor accommodated ships of fifty tons; afterward it was useless except for small boats. Since that year (1755), Alvôr has been of minor importance in the affairs of the south coast. After the earthquake a small group of fishers and farmers re-established the settlement, and before the end of the eighteenth century eighty fishermen registered at the settlement were reported to be skilled in fishing along the coast and also on the high seas.[119] Since that time, other Algarvian ports have appropriated its place in fishing. Now it is a dispirited village. Most men of the

[118] John Stevens, *The Ancient and Present State of Portugal,* p. 241.
[119] Constantino Botelho de Lacerda Lobo, "Memoria sobre o estado das pescarias da costa do Algarve," *Memorias económicas,* Vol. V, p. 107.

A fish trap at Alvôr.

area are fundamentally and exclusively farmers; few are exclusively fishermen; many farm when they can and fish when it is profitable, using traditional gear, both nets and lines. During the winter, when there is no employment in farming, some row out several miles from shore where they put out lines to catch demersal fish. During all months of the year they gather shellfish, especially clams (species of *Tapes* and *Donax*). Cockles (*Cardium edule*) are eaten locally and the razor shell (*Solen marginatus*) is gathered to be eaten in time of dire need, but otherwise to be sold to sports fishermen in the summer for bait. The spinous spider crab is caught to be sold.

A hand net on a stiff frame is used to scrape the bottom of the estuary for shellfish. The channel net is used openly when not forbidden by the government, and clandestinely when it is prohibited. The same is true of another net, similar in purpose but not fixed; it is drawn by two men toward the narrowing river mouth when the tide is receding. The fish spear, of some use in earlier days, is hardly known now. Also used are trotlines, weels, trammels, and seines.

Ferragudo, across the bay from Portimão, is a town sharing the common heritage of Algarvian coastal towns, a long tradition of fishing. At the end of the eighteenth century the two hundred fishermen then recorded in the settlement were reputed to be even more daring and skilled in various methods of their profession than the noted fishermen of Lagos. Versatility was obviously one of their qualities, for they divided the year into four quarters, each of which was largely devoted to a type of fishing differing from those of the others: during the first quarter line fishing at sea was the major preoccupation; during April, May, and June the majority of the fishermen worked on a great fixed tuna net; from early July through September a variety of demersal fish were caught by the use of weels; and the activity during the last three months of the year was concerned with the shore-seine catch of sardines. Not only were fish sold fresh for local consumption but part of the catch was salted for sale to the pack trains from the Alentejo. The settlement was one of the economic leaders among Algarvian fishing towns at that time.[120]

Ferragudo's position of importance was changed, however, with the emergence of Portimão, in the twentieth century, as the major fishing port of the western Algarve. Now, as at the small ports to the east—Carvoeiro, Benagil, and Senhora da Rocha—the few remaining fishermen use traditional devices; but these techniques are diminishing in importance. Such men as remain in the profession are apt to go to Lisbon to sail with the cod fleet or to take employment in the canning plants of Portimão.

Minor centers of the Sotavento. About equidistant from Tavira are another pair of small fishing towns, Santa Luzia on the west and Cabanas on the east. Both are known for their catch of octopus, but Santa Luzia usually records the largest tonnage of any settlement on the Algarvian coast, and the number of its *alcatruzes*, the devices with which

---

[120] The *concelho* of Lagoa paid the third highest tax upon fishing boats in the Algarve at that time. This must have been levied against the boats of the settlement of Ferragudo. See Constantino Botelho de Lacerda Lobo, "Memoria sobre o estado das pescarias da costa do Algarve," *Memorias económicas*, Vol. V, p. 109; also João Baptista da Silva Lopes, *Corografia*, p. 297, Map. 11.

the molluscs are caught, is the highest of the province. The so-called *alcatruz*[121] is a long line of clay pots tied together by a quarter-inch cord. Each pot has a height of about ten inches and a maximum diameter of about eight inches. The cord is tied around the relatively narrow neck below the flaring upper edges. Separated from each other by about three yards, the pots are tied to the "mother-line" by yard-long cords. An ordinary apparatus will have two hundred pots to be laid on the sandy bottom of the sea. In the summer, when weather is calm, they are put out in about twenty feet of water; in winter, with a turbulent sea and greater danger to the pots, they are put out farther, in water of seventy-five to one hundred feet, up to four miles from shore.[122] In the last few months of the year, when the catch is good, they may be taken up each day so that salt can be put in to drive out the occupant. In other months, the apparatus may be left for several days without lifting it. Usually involved are a small boat and four or five men who divide the value of the catch so that the men and the boat get one part each and the *alcatruz* two.

Although its claim to distinction is in the catch of octopus, Santa Luzia also records the catch of several other species, chiefly short-finned tuna, Spanish mackerel, and horse mackerel.

Until the last quarter of the eighteenth century the important settlements near the mouth of the Guadiana River, in the eastern Algarve, were Castro Marim, Monte Gordo, Cacela, and, a little earlier, Santo António de Arenilha. The first, possibly the site of Roman Baesuris, now encircles a hill which was fortified by the Arabs when they controlled the territory and later was strengthened by Christian conquerors. For some generations after the reconquest, it was considered to be the strongest center of defense in the Algarve.[123] It became the seat of the

[121] Properly, it should be called "apparatus of *alcatruzes*" (*aparelho de alcatruzes*). The word *alcatruz*, taken from Arabic, refers to the type of clay pot that was tied to the wheel of a *nora*. It was this same type of pot, apparently, that was put to service in catching octopods.

[122] Raquel Soeiro de Brito, "Um pequeno porto," *Comptes Rendus du Congrès International de Géographie*, p. 241.

[123] Gaetano Ferro, "Ricerche di geografia urbana nell' Algarve," *Annali di ricerche*, X, No. 2, 60.

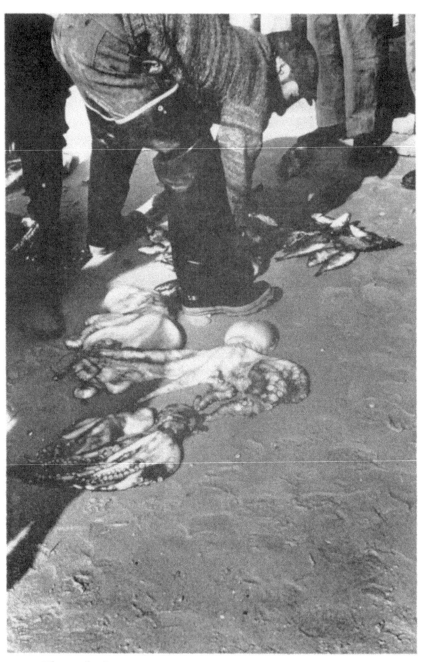

The catch of octupus.

famous Order of Christ in the fourteenth century, and even prior to that time its salt beds had been of sufficient importance for the Portuguese king to reserve them for the crown.[124] It was one of the earliest of Algarvian settlements to receive a charter from the king, roughly at the same time that Tavira, Faro, Loulé, and Silves were so recognized.

After the troubled times following the reconquest of the Algarve, however, the need of a stronghold against Moslems and Spaniards declined; and by the early nineteenth century only a part of the salt beds were being used.[125] With the increasing importance of Vila Real de Santo António, both in the last century and in this century, Castro Marim has grown ancillary to it, supplying salt for fish packing and labor for the factories and ships. Such is its present, modest function.

The complete history of Monte Gordo, a fisherman's center situated just to the west of Vila Real, is not recorded, but it is known to have been an important place of fishing in the fifteenth century; in 1443 Prince Henry received a grant of one-tenth of the fish caught there.[126] That it continued in the same type of economy is obvious from a manuscript of 1577, which relates that the fishermen of Monte Gordo supplied fish to the nearby settlement of Cacela.[127] Its decline probably followed directly after that date, as did that of all of the Portuguese coastal settlements while the country was under Spanish control. However, the effect of Spanish control seems to have been more disastrous for Monte Gordo than for most other settlements; there was no fishing at the site in the early eighteenth century and it is recorded that a man from Castro Marim re-established the industry in 1711. Then a few Catalans came; they were followed by Andalusians, French, and other Catalans in numbers. They fished and built huts.[128] By 1774, they comprised a busy group, living in makeshift straw huts and evading the pay-

[124] Henrique da Gama Barros, *História da administração pública*, IX, 296.

[125] However, it still was a far more important producer than any other settlement of the Algarve in 1790–1791. See Adrien Balbi, *Essai statistique sur le royaume de Portugal et d'Algarve*, I, 138.

[126] Henrique de Gama Barros, *História da administração pública*, IX, 296.

[127] Francisco Xavier d'Athaide Oliveira, *Monografia do concelho de Villa Real de Santo António*, p. 65.

[128] H. F. Link, *Voyage en Portugal*, II, 158; Francisco Xavier d'Athaide Oliveira, *Monografia do concelho de Villa Real de Santo António*, p. 73.

ment of taxes to Portugal by taking their catch to Spain. In total, about one hundred boats with seines were based upon the settlement.[129]

These settlers and their activities were one of the important reasons for the establishment of Vila Real by the Marquis de Pombal. His determination to remove the political danger that they might present and the economic loss that was occasioned by their delivery of fish caught off the Portuguese coast to Spain led him to insist that they move into the new city. Most of them refused and a considerable proportion moved into a settlement on the Spanish side of the mouth of the Guadiana. The settlement of Monte Gordo was obliterated when Pombal ordered the huts burned.

But the site is too valuable to be neglected. This area near the mouth of the Guadiana River is a feeding area for fish of many species. Now again it has grown and is the home of a thriving industry for its inhabitants. They still use traditional gear, but with it they maintain a better standard of living than do the men hired by the commercial companies in nearby Vila Real. By the use of shore seines and sardine nets, they catch pelagic fish that are sold for canning. With trammels they catch the high-priced mullet and sole. They catch other highly valued fish, in smaller amounts, on lines and with a miscellany of other traditional types of gear. Many a man working for the commercial companies of Vila Real wishes that he were a member of the Monte Gordo community.

Cacela, about five miles west-southwest of Monte Gordo, was once an important stronghold. Taken from the Moslems by the aid of the

---

[129] One source states that twenty-five hundred fishermen normally worked at Monte Gordo (see Constantino Botelho de Lacerda Lobo, "Memoria sobre a decadencia das pescas," *Memorias económicas*, Vol. IV, p. 350), and that five thousand people lived in the settlement, some fishing and others preparing the fish for transport and sale, living in a "large city," with huts along a series of streets that reached from the Guadiana River almost to Cacela. See Constantino Botelho de Lacerda Lobo, "Memoria sobre o estado das pescarias," *Memorias económicas*, Vol. V, pp. 129–130.

Some later authors were dubious of these figures and there are no official statistics to support Lacerda Lobo. However, the number of fishermen must have been large enough to cause perturbation, or Pombal would not have acted as he did.

Knights of Santiago, it was given into the control of that order.[130] The Knights were reasonable and retained Moslems to work on the land. Because of their tolerance, disruption of the economy was not great. For a while the settlement became the residence of the Master of the Order;[131] it was sufficiently important in the early years after the conquest to receive its charter from the king, in 1283. The decline that followed shortly thereafter was caused, in part at least, by the fact that it was in a position exposed to the Moslems, who were persistently raiding the coast. To escape this danger, the local administration was moved to Castro Marim, and by 1750 its inhabitants numbered fewer than five hundred. Its virtual ruin was caused by the earthquake of 1755, when not only were the buildings of the town mostly shaken into rubble, but the changes made along the coast caused blocked drainage and stagnant pools, which became breeding places of malarial mosquitoes.[132]

At the present time, with malaria control effective, a few fishermen live on the site and support themselves through the use of traditional gear. Their only claim to distinction is found in the fact that their beach is one of two in the Algarve where commercial quantities of clams are gathered.

Santo António de Arenilha, a loosely agglomerated settlement on the right bank of the Guadiana River, seaward from the present site of Vila Real, was recorded in a document of 1577 as a small "*villota*." In another century and a half it was "swallowed by the sea," the phrase apparently indicating a change in relative levels of land and sea. By 1722, only ruins were left and all that has come down to the present is that part of its name used by Vila Real de Santo António.[133]

[130] H. V. Livermore, *A History of Portugal*, p. 135.

[131] Francisco Xavier d'Athaide Oliveira, *Monografia do concelho de Villa Real de Santo António*, pp. 62, 66, 118.

[132] Changes, both sudden, as in the case of the earthquake, and secular, have changed the levels along the Algarvian coast and caused the elimination of several settlements. See Francisco Xavier d'Athaide Oliveira, *Monografia de Alvôr*, pp. 99–100.

[133] Francisco Xavier d'Athaide Oliveira, *Monografia do concelho de Villa Real de Santo António*, pp. 65, 69, 71,

Such are the aspects of towns and of life among Algarvian fishermen as I observed them. The willingness to accept productive change is shown in the differential specialization of the towns. The differences between these settlements demonstrate an intelligent resiliency and a capacity to grasp local opportunities. In spite of such qualities, however, there is also a deep-seated conservatism, shown, not unsurprisingly, in inverse ratio to the economic prosperity of the settlement. The poorest groups cling most tenaciously to their accustomed ways; the nearer they live to minimum subsistence the greater is their devotion to ways that have long proved to be useful. Before abandoning known methods these people ask for assurance that other methods will be better. No doubt since antiquity they have repeatedly heard that change was desirable, essential, and inevitable, yet they have rejected many developments that, to other parts of the world, have seemed essential and inevitable.

Two strong currents run through this stream of culture: one, alert and energetic, directed toward change, the other, fringing and cautious, an eddying movement directed toward protected, quiet backwaters. In view of the record it is safe to say that great changes will take place in these towns and among these fishermen; but it is also indicated that a visitor to the region three—or five—hundred years hence would find familiar accents in this account of men pursuing time-tested ways.

4. The Limestone Zone

▞▚▞

T HE LENS-SHAPED Limestone Zone, narrow at the Cape, about a dozen miles wide in the center, and virtually pinched out at the other end just north of Tavira, lies between the schist mountains on the north and the Coastal Plain to the south. Made up of Jurassic limestones, dolomites, and marls, and broken by faults, it appears as a series of linearly disposed crests, subparallel to the sea, and separated by fertile, green valleys. Through almost all of its length, the Zone is separated from the schists by a thin edge of red Triassic sandstones and conglomerates. This line is indicated by the route between the towns of Vila do Bispo, on the extreme west, through Budens, Bensafrim, Silves, S. Bartolomeu de Messines, Salir, then along a fault line to Alportel, after which it turns east to follow another fault line, continuing eastward to beyond and just above the city of Tavira.[1] Each interior crest, usually of

[1] See maps: Towns of the Algarve (p. 2) and Physical Regions of the Algarve (p. 15).

167

dolomite or compact limestone, is higher than the preceding, until the highest, in its center section, is above the level of the nearby schist mountains. The valleys, broad on the seaward edge and increasingly narrow toward the mountains, have been cut by streams into soft marls.

THE LANDSCAPE

The Limestone Zone has acquired some of the cultural qualities of both the Caldeirão Mountains and the Coastal Plain area, but the addition of traits exclusively its own gives it a distinct personality. Coming to it from the mountains, one notices its special landscape. No longer does one have the lonely sensation of bleak spaces and the feeling of stern necessity for struggle and frugal living. The Limestone Zone has the appearance of more intimacy and greater amity between men and the land; not that the area gives the impression of lush prosperity, as do certain parts of the Coastal Plain, for exposed over much of the surface are grim, grey outcrops of limestone or uncultivated areas of natural scrub typified by the dwarf palm (*Chamaerops humilis*), the low, bush-like oak (*Quercus coccifera*), cistus (*C. albidus* and *C. monspeliensis*), asphodel (*Asphodelus lusitanicus*), mastic (*Pistacia lentiscus*), the wild olive (*Olea oleaster*), lavender (*Lavandula stoechas*), holm oak (*Q. ilex*), and carob (*Ceratonia siliqua*). Eighty per cent of the woody species are Mediterranean and the rest are species limited to Iberia or Africa. Of the nonwoody species, 68 per cent are Mediterranean. Middle European species are virtually absent.

The vegetational borders are sharply drawn. The members of the Limestone Zone floristic complex are scarcely seen either on the Coastal Plain or on the schists of the mountains; and the gum cistus (*Cistus ladaniferus*), the dominant member of the mountain complex, is seldom seen on the limestone. Rarely to be seen are any of the few still-existing species of the natural vegetation of the Coastal Plain.

It is not a plant complex that would recommend the land to an observant farmer of most lands of the world. So it is not surprising that a considerable proportion of the Limestone Zone is not cultivated. The amazing fact is that so much of it is used at all. Here, on the most unpromising-looking rocky hills, Algarvian farmers have broken the surface

Fence of rocks taken from the land in the Limestone Zone.

and planted carob, olive, almond, and fig trees, often with grains beneath. To do so they have worked for generations to clear the fields of the larger stones, piling them up into rock fences at times six feet high and from eight to ten feet broad. Only in the valley bottoms, separated by wide areas of calcareous upland, is there good soil to be cultivated without laborious preparation.

Different from its bordering regions, that can be divided into western and eastern economic subareas, the Limestone Zone is essentially the same throughout its length. The hardy plants growing on the uplands are not sensitive to minor differences of temperature and rainfall and the irrigated crops of the valley bottoms are largely protected against outbreaks of cold by the mountains to the north.

Climatic differences within the region are due mostly to variations in elevation and distance from the sea. Such facts can be recognized by comparison of the length of the growing season and the date of maturation of the crops growing in the low valleys of the southern border near the sea with those of the northern, higher valleys. These facts, however,

The Limestone Zone, with schist mountains in the background.

cannot be given conclusive statistical support because there is only one climatologic station in the area (and with a broken record) and two other stations which record only rainfall. From the records of these three stations it appears that the rainfall of the Zone, on the average, is as low as twenty-five inches per year (Loulé) and at least as high as thirty-one inches (São Brás) elsewhere.[2]

Settlement

Unlike the Caldeirão Mountain area, where the population is concentrated in villages, about half of the inhabitants of the Limestone Zone live in small houses which are dispersed over the slopes and valleys. This dispersal took place after the Christian reconquest of the Algarve. The land, except for favored locations like Loulé and a few others,

[2] Loulé received an average of twenty-five inches per year from 1931 to 1950; S. Bartolomeu de Messines received an average of twenty-seven inches, 1932–1950; São Brás received an average of thirty-one inches during the years 1912–1941. *O Clima de Portugal*, Pt. VII, "Baixo Alentejo e Algarve," Maps 24, 26.

mostly those that were in convenient contact with coastal settlements, was probably unused for agriculture before the Christian reconquest, especially during the final generations of Moslem control. In spite of choice small areas where irrigated crops are now successful, there are no reports from the earliest years after the defeat of the Moslems to show that settlement had been made in desirable locations such as São Brás, Alte, and Salir. Castles are recorded; Paderne apparently was a fort of great strength,[3] but towns and agricultural exploitation of the remote oases are not mentioned. Such a condition is not surprising in view of the methods of warfare practiced by both antagonists of the time. Noting the destruction of Spanish lands during this period[4] one must assume that the same treatment was accorded to southern Portugal.

Thus it seems that settlement of the Limestone Zone was not made early in the period after the reconquest. The earliest known report mentioning the present settlement of São Brás is one of 1517, and the total population of the county (*concelho*) of Alportel was between 500 and 750 in 1565. The areas of Salir and Boliqueime were not established as parishes until 1589.[5] But slow development of both settlements and dispersed homesteads took place prior to the middle of the eighteenth century. In 1757 a report concerning the county of Alportel described a scattered population, partly in villages and partly in individual homesteads. It seems from the wording of the report that the population lived in irrigable areas where they planted vegetable gardens as well as cherries, plums, peaches, apricots, quinces, apples, and "other trees." Vines, frequently mentioned, have subsequently disappeared, presumably at the end of the nineteenth century, when phylloxera destroyed most of the vineyards of Portugal. Figs and carobs were the most-mentioned crops, and without doubt the most-valued unirrigated trees. Almonds were cultivated, but if number of references indicates their importance they were not widely spread. Total population at that time was low. As Estanco Louro says, "During one hundred and sixty-seven years from

---

[3] "Chronica da conquista do Algarve," *Portvgaliae monvmenta historica*, I, 418.
[4] Dan Stanislawski, *The Individuality of Portugal*, pp. 157–161.
[5] M.F. do Estanco Louro, *O Livro de Alportel*, pp. 55, 68–69.

1757 to 1924, São Brás progressed far more than it had in the four hundred and fifty-seven years between 1300 and 1757."[6] Progress has meant not only increased population but accomplishment; it is obvious from the appearance of the houses that the present inhabitants are not living without amenities. These dwellings, made of the country rock with mud mortar and a coating of clay daub, are calcimined frequently. The woman of the house puts a coat of white or tint on her dwelling at least once a year and in most cases she persistently keeps watch for any small areas in need and immediately covers them. Often a wide band of bright blue is painted around the top, and around the doors and windows.

The plan of the house is simple: it is a rectangle, more often than not with a two-slope roof, the ridge of which usually parallels the road—if the house is placed against the road. The one-slope roof is also used, but less frequently, and the four-slope roof is rare. Many of the houses that border the roads are built with the front wall continuing a few feet above the level of the lower tiles of the roof so that the roof and its form are not seen by a traveller. This high, front wall is less frequently used for houses dispersed in the fields; more commonly, the tile roofs of these houses surmount the walls and project slightly beyond them. In virtually all cases the interior plan of houses is uncomplicated, ordinarily with a minimum of two small rooms for multiple uses. With increasing economic status of the owner, the number and size of rooms is greater. Crowning the structure, in most cases, are Algarvian chimneys, delicately fashioned structures that are not always functional; sometimes they are put on houses just for decoration, even when there is no fireplace within the dwelling.

Next to the house there is typically a small, walled garden area, where fruits and flowers are planted at the edges and where figs, maize, carobs, and other crops are laid out to dry in summer. Commonly, there is a threshing floor nearby. It may be paved with stone for the threshing of wheat, or it may be of packed earth, hardened while damp by driving a

[6] *Ibid.*, pp. 22–29, 68–69, 75. This sparcity of population is a matter of the interior and remote areas of the Limestone Zone; Loulé continued to be, as it had been under the Moslems, an important center, and Silves, even though badly deteriorated, continued to exist, as did other towns nearer the Coastal Plain.

Threshing with the *trilho,* a wooden sledge with cutting stones—and some-times, now, pieces of metal—set in the bottom.

flock of sheep or goats back and forth over it for several hours. The latter floor is suitable for husking broad beans and other products of large kernels or seeds. Here from one to four or five mules (or other animals) are driven over the grain; or, less frequently, some form of the *trilho,* the ancient Roman *tribulum,* may be used. If there is not a well near the house, a cemented floor may be built with a slope toward an orifice leading to a cistern, for collecting rainwater. On the crests of some of the hills above the villages one can still see the circular buildings with conical roofs for wind mills.

AGRICULTURE

The agricultural aspect of the Limestone Zone is twofold: irrigated bottomlands in the valleys, and nonirrigated tree crops and grain on the slopes. The valleys on the south, in general, are broad and relatively low, and their exploitation is similar to that of the nearby Coastal Plain; a

173

varied horticulture with two or three crops each year is the result of intensive cultivation and fertilization. However, toward the northern edge of the Limestone Zone the valleys are smaller, higher, and farther from the tempering effect of the sea. The yearly range of temperature is greater. Summer mean temperatures are only slightly higher than those of the Coastal Plain stations, but the winter temperatures are critical and impose limitations upon agriculture. For example, Faro, on the Coastal Plain, rarely has a freezing day (one day when minus one-fifth of a degree F. was recorded in the period 1912 to 1941, and one day with a temperature reaching to one and a half degrees below freezing in 1956). São Brás, almost directly above it in the Limestone Zone, is threatened with nights of sharp frost in each of the three winter months. Orange trees that produce a more satisfactory fruit in the higher valleys than those grown nearer the sea are threatened by such frosts. During the cold winter of 1956–1957, when temperatures of twelve degrees F. were recorded in the upper Limestone Zone,[7] all of the oranges grafted upon the ordinary bitter-orange stock were killed. Only those grafted onto the cold-resistant *Citrus triptera* (an experimental variety developed at Kew Gardens and interplanted with those of the bitter-orange rootstocks near Alte) survived.

In general, horticultural products of the upper Limestone Zone valleys are three weeks later in ripening than those at Faro or Tavira on the coast. Nevertheless, the upper valleys are still premium areas with a thriving agriculture and horticulture, commonly with two crops each year or, with some rotations, five crops in two years. A frequently used rotation is that of wheat in the winter followed by maize in the summer, then sweet potatoes, which stay in the ground during the early part of the following year. Lima beans, which grow especially well in the higher valleys, follow the sweet potatoes; then maize is planted again, to be followed by string beans or cabbage, completing the cycle. Another cycle will begin with one of the small grains.

Important and fertile as they are, the irrigated valleys do not create the special character of the Limestone Zone; it is the unirrigated slopes

[7] *O Clima de Portugal*, Part VII, Maps 11 and 18; *Anuário climatológico de Portugal*, Vol. X (1956), Part 1, p. 90; Vol. XI (1957), Part 1, p. 86.

with their groves of figs, almonds, carobs, and olives—usually with wheat, but at times any other one of the small grains, chick-peas, or broad beans planted beneath them—that best typify the area. And it is the product of these trees that have yielded cash from exports. Even in the river valleys the characteristic association of trees and grain may be maintained. In the lower part of the Zone, where the hills are gently rolling, most of the land is covered with one or more of the trees, or, indeed, with all four intermixed, with underplanting as well. In the upper part of the Zone near the schist mountains, almonds and figs are few and olives and carobs appear sporadically with large tracts of uncultivated land between the clearings made for them.

The dominant man-land association in the Limestone Zone is that of farmers working their own properties. The percentage of such ownership is higher than in the Coastal Plain (but not as high as that in the Caldeirão Mountains). Both share-working and renting of properties is comparatively low. In the counties of Loulé and Silves almost three-quarters of the farms are worked by their owners; of the balance, more are rented than worked by shares.[8]

THE FIG

The fig is hardy and can be seen on rocky soils and even growing out of rock walls, but it produces well only on relatively good and fairly level land. The traditional belief of local farmers that it must have its roots wet and its leaves warmed by the sun is well based. In the upper Limestone Zone, where its roots may not be able to reach water except in favored locations, it is limited to the river valleys and dells. In lower parts of the Zone it is more widespread, even on the interfluvial slopes. It is found from extremes, east and west, in the Algarve.

The fig is, possibly, one of the earliest domesticated plants introduced into the Algarve. Victor Hehn has shown that it was not known to the Greeks of the earliest Homeric times, yet it is commonly mentioned in the Old Testament. Like many other important economic items, it may have been introduced into southern Iberia by the Phoenicians prior to

[8] *Inquérito as condições de habitação da família, anexo ao IX Recenseamento geral da população* (em 15 de Dezembro de 1950), pp. 8–9.

175

the time of its acceptance by the Greeks.[9] Certainly the fig groves were famous under later Semites, for Edrisi, of the twelfth century, reported that the area of Silves was famous for its figs which were of exquisite flavor and were exported to all countries of the Occident.[10] In the same century (or perhaps slightly later) another Arab described the method of caprification that is still followed in South Portugal.[11] From the context one may infer that his description is similar to that of an early Chaldean source. It seems that not only figs, but the caprification necessary to produce good fruit was an ancient Semitic discovery.

The process of caprification ordinarily involves planting about one nonedible-fruit-producing fig tree for each twenty producers of edible fruit. It is in the former that the insect called a fig wasp (*Blastophega psenes* L.) develops. In June it leaves the host tree and fecundates the female, edible, fruit-producing fig. Without such fertilization, fruits do not properly mature; they are small, low in sugar content, and may fall from the branch before fully developed. With caprification, the choice fig of the Algarve is produced, an oblong, black fruit with yellow flesh.

In the Algarve figs are started by cuttings, which are watered and cultivated carefully during the two years following planting. After five years they begin to bear. Ordinarily, there are three periods of harvest after mid-August. The product of the first is exported or made into regional confections. That of the second is mostly used for the diet of the ordinary people, who depend upon dried figs as a standard part of their winter diet. For the poorest people figs may be the only food that they eat for breakfast. At harvest time the owner of the property may give the workers toasted figs in the mid-morning. Country people put figs in the oven after bread has been baked to use the remaining heat. The fruit is left for two to three days, and after such dessication it can be stored through the winter. The last harvest, beaten down with branches

[9] Victor Hehn, *The Wanderings of Plants and Animals from Their First Home,* pp. 85–86.

[10] Abu-Abd-Alla-Mohamed-al Edrisi, "Descripción de España," *Viajes de extranjeros por España y Portugal,* (ed. J. García Mercadal), p. 188.

[11] Abu Zacaria Iahia aben mohamed be ahmed ebn el awam, *Libro de agricultura* (trans. and annotated by Josef António Banqueri), I, 573.

(an unfortunate practice which damages the trees), is largely used to feed cattle or to distill into alcohol.

Figs are often planted in the same field with almonds, an association that is satisfactory to the figs, but certainly is detrimental to the almonds. Occasionally vines are planted with figs, but this combination seems to be unsatisfactory to both. The trim of the fig is valuable for firewood, and the leaves, either dry or green, are mixed with straw to be fed to cattle.

THE OLIVE

Hesiod, in Greece of the eighth century B.C., does not refer to the olive. Three centuries later Pindar adopted the legend that the wild species (*Olea oleaster*) was brought to Greece from the extreme west by Hercules. But the cultivated olive is a product of lands to the east of the Mediterranean Sea and Hercules can in many ways be equated with Melkart, the Tyrian god. It seems probable that early Semites were involved in the spread of the plant and that they took the cultivated variety into Iberia, where it was picked up by the Greeks.[12]

In Portugal, after the reconquest of the country by Christians, either olives were absent or their cultivation was negligible in the northern territories; in the territories of middle Portugal, conquered in the twelfth century, they were observed but references indicate that the crop was considered of little importance.[13] Even thirteenth-century documents take so little account of olive cultivation that one might conclude that the trees were not widespread, a situation due probably to destruction of groves during the centuries of warfare. The tree had certainly been esteemed by the Visigoths; their legal code specifies a severe penalty for wanton damage to it.[14] Visigoths had, at best, modest agricultural propensities; it would be difficult to believe that they introduced the tree into Iberia; it must have been part of their inheritance from the Romans.

[12] This interpretation is made on the basis of material and ideas of Victor Hehn, *The Wanderings of Plants and Animals*, pp. 89–93.

[13] Henrique da Gama Barros, *História da administração pública em Portugal nos seculos XII a XV*, IX, 97.

[14] *Fuero Juzgo*, Madrid (Ibarra), La Real Academia Española, 1815, p. 138.

Abu Zacaria describes care of the tree at some length in speaking of his native area of Seville, and Edrisi documents the importance of shipments of olive oil from that city.[15]

Edrisi's neglect of the olive in his description of the Algarve indicates its lack of importance to this region in the twelfth century; and it may be assumed that its later importance was chiefly a matter of the general development of agriculture and the spread of population into the Limestone Zone during the last two centuries. Now it is widespread in the Lower Algarve and until recently had been considered to be the most dependable tree of all on the unirrigated lands; many farmers still maintain that it is the most desirable for a farmer to cultivate. Two counties (*concelhos*) of the Limestone Zone, Silves and Loulé, produce nearly half of the Algarvian total. The oil is not of high reputation in Portugal but this is more a matter of lack of care in processing than in the quality of the original product.

THE CAROB

The carob (*Ceratonia siliqua* L.) is commonly said to grow "spontaneously." However, although it is now found in the countries of northwest Africa and in all of the Mediterranean countries and islands of Europe, its "spontaneity" seems to have had its origins beyond the eastern Mediterranean Sea, probably among the Semites; and its Arabic-derived Portuguese, Spanish, French, and Italian names indicate that its spread into Western Europe is to be credited to Arabs.[16]

In many countries bordering the Mediterranean Sea, and in Portugal, it has served as food both for men and for cattle. It grows vigorously on the rocky lands of the Limestone Zone. In the Algarve of the nineteenth century poor people toasted it for food and made reputedly good

[15] Abu Zacaria Iahia aben mohamed ben ahmed ebn el awam, *Libro de agricultura*, pp. 428, 430, 437, 439; Abu-Abd-Alla-mohamed-al Edrisi, "Descripción de España," *Viajes de extranjeros por España y Portugal* (J. García Mercadal, ed.), p. 187. Alonso de Herrera, a Sevillano of the fifteenth century, rhapsodizes over the virtues of the tree and its product. The space that he devoted to it in his book is his tribute to its importance. See his *Agricultura general*, p. 158.

[16] Victor Hehn, *The Wanderings of Plants and Animals*, pp. 341–342.

Carobs in the Limestone Zone.

brandy from it, and its hard wood was recommended for grist mills and for *noras*. Now it is rarely eaten, although one hears occasional references to such use; but, in the opinion of a large number of Limestone Zone farmers, it is the most profitable tree to have on their land. It can be started by seed or by slip. It thrives, with little or no care, on lands where none of the other commercial trees of the Algarve will grow; and climatologically it is well suited to all parts of the Algarvian Lowland except the foggy region of Cape S. Vicente. Reaching its full production when it is fifty years old, it lasts, so say these farmers, "forever." The shells of the pods, prized because of their high protein and sugar content, are used to make syrup in one plant, but mostly they are broken up to sell as high-value cattle feed. Within the last generation the chemical industry has learned to process the seeds for weighting fabrics and for use in bakeries, both to make high-protein flour, and, in small amounts, to keep bread fresh.

THE ALMOND

The almond is probably the most recently introduced of the four chief unirrigated trees of the Algarve, and, in fact, a relatively recent addition to general Mediterranean agriculture. There was no cultivation of it in Italy at the beginning of the second century B.C. and the first mention of sweet and bitter almonds is in the first century A.D.[17]

Of the four unirrigated trees of Algarvian commerce, it is the least rugged; it requires soils of relatively good quality; they should be deep and with a good deal of lime. The best locations for the tree are those at low elevations, in regions of bright sunshine, with light spring rainfall. In the Algarve the root stock planted is usually that of the bitter almond, upon which one of several varieties is later grafted. As the tree is not a dependable producer, farmers prefer not to have too high a percentage of their lands given over to it. The crop, either in raw form as nuts or in processed form as confections, is mostly exported.

ANIMALS

The natural vegetation of the Limestone Zone does not make good pasturage, except for a short part of the year; in the main, flocks must either be fed with more concentrated fodder at home or taken elsewhere to be fattened. Herding is on a small scale and is quite ancillary to farming. Those few herds of sheep or goats that do exist graze along the roadsides or at the fringes of the cultivated fields during the growing season and are turned into the stubble of the wheat fields after it is cut. The owners of farms are glad to allow the animals to graze, for if the flocks are shifted regularly during the day and their rope folds are changed each night manure will be distributed widely. Sheep are by far the most important grazing animals, and herds up to two, or even at times three, hundred animals may be seen grazing under the care of a shepherd, his helper, and dogs. Sometimes small herds will be tended by a boy. The common sheep of the Limestone Zone is the long-haired sheep. In spring (March and April) specialized shearers make their rounds and clip the fleece in one piece.

[17] *Ibid.*, pp. 294–296.

The milk of both the sheep and the goats is prized. That of the sheep is available for about eight weeks and is mostly made into cheese. Goats are less important in total, but occasionally relatively large herds—to 125 animals—can be seen; they, too, are migratory. As in other areas of the Algarve, there are no herds of pigs, but most households have one or two animals in a pen adjacent to the dwelling. Small flocks of chickens are commonly kept near the house or its yard enclosure. Both oxen and horses are relatively rare, as the former is too cumbersome for the slopes and the latter is not a sufficiently hardy work animal. The cow, however, is commonly used as a work animal although it is not as important as the mule—which is the most highly valued for work—and the donkey, which, as an animal with various functions, is perhaps the most generally useful of all. The donkey may be used for draft, either for carts or plow, but more commonly it is used for packing and by women for riding and carrying burdens to and from the market.

TOWNS

The towns in the Limestone Zone appear in three main lines roughly parallel. The most northerly follows the contact between the schists of the mountain area and the Mesozoic rocks of the Limestone Zone; here water flowing over the surface of the relatively impermeable schists is collected in low drainage lines and used before it is lost in the limestones. Another line of towns is on or near the southern edge of the limestones, and a third line runs through the center of the area.

Prior to the development of modern trucking, the towns near the edge of the schists (Budens, Bensafrim, Silves, S. Bartolomeu de Messines, Alte, Salir, Querença, and Alportel are the chief ones) had greater relative importance than now. When transport by pack animals was fundamental, they fulfilled a function presently diminished. After the long and dreary trek through the Alentejo and the mountains of the Algarve on the routes from Lisbon to the south coast, the towns along the base of the schists were welcome oases where there was ample water and pasturage for animals. Here, too, were fertile valleys where population was relatively dense and the settlements served as distribution points for parts of both mountain and lowland. Latitudinally, the spac-

181

ing of these towns was made partly in terms of agricultural possibilities and availability of water but also to serve the needs of a scattered and relatively dense rural population; from five to eight miles apart, the little centers could be readily reached by walking or on donkey back, and after making purchases one could return home within the day.

The towns along the southern edge of the Limestone Zone (Sagres, Mexilhoeira Grande, Boliqueime, Loulé, Sta. Bárbara de Nexe, Estoi, Pereiro, and Sto. Estêvão) grew up as service centers at the meeting place of two different physical environments. Even today, with all of the improvement that has been made in transport, the Coastal Plain is dominantly a place of cart traffic and the Limestone Zone notable for its use of pack animals. These towns, like those at the upper edge of the Limestone Zone, are spaced to serve the requirements of a relatively well-settled area.

The third series of towns is located in the center of the Zone; no single reason can be given to account for distribution except local productivity. In at least two cases, however, there was also an advantage of cross-roads position. The latter boon is still enjoyed to such an extent by São Brás de Alportel that it requires the description given later. Another member of this series of towns enjoyed the same advantage at the time when packing by animals was the dominant form of transport: Sta. Catarina de Fonte do Bispo was described over a century ago as being both an agricultural center and a place in which many mule trains were based so that they could transport almonds, olive oil, and partridges to the markets of the north. The same account described the inhabitants as being "turbulent" and given to smuggling,[18] a description frequently applicable to such distributing centers at that time. Included in this series of towns, in addition to São Brás de Alportel and Sta. Catarina de Fonte do Bispo, are Paderne, Ator, and São Romão. Paderne and Ator are in the important and fertile Algibre River valley, but they have little relation to each other; both have their economic connections with Loulé or with cities of the Coastal Plain. Part of the route between São Romão, São Brás, and Sta. Catarina now, with the high development of

[18] João Baptista da Silva Lopes, *Corografia ou memoria económica, estadística e topográfica do Reino do Algarve*, p. 377.

182

irrigated agriculture, is almost a *Strassendorf*, so closely spaced are the dwellings along this important road that connects Loulé on the west to Tavira on the east.

Four urban centers of the Limestone Zone—Silves, Loulé, São Brás de Alportel, and S. Bartolomeu de Messines—take precedence over others and their relative importance is increasing. All are at the edge of, or in, fertile agricultural districts with relatively dense dispersed populations. Each is in a crossroads position so that it serves territory all around it.

Silves. Silves, on the Arade River, and just above its confluence with the Odelouca, has the boon of fertile river-bottom lands with abundant water for irrigation; with Algarvian climate added to these advantages, the area is one of obvious attraction. It is hardly conceivable that the Romans neglected to take advantage of such a productive area and, although record of their exploitation is lacking, the name suggests Latin derivation; it is an unlikely name for Arabs to have chosen. Nevertheless, only under Moslem control is the record clear; then Silves became a famous city and the capital of an area which included the present province of the Algarve.

The best account of it during the period of Moslem control is that of Edrisi, in the twelfth century, who described it as a beautiful city, inhabited by Yemenite Arabs, with handsome buildings and markets providing a great abundance of merchandise, all encircled by strong walls. It was a port with docks and dockyards and beyond the city itself the environs were covered with orchards and gardens that produced famous figs which were shipped to all of the countries of the Occident. From the mountains nearby great quantities of wood were cut for export to distant places.[19] It was an excellent port for Moslem needs, and served, at the junction of the Limestone Zone and the mountains, as a meeting place

[19] Abu-Abd-Alla-Mohamed-al Edrisi, "Descripción de España," *Viajes de extranjeros por España y Portugal,* p. 188.

Edrisi's comments with regard to building was no doubt in reference to those of a small proportion of prosperous merchants and administrators. A slightly later report (of 1189) described the city in terms that might be expected for an Arab city: tortuous, narrow streets and tightly packed structures. See João Baptista da Silva Lopes, *Relação da derrota naval,* p. 73.

of land and sea routes. A port at the mouth of the stream would have been less advantageous for mountain products and open to attack by Christian marauders, whereas Silves not only served the needs of a flourishing farming area but, because of its distance from the coast, could have timely notification of danger; and protection was provided by the fortifications along the stream. When the city fell to a group of north-European crusaders in 1189 it was surrounded by four great lines of tamped-earth walls and by moats. A report, written by a man who took part in the siege, described the city as being much stronger than Lisbon and ten times richer. At the end of the siege, when the city fell after dreadful hardships, nearly sixteen thousand people were alive within it.[20]

Although it was damaged then, and perhaps again when the final conquest of the Algarve took place in the mid-thirteenth century, the Christians made it their capital for both public and ecclesiastical administration. A bishopric had been established with its see in Silves during the two-year period of temporary Christian control in the years 1189–1191[21] and this was re-established in the mid-thirteenth century when final domination was achieved by the Portuguese king. It was reasonable to establish the civil administration in the former Moslem capital, for psychological reasons if no other. However, decline began almost immediately; a position that had served the Arabs well did not do so well for the conquerors. For the Portuguese kingdom, with its capital in Lisbon and most convenient connections with its newly acquired province by sea, a coastal city had advantages beyond those of Silves.

With the changes brought about by war, defeat, new rulers, and economic adjustment, another problem arose to plague the area: the site of the city became unhealthy. It is unclear from the reports that have come down to us whether the cutting of the forests back of Silves had reached a point where erosion of the mountains and choking of the river channel would have caused the same difficulties for the Moslems in the same

---

[20] João Baptista da Silva Lopes, *Relação da derrota naval*, pp. 65 *et seq.* and p. 36 of document cited by Lopes.

[21] J. Leite de Vasconcellos, *Etnografia Portuguesa*, II, 473; III, 616.

period of time or not. Certainly such a situation might have been brought about by deforestation. However, with Christian interest centered upon coastal cities, the delicate economic organization necessary to the support of the city broke down. After such events disintegration could well be almost absolute without other contributing circumstances; and with neglect of dikes and dams that had formerly controlled the flow of water, the area became malarial; from that time on its problems were multiplied by abandonment of the area by all persons who could leave.

In the fifteenth century all of the small remaining population who could abandon the city during five months in the mid-year did so. The bishop requested that his see be changed because of the insalubrity and poverty of the region; the transfer was made in the mid-sixteenth century.[22] Soon after that time, the civil administration was changed also, to Lagos. The formerly beautiful and thriving city became virtually a ghost town and so remained throughout the seventeenth, eighteenth, and early nineteenth centuries. In 1705 John Stevens reported that it had but forty houses and the area offered little wine and less grain.[23] The earthquake a half century after Stevens' report demolished all but twenty structures.[24] A turn in affairs took place in the nineteenth century; new vigor was reported for the city. General economic conditions and agriculture were improving, and, although only small boats could come up the stream from the sea, cork was brought to the city from the Alentejo for shipment.[25]

Cork shipments were the reason for Silves' commercial re-establishment, and, as is usual at the place where the mode of transport is changed, processing was begun. In spite of the continuance of malaria,[26] this commerce and the beginning of manufacture (and general improvement in economic conditions in the Algarve) led to increased population in the area and in the city itself. By the early twentieth cen-

[22] A. de Sousa Silva Costa Lobo, *História da sociedade em Portugal,* pp. 140–144.
[23] John Stevens, *The Ancient and Present State of Portugal,* p. 208.
[24] João Baptista da Silva Lopes, *Corografia ou memória económica,* p. 279.
[25] *Ibid.,* p. 280.
[26] Charles Bonnet, *Algarve (Portugal) Description Géographique,* p. 100.

Cork barge on the Arade River, with Silves in the background.

tury there were nearly thirty-two thousand people living in the county and five thousand in the city.[27]

Between the nineteenth-century period of growth and the middle of the twentieth century little change took place in the Silves area. Processing of cork, one of the chief bases of improvement at the outset of the period of resurgence, has not improved with the years; Silves does not make the full list of articles that are made in the more modern plants of Faro and, especially, in those near Lisbon. In Silves bottle corks are the chief product, most of them the simple tapered type or that with the flange on top. Most of the work is done by hand operation; each cork is handled by eight to a dozen people from the time that the large pieces of bark are cut by a table saw, through the punching, bevelling, grinding (in the sun or in ovens), washing, rotating, second drying, and sacking operations. The scrap from these various processes is sent

[27] Aristides de Amorim Girão and Fernanda de Oliveira Lopes Velho, *Estudos da população Portuguesa*, I, last statistical chart; Gaetano Ferro, *L'Algarve*, p. 110.

The valley from the castle at Silves.

to other parts of Portugal to be made into agglomerated cork, or sent in power-propelled barges down the Arade River when the tide is full (when the tide is out the Arade is a mud-puddle at Silves) to be loaded onto boats lying off Portimão. From there it is taken to the United States or other industrialized countries to be used mostly for insulation.

The railroad line that reached the south coast in 1922 passed several miles to the east of Silves and put the city at a relative disadvantage with other settlements of the province. As a cork-manufacturing center Silves is losing out to the plants near Lisbon and even to those of Faro. Although it was second in production in the Algarve at the end of 1957, it was a poor second to Faro and employed a disproportionately high number of men and women in the manufacturing process.[28] Its plants are relatively small and relatively inefficient. Its hope now lies in the development of agriculture. The earth dam on the Arade above Silves

[28] *Inquérito industrial . . . Faro*, 1957, pp. 98, 100.

was completed in 1956 and new lands are now being put under irrigation; electricity will at least bring to the city amenities formerly lacking.

Loulé. The villa of Loulé, greatly favored in the soils of its region and also by hydrologic resources (rivers converge toward it from the northwest, the north, and the northeast, and the water table is near the surface of the land) is one of two settlements of the interior comparable in population with cities of the Coastal Plain. Its neglect by Edrisi seems strange, although this may indicate that it had less importance to the Moslem Algarve than had Silves and the coastal settlements. Possibly, however, its interior position and less spectacular countryside militated against its prominence. At the time of the final defeat of the Moslems in the mid-thirteenth century, it was one of the four most important settlements of the Algarve, for it received its town charter in the same year as did Faro, Silves, and Tavira.[29] The most important Moslem group of the Algarve lived in its territory in the late fifteenth century; and they owned three-quarters of the land in the county.[30]

In a way, it has had a history like that of Tavira. Agriculture has been the basis of its well-being but its citizens have also been aware of the profits of trade. In 1843 its population was estimated to be larger than that of any other settlement of the Algarve. It was not only the center of its agricultural region but also a craft center and distribution point for the products of the crafts in the smaller towns around it.[31] Since that time it has absorbed, commercialized further, and somewhat rationalized most of the crafts that had a wider distribution through the Limestone Zone a century ago. Palm leaves are imported by dealers in Loulé and turned over to the women of the countryside or of the small villages for plaiting. After having done that, the craft workers may turn the strands over to Loulé dealers or they may stitch the strands together into containers which will be sold by the same dealers. Loulé is the unquestioned center of all such work. Copper working, formerly so important in Alte, is now dominantly the product of artisans in Loulé, who

[29] João Baptista da Silva Lopes, *Corografia ou memória económica*, Map 1.
[30] A. de Sousa Silva Costa Lobo, *História da sociedade em Portugal*, p. 38.
[31] Charles Bonnet, *Algarve (Portugal) Description Géographique*, pp. 72, 107.

Plaiting strands of palm fibers.

import the raw material, mostly in the form of old copper wire, and who send their wares to compete in Alentejo and Lisbon fairs, recently having had exhibits as far afield as Munich. Their work is of high quality, and, as it mostly duplicates designs refined through generations of peasant production, it is also of good taste. Loulé continues its age-old crafts appertaining to towns established at crossroads—the fabrication of trappings for horses, mules, and donkeys. The remnants of the sisal production contribute to this specialization; the multicolored ropes that are made for tying down the shafts of the carts to the mules are made of it. Bridles, saddles, and various other parts of the equine trappings are on display in its shops. A factory making brooms from palm fronds bound to a short handle of oleander wood works with a small permanent staff of laborers throughout the year; and the Loulé pottery factory continues to turn out ordinary wares which are sold to the poor who cannot afford to buy what is imported from the Alentejo.

Of all Algarvian towns, both on the Coastal Plain and in the interior,

Loulé seems to have been most sympathetic to change in recent years. Its wide, parked esplanade, along which one enters the town from the east, is a much more impressive street than the entryways of the larger cities to the south. Its shops have been spruced up remarkably in the late fifties and its merchants are attentive. Its present situation is obviously partly a product of its own energy and resourcefulness. Certainly it has not been aided by tourism; there is no hotel.

São Brás de Alportel. São Brás de Alportel was of little importance in the early years after the Christian reconquest of the Algarve, yet its name, using the Arabic *al* with the Latin-derived *portel*, suggests that the Romans used this location for a settlement on the best route through the mountains to Lisbon from the Algarve and that the Arabs later continued to use it. The line of towns to the north of the pass, including Almodôvar and Aljustrel, strengthens such an opinion. If such was the case, however, the site was neglected in later Moslem times (for reasons pointed out above); but once the area was at peace again and population increased in the Limestone Zone, growth of a settlement in this location again was inevitable. The important route from Loulé to Tavira here crosses that from Faro toward the pass. Trade advantages, particularly in a time of primitive transport, were manifest. But with the advent of trucking and the concentration of industries in larger centers, São Brás has suffered a relative decline.

It still serves as the market center for an important agricultural region, but the cork industry tends to migrate either to Faro or out of the Algarve to the banks of the Tejo River, near Lisbon. In 1957 São Brás held a weak third position in the Algarve with regard to cork processing, following Faro and Silves. While the seventy-two plants in São Brás which were occupied in such work in 1957 were almost three times the number of those in Faro, they produced only a little over one quarter of the product by value.[32] They are small plants and mostly obsolete, where virtually all of the work is done by hand.

S. Bartolomeu de Messines. In 1189, when the Christian armies took temporary control of the Algarve, the castle of Mussiene was cap-

[32] *Inquérito industrial . . . Faro, 1957*, pp. 29, 31; *Estadística industrial, 1951*, p. 222.

tured.[33] Like other castles in the interior of the Limestone Zone, it was a strategically placed fort but not a center of settlement. The fact that the area to the north of the S. Marcos Depression is lacking in names of Arabic origin (unlike the routes to the north of São Brás and Lagos) may indicate that the route had never been of importance to the Moslems; and the fact that there was no settlement at the site of present S. Bartolomeu at the time of the permanent reconquest seems to be borne out by the lack of a town charter for such a settlement at that time.

The necessity for a crossroads gathering and distributing center at the juncture of the east-west route running along the contact between the mountains and the Limestone Zone with the north-south route from Lisbon to the south coast came with the settlement of the Zone. By the early nineteenth century the route running from Faro through S. Bartolomeu and thence through the S. Marcos Depression to the north was reported to be the only satisfactory road for carts through the Limestone Zone.[34] This road was eliminated by the completion of the railroad from Lisbon to the south coast in 1922, and was re-established only in 1959. Today, S. Bartolomeu energetically functions as the distributor for manufactured goods from the capital to the countryside for a radius of several miles on each side of the town as well as the collecting point for goods to be sent either to the capital or to the cities of the south. Inhabitants in parts of both the mountains and the Limestone Zone look to it for their saddles, other trappings, and their general supplies; to it they bring their agricultural products either for immediate shipment or for processing. Two plants in the town separate carob beans from the shells, shipping the former to Switzerland, where they are made into high-protein flour or processed for weighting of fabrics, or for other industrial uses. The shells are broken up to be shipped into other parts of Portugal and abroad as high quality fodder for animals. Another plant handles almonds and figs and prepares them for shipment and sale. Two olive presses handle the crop of the local region.

But S. Bartolomeu merchants are not content to let trade come to

[33] João Baptista da Silva Lopes, *Relação da derrota naval*, p. 42.
[34] João Baptista da Silva Lopes, *Corografia ou memória económica*, p. 75.

An itinerant vender in a village.

them; itinerant venders, with a miscellany of merchandise but chiefly drygoods, go with loads packed on the backs of animals (and now, with trucks) into the remote areas of the Limestone Zone and the mountains to reach the small isolated settlements, where they purvey to people who cannot conveniently make the trip into the lowland.

Surprisingly, in face of the energy displayed by its merchants, the town is without running water. Several men make their living by filling jugs at the well near the edge of town and selling the water from house to house for half an escudo (about $.02 U.S.) for approximately five gallons.

The functions of villages. Small towns of the Limestone Zone, for the most part, are centers supplying the needs of simple agricultural communities. Many of them have not changed greatly in recent years except to gradually lose part of their former function, by reason of improved communications and more intimate contact with cities. They are now essentially residential, but they perform some limited services for the immediate hinterland. Improvements have been slight. One does notice that in the last half-dozen years the function of the windmill for grinding wheat and maize has largely been taken over by small motor-driven milling plants in each of the more important towns. Buses and trucks make regular calls, and inhabitants can either select from a large assortment of goods brought in or go to the larger cities of the coast to make their purchases. However, a conservative group does not alter its ways casually and, in an area where the equivalent of $.70 U.S. is the going daily wage for a family-head, casual trips cannot be taken.

The crafts that formerly were a part of the life of many of the villages have almost completely disappeared. The industry using esparto grass (*Stipa tenacissima*), in which the Phoenicians acted as intermediaries between Iberia and the Near East long before the time of Xerxes,[35] shows remnants of its former importance. Salir is now the most important center making heavy work baskets for carrying dirt and rocks, muzzles for animals so that they will not eat the grain that they are hauling or threshing, and almost indestructible ropes. When copper was mined near Alte a craft industry for the production of copper utensils was started. Even though mining is no longer continued there, the skills are maintained by a few individuals; but it is clear that Alte is going out of the business. A common household enterprise among the women of the Limestone Zone is the plaiting of strands of the leaves of the dwarf palm. Although the plant grows in the Algarve, its fibers are not as good in color or strength as those imported through Spain from Morocco. Women plait it into long strips to be made into baskets, panniers, and other such receptacles.

The sisal industry, important some generations ago, has almost died out. One occasionally sees the plant and leaves being beaten and scraped or the fiber drying in the sun, but today the craft has almost no importance.

WESTERN SUBREGION: THE SÃO MARCOS DEPRESSION

A narrow area, Algarvian in latitude and administration, lying between the mountains of Caldeirão and Monchique, is called the São

---

[35] Victor Hehn, *The Wanderings of Plants and Animals*, p. 134.

Marcos Depression. The village of S. Marcos, on the railroad which connects Lisbon with the south coast, serves nearby inhabitants of both mountain areas.

Along the Depression grains are planted on the rolling hills on either side of the gap; and where water is available from small streams coming from the hills or where the water table is close enough to the surface for use of the *nora* or sweep, there are oases of cultivation. Houses are dispersed and the fact that many have decorative chimneys gives the area a certain Algarvian quality. Yet, in spite of such traits, one has the sensation of being in the Alentejo rather than in the Algarve. Perhaps this feeling is due to the sight of low rolling wheat land dotted with cork oaks, or perhaps it is due to the appearance of red-brown Alentejano-type cattle, which draw the plows in place of the mules common to most of the Algarve.

Toward the north of the Depression the garden plots, irrigated by *noras* and sweeps, are more numerous and larger than those of the south. Especially around the town of S. Marcos itself, which is situated on the top of a hill above a meander of the Odelouca River, the valley is intensively used for the cultivation of grains, vegetables, olives, and citrus. The sweeps and *noras*, formerly fundamental to this irrigation, are still to be seen and occasionally are used, but in late years motors have taken over their function.

To one familiar with the Algarve, the Limestone Zone has a transitional quality. It is much like the Coastal Plain in the vigor of its present exploitation of resources, in its trading centers and the easy volubility of their citizens, in the bright neatness of its houses, and in the intensive use of garden techniques wherever irrigation is possible. But even a quick view of the predominantly large areas of uncultivated land, covered only with the scrub that is capable of spontaneous growth on such raw limestone slopes, makes one realize that this area is set apart from the Coastal Plain both by its physical nature and by the choices men have made for its use. The intimacy of the closely spaced houses in the Coastal Plain is mostly lacking. Away from the towns one has a sense of isolation. He feels that if he strained his ears he might hear the clack

Algarvian chimneys in the Limestone Zone.

of mule trains on the roads and trails—as he still does in the Caldeirão Mountains. And mule trains are not entirely foreign to the Zone. Part of the quality of its life is still derived from its intermediary position between coast and mountains; the termini of the routes of primitive transport which serve the mountains lie in the Limestone Zone. Position, function, rock, topography, and persistent ways of life conspire to make this area transitional and to keep it so.

5. The Caldeirão Mountains

▪▪▪

THE DISTINCT CULTURE AREA of the Caldeirão Mountains has been mostly overlooked during its several thousand years of existence; accepting change but slowly, it has followed traditional ways.

THE PAST IN THE PRESENT

Some of its present techniques and attitudes have come down from pre-history only partly changed, either by local developments or by intrusive ways and values that have been accepted (perhaps grudgingly) during this long time span. This area is a museum of things of the past; in a land of little return, people have lived frugally, according to modes that in some cases extend back to the time of the arrival of Neolithic peoples in Portugal. Even though today's roads put the area into intimate relation with the commercial towns of the southern coast, acceptance of new ways is cautious at best; these

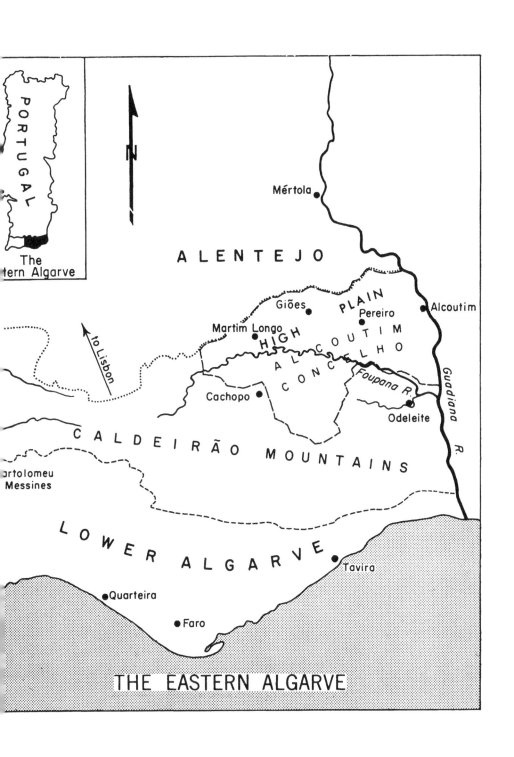

PORTUGAL

The
tern Algarve

N

Mértola

A L E N T E J O

HIGH   PLAIN

Giões
Pereiro   Alcoutim
Martim Longo
A L C O U T I M
to Lisbon   HIGH   C O N C E L H O
Foupana R.
Cachopo   Guadiana R.
Odeleite

C A L D E I R Ã O   M O U N T A I N S

artolomeu
Messines

L O W E R   A L G A R V E

Tavira

Quarteira

Faro

THE EASTERN ALGARVE

Harvesting grain with sickles in the Caldeirão Mountains.

people, with their cultural continuity of several thousand years, accept changes selectively, if at all. Their region is a parenthesis between the active, commercial Lower Algarve, to the south, and the conservative, somewhat medieval, but dynamic Alentejo province, to the north, whose great landowners still exert power in Portuguese political affairs. The Caldeirão area is a largely self-sufficient and unmodernized world of its own with a sparse population of villagers living from the product of grains and flocks.

Their neighbors consider them to be backward and resistant to improvement; but perhaps they have their reasons for refusal to accept changes that to others seem to promise obvious benefit. Perhaps the people of the Caldeirão have learned the limitations of their area and are wise in refusing to gamble with tested ways of life. When people are living next to the boundary of minimum subsistence, gambling may mean extinction. In the Caldeirão a conservative, rather primitive, economy has at least maintained the population even though parsimoniously. A way of life has taken form that is satisfactory to the inhabitants

The deforested slopes of the Caldeirão with piles of wheat.

of the area, but different from anything that most western Europeans or Americans could accept.

The Caldeirão presents an obstinate milieu for its villagers. For the largest part the basic rock is sedimentary schist, which tends to break down into clayey soils relatively impenetrable to water. As a consequence, rainfall scours the land surface, each year removing a thin mantle of disintegrated material that might otherwise become soil. Little support is left for crops.

Such progressive destruction, however, has not always obtained. Less than a century ago a protective cover of oaks, and of cistus, heather, gorse, and other species of scrub, extended over at least four-fifths of the surface, and only a few favored and relatively level parts of the High Plain, extending from south and west of Martim Longo to east of Pereiro, were cultivated. Then, less than a half century ago, the knowledge of chemical fertilizers reached the mountain dwellers, and the high price for wheat during World War I was an additional stimulus to clear the natural vegetation from the land. More than four-fifths of the formerly scrub-covered area was cleared and became grain land.[1]

The vegetation complex that then existed is shown now by remnants of *Cistus ladaniferus* (by far the most important of the spontaneous plants), *C. populifolius* and *C. Monspeliensis* (which in the area near the Guadiana River becomes more important than the *C. ladaniferus*), *Erica australis, E. lusitanica, E. scoparia, Genista polyanthus, G. lobeli, Ulex spp., Pterospartum laciantum, P. tridentatum,* and *Lavandula stoecha.* The holm oak (*Quercus ilex*) is still widespread on some of the lower slopes and the cork oak (*Q. suber*) at somewhat higher elevations. Common in the valley bottoms is the lovely pink (or white) blooming oleander (*Nerium oleander*).

Entering the area along the main highway from Lisbon to Faro, one gets a false impression of the vegetation cover in the mountains. The large cork oaks represent a remnant of forests existing at the time of the printing of the Agricultural Map of Portugal in 1902.[2] In addition to such remnants of the former forest, there are eucalyptus trees along the roadside, occasional groves of young maritime pines, and young cork oaks that are the product of relatively recent replanting. These trees, seen from the road, make the countryside seem better forested than it actually is. One does not have to go far from the highway on either side to see a landscape of stripped slopes.

The first few harvests from this cleared area sometimes returned the seed grain twentyfold and commonly better than tenfold, but this situation was quickly changed. With the elimination of the vegetation cover, sheet wash stripped the surfaces,[3] and the average return now, in good years, is only five times the amount of the seed grain. In poor years, the return may be only twofold. The effect of cultivating, sowing, weeding,

[1] Mariano Feio, *Le Bas Alentejo et L'Algarve: Livret-Guide de l'excursion E, Congrès International de Géographie,* p. 95.

[2] M. Gomes Guerreiro, *Valorização da Serra Algarvia,* p. 9.

[3] Observations made during the ten-year period 1940–1949 show that the river flowing into the sea at Tavira deposited at its mouth the equivalent of a four-inch (10-cm.) depth of soil stripped from its watershed (M. Gomes Guerreiro, *Valorização da Serra Algarvia,* p. 13).

and harvesting by sickles may, in the worst years, return nothing more than the amount of the seed grain itself.

Burning of the cistus, the almost exclusive occupant of many of the slopes, is common in the fall. The planter may realize that this practice leads to further deterioration, but what shall he do? Hunger is never far off and the ashes left on the soil, with good rainfall, will produce enough grain for another season's food. The farmer constantly gambles with weather, for he is at the border of hazard. If other conditions were favorable the total rainfall would be sufficient for successful agriculture,[4] but unfortunately the rain comes in quick bursts, mostly in the cool, winter season, and runs off the surface of the schists with almost no penetration; the summer drought lasts for almost half the year.

Crops

Wheat, oats, barley, or rye—in that order of importance—are planted in the ashes of the burned scrub in December or January, and the harvest is completed in June. In the typical mountain *concelho* (roughly comparable to our county) of Alcoutim, less than one-sixth of the surface was planted in 1957. Of the cultivated area, approximately 96 per cent was planted to grains and 60 per cent of that in wheat. Oats occupied 30 per cent of the grain lands, barley 6 per cent, and rye 3 per cent. The return per acre for these grains is poor in comparison with that in other parts of the Algarve; in wheat production this *concelho* stands in last place. The position with regard to the other grains is better but never very good.[5]

In the area that is known to the mountain people as the High Plain, the premium grain area of the mountains, the land is relatively level and the erosion apparently is not serious, for much of the land has been cleared and cultivated since the early nineteenth century. Here, in the harvest season, the sheaves of wheat or of other small grains are stacked in the fields as far into the distance as one can see, waiting to be carried either to the threshing floor, where mules or other animals will tread

[4] Ranging between twenty and forty-two inches (*O Clima do Portugal, Part VII, Baixo-Alentejo e Algarve*, 1952, Maps 24 and 25; *Anuário Climatológico do Portugal,* Part I, 1951–1959).

[5] See *Estatística Agrícola 1957*, p. 82.

Cangalhas (wooden frames for packing grain). The upright staves can be lowered for transporting grains until they are nearly horizontal.

out the grain, or to the modern, ambulant threshing machines. The grain is transported by tying sheaves on either side and on top of a pack animal, or in carts. *Cangalhas*, grain packsaddles, are still seen occasionally, but are going out of use as a result of road improvement. After threshing, the grain may be taken as of old to one of the windmills, but now it is more apt to be taken to a motorized mill. As most of the small towns have acquired modern mills in the last few years, windmills may be doomed. Each year they become fewer, but some are still to be seen on the hilltops. Unless the government subsidizes them, as it has done in some cases for aesthetic and touristic reasons, they will not be able to compete with the modern mills.

At the edge of the High Plain, where the slopes begin, one notices the destructive effect of erosion. The village of Giões, in this position and on the main route between Lisbon and Tavira, was described a century ago[6] as prosperous because of its income from agriculture as well as

[6] João Baptista da Silva Lopes, *Corografia ou memória económica, estadística e topográfica do Reino do Algarve*, p. 398.

202

that from mule-driving. Now the mule trains are no longer employed, and the elimination of this source of income may be the reason for the present dispirited aspect of the village. However, the ragged upper edges of the sharply dipping layers of schist project through the soil cover in such fashion as to make it seem probable that man's damage to the land has also played its part.

On much of the mountain land grain cannot be planted each year, even with the use of chemical fertilizers. Rotation with fallow, such as the following, is essential:

First year: preparation of the land and broadcasting of chemical fertilizers
Second year: wheat
Third year: land worked after first rains, barley planted about Christmas
Fourth year: oats
Fifth year: a lupine
Sixth year: fallow
Seventh year: fallow
  or
First year: preparation and fertilization
Second year: wheat
Third year: oats
Fourth year: fallow
Fifth year: fallow
Sixth year: fallow (sometimes eliminated)[7]

On lands at the lower limit of productivity, the burning of cistus and planting of one crop of wheat must be followed by ten to fifteen years of reversion to wild growth.

The meagre production of the grain lands is supplemented by that of small garden plots in any of the canyons that have sufficient terrace at the bottom and water available to the sweep or *nora*. Maize is the crop most prized in these canyons and is always present in summer, but other things are customarily planted as well: squash, cabbage, tomatoes,

---

[7] Feio, *Le Bas Alentejo et L'Algarve,* pp. 95–96.

Newly cut cistus in piles on the Caldeirão.

beans, chick-peas, sweet potatoes, and, in some places, oranges and tangerines. Running up the shallow dells above the vegetable gardens, may be a line of fig trees and a few almond or olive trees. For example, the inhabitants of Cachopo, at the edge of the High Plain, cultivate grains on the hills around the town, while on the low terraces along the stream running through town and in the small tributary canyons in a narrow area extending on both sides of the settlement for over a mile in length, one sees the crops mentioned above as well as a variety of fruit trees, white as well as sweet potatoes, broad beans, and onions. Trailing grapevines bearing table grapes extend along the edge of the canyons, while vines for red wines and vines for white wines have climbed re-spectively the cork and holm oaks.

The garden plots of such a canyon, even though the whole area is relatively small, are almost invariably the property of many owners who live in one of the nearby villages. Inheritance has led to splitting up of the properties into tiny plots; one fig tree may belong to five heirs.

A canyon garden in the Caldeirão Mountains. In this plot the following products are normally grown in one year: olives, sweet potatoes, onions, almonds, plums, maize, broad beans, trailing grape vines along edges of plot, climbing grape vines on both holm and cork oaks (*Quercus ilex* and *Q. suber* respectively), white potatoes, squash, beans, and wheat. Cork oaks and eucalyptus trees can be seen on the hills behind.

Relation of people to the land. Although the mountain people of the Caldeirão belong politically to the province of the Algarve, and economically as well, insofar as there is connection, they do not consider themselves to be Algarvians. They speak of "the Algarve," meaning the lower country, and some of the road signs still read "to the Algarve." In their folklore a clear and invidious distinction is made when the mountain people sing of the superiority of their bread and meat-eating population over the lowland "carob-eaters":

> Se dizem que a serra e serra,
> A serra também da Pão.
> Também na serra, se criam
> Meninas de estimação
>
> Sou da serra, sou serrenho,
> E vendo carne as arrôbas
> Eu não sou como vocês
> Que só comem alfarrobas![8]

In spite of their pride in meat-eating, their total consumption is low, although perhaps higher than that of simple people in most other parts of Portugal, and carobs are not part of the diet of the lowlanders. Nevertheless, inaccurate as it may be, this song does express their feeling of distinction. Isolated until very recently, the mountain folk still harbor considerable distrust of the people and the ways of "the Algarve" below. Only occasionally do they make journeys downslope to sell their products. Once a year, on St. John's Day, they make a pilgrimage to the beach at Quarteira for their ritual bath. Other beaches are also used, but Quarteira is preferred. This custom is a vestige of an ancient water-cult, important in the remote prehistory of Portugal.[9] Mostly, however, these hill people are not only content, but also proud, to remain in their mountains. Poor as the land may be, most *serrenhos* like their way of life, in spite of the fact that only slightly over half of them derive enough income from the land to support their families.

[8] Quoted by Mario Lyster Franco, *O Algarve: Exposição Portuguesa em Sevilha,* p. 7.

[9] See Jorge Dias and Fernando Galhano, *Aparelhos de elevar a água de rega,* p. 180.

Figures relating to the *concelho* of Alcoutim may be used to indicate "mountain" economic and social conditions, since the county lies wholly within the mountains and is unique in this respect; all other *concelhos* that include Caldeirão territory also stretch into the Lower Algarve. Containing 11 per cent of the total area of the Algarve, Alcoutim has but 3 per cent of the population. Its most important economic activities are related to grains and grazing. Over half of its families live exclusively by farming, but of this group over one-third do not own the land upon which they work. On the other hand, 40 per cent hire aid.[10] An inquiry into housing, as a part of the 1950 census,[11] shows that 82 per cent of the families of the *concelho* live in their own houses.

Nevertheless, and in spite of statistics, it is virtually impossible to estimate accurately the number of people or the areas involved in the various systems of working the land: as owners, sharecroppers, or renters. The Portuguese statistics do not make a distinction between share-workers and renters in the Algarve, and no acreage figures are available for owner-worked farms. My inquiries in various parts of the mountain area led as much to confusion as to enlightenment. In some areas the answers indicated that mostly owners were working their own plots; in other areas share-working seemed to be dominant. It is a vexing problem which only a cadastral survey will resolve. However, two facts emerged from my efforts: one, that renters were uncommon everywhere and, two, that absentee ownership was not important. In the Caldeirão there are no great estates and virtually all absenteeism is that of owners living near enough to their properties so that their supervision is continuous.

On most of the farms it would be impossible to use machines, as frac-

---

[10] *Inquérito às explorações agrícolas do continente, 1952,* Instituto Nacional de Estatística, Lisboa, Bertrand (Irmãos) Lda., Vol. I. pp. 3, 9–11. The same statistical institute has issued several other useful volumes which have been used for this chapter: *Estatística Agrícola,* 1957; *Estatística Industrial,* 1957; *Gado e animais de capoeira,* 1955; *Inquérito Industrial, Distrito de Faro,* 1957; *IX Recenseamento Geral da População, 1950, Tomo II.*

[11] *Inquérito às condições de habitação da família,* Anexo ao *IX Recenseamento Geral da População* (em 15 de Dezembro de 1950), p. 8.

tionalization has been carried to an extreme degree. Only one in twenty-five of the farm enterprises[12] is of one piece. Nearly two-thirds are made up of from three to ten separately owned plots, and almost one-fifth are made up of eleven or more. To the difficulties of multiple plots is added the fact that the total size of most enterprises is small for grain and grazing country: over one-quarter of them total between 12 and 25 acres in size, another quarter are between 25 and 50 acres, and those larger than 125 acres are few, no more than twelve enterprises being larger than 250 acres each, and only one containing over 500 acres. Although a few properties are called "large" by the local folk, there is no *latifundismo* in this *concelho* such as that to be found in the province of the Lower Alentejo just to the north, where there are nearly nine hundred enterprises of more than 500 acres each and many of several thousand acres each.[13]

ANIMALS

Work animals account for 90 per cent of the power used on farms (actually 100 per cent, for another animal—man—supplies the other 10 per cent).[14] No farm machines are recorded for the *concelho* of Alcoutim. Among the equines, donkeys are the most numerous; they are used for a variety of chores: packing, riding, plowing, turning of *noras*, and many others of lesser importance. Mules, however, although fewer, are more important in farming and even in transport. They are the best animals for plowing, for the transport of wheat and other burdens, and for threshing. Horses are not numerous anywhere in the Algarve, but over half of the total are found in the mountain areas and the regions adjacent to them—presumably as a relic of pack transport. For power on farms, cows follow mules and donkeys in importance; milk is not considered to be of importance.

[12] Portuguese statisticians use the term *explorações*, which can be translated as "enterprises." To use the word "farms" might be misleading, as it would suggest, to some persons, a continuous geographic unit.

[13] *Inquérito às condições de habitação da família,* pp. 66–67.

[14] *Gado e animais de capoeira,* pp. 86–87; *Inquérito às condições de habitação da família,* p. 106.

208

Sheep are important to the Caldeirão.[15] Herds average less than one hundred, but in 1959 there was at least one herd (that is, total sheep belonging to one owner) of nearly three hundred, and three others with over two hundred each. The larger herd was handled by one shepherd, one helper and dogs. Frequently herds of several owners are tended together. One herd of over three hundred sheep belonged to three owners. The animals were mostly a crossbreed, but a few long-haired sheep, Merinos, and goats were included.

Most flocks are made up of a type of sheep that is a cross between the long-haired sheep of the Lower Algarve and the wool sheep of the Alentejo; small animals, and not of great value either for wool or meat, they are turned into the stubble of the grain fields after the harvest. During the nights they are confined either in the ancient round (and occasionally square) rock-wall enclosures or in rope folds. Sheepskins, in the form of a crude coat, are worn by shepherds as a protection against winter cold, and sheepskins are sometimes used as bedcovers.

Goats, a breed with short legs, short horns, long hair, and hanging ears, are said to be the product of an Algarvian-Moroccan cross of the mid-nineteenth century. Nearly 12 per cent of the goats of the Algarve live in the *concelho* of Alcoutim; other mountain areas also support goats in large proportion as compared to their human populations. In a sense, they are refugees from the lowland, where people do not like them and say that they "burn the vegetation." Indeed, they are at odds with cultivation. In the mountains, on the contrary, the goat is not a competitor of the cultivator, but a welcome guest, for it grazes upon gum

---

[15] Using the animal census (*Gado e animais de capoeira* [1955], pp. 86, 88) as a source, and dividing the figure in half for these parishes that straddle the Limestone and Caldeirão areas, it seems reasonable to assume that over half of the total sheep of the Algarve belong to the Caldeirão.

The *concelho* of Alcoutim probably grazes about one-quarter of the Algarvian total. The *Inquérito* of 1952 credits it with 25 per cent (*Inquérito às condições de habitação de família*, pp. 76–77, 106–107), but the animal census of 1955 (*Gado e animais de capoeira*, p. 86) shows only 22 per cent. However, the *Estatística agrícola* of 1957, pp. 122–123, lists 27 per cent as being within the *concelho*. No doubt it is dubious practice to average out 22, 25, and 27 as 25 per cent; however, the proportion is reasonable and about as close as an estimate can be made.

Wood to be made into charcoal.

cistus and the heather. Mountain herds are relatively large; as many as 125 goats may be herded by one specialized herder. He is not specialized in this work because he is ignorant of agriculture or finds it distasteful, but because he has no land to work. "Only he who has no land has flocks," it is said. Although most goats are owned by the herders, in some cases animals of one owner may be included in the flocks of another by an arrangement with regard to the offspring, the milk, and also usually some cheese. Most of the milk is made into cheese.

Pigs are kept in pens near the houses, not herded. In some cases chickens are kept in pens, or they may be housed in crude open shelters and allowed to forage around, and in, the house. Chickens and eggs, however, are seldom eaten by the local people; they are too important as a source of cash. Both pigs and chickens are relatively numerous.[16]

[16] *Gado e animais de capoeira*, pp. 86–87.

A charcoal mound before firing.

With such meagre resources, many families find it impossible to live upon the yield from the land. In this essentially farming area over 40 per cent of the population must supplement its income from the land by means of some other economic activity.[17] Many men go to the Alentejo or to other regions of the Algarve to work for wages at times of demand. Other men busy themselves with activities such as making charcoal, which requires considerable patience, but no great skill. Usually the charcoal pits are on distant slopes. After the pit is dug, a kindling of cistus twigs and strawberry tree branches is laid. Over this pile are placed larger limbs of cork or holm oak, or of olive or the strawberry tree, and, at times, the heavy roots of cistus and of the strawberry tree. Over the whole mass of kindling and wood a mound of earth is made. The mass of wood is ignited and the fire smoulders for ten to fifteen days,

[17] *Inquérito às condições de habitação da família*, pp. 3, 9–11.

211

Cork oaks after trimming.

Beehives in the Caldeirão Mountains. Those on the left are modern frame
hives; those on the right are the ancient cork type.

by which time the wood has become charcoal. Charcoal, which is expensive, is not made for local use; it is a trade item to be sold to prosperous city people for use with special purposes or in homes.

Cork oaks are found around most of the villages. The small proprietor
may cut the cork himself, but usually the job is turned over to a man
skilled in such work, who receives a high wage, twice that of the ordinary agricultural laborer. Trimming can be done only according to rules
laid down and firmly maintained by the government. There must be a
period of at least seven years between seasons of trimming, and only
cork from specified parts of the tree can be removed.

The use of cork is of ancient lineage. Two thousand years ago Varro,
the Roman authority on agriculture, wrote of the superiority of cork
beehives above others by reason of the even temperatures that were
maintained within them.[18] Today a large proportion of the Algarvian

[18] Lloyd Storr-Best, *M. T. Varro on Farming*, p. 330.

A donkey transporting cork beehives with honey.

hives are simple cylinders of cork taken from the tree and used without further elaboration except for fixing crossed sticks inside to support the honeycomb. They represent, no doubt, the direct and unchanged descendants of the hives to which Varro referred. Early in this century virtually all hives of the Caldeirão were of this type; only within the last few years the wooden-frame hive has begun to replace them.

With increasing import of sugar the use of honey has diminished, especially in the Lower Algarve, which was once a profitable market for the gathering industry of the mountains. When honey was the basic sweetening substance for the Algarve, the mountains were the best gathering field for the bees. This condition was radically changed in the twentieth century when the natural vegetation was cleared from the mountains for the planting of wheat. However, honey is still important to the mountain folk, who can hardly afford to pay for imported sugar, and both cork and frame hives are used in considerable numbers.[19] Processing is a simple matter; after the bees are smoked out of the hives, the honey is simply pressed out of the combs with the hands.

A few men make additional income by gathering various species of natural vegetation to be sold for fuel or as raw material for craftsmen, who, while competing poorly against imported factory products, continue to produce articles for sale.

The "industries" of the *concelho* would not have the name applied to them in some other parts of Portugal nor in any of the so-called industrialized parts of the world. The *Inquérito industrial* of Faro shows eighty-five "industrial establishments" with 120 workers in total, of whom 72 work in establishments having only one worker each (which leaves 48 workers for the thirteen "big industrial plants"). In total there is a fixed capital equal to $50,575 U.S. Of this total, milling and other processing of food products account for 43 per cent.[20] Nine windmills and twenty-six water mills were listed for the *concelho* in 1952[21] but by 1958 many of these mills were temporarily—and probably permanently —out of use. Within the last three or four years most of the small towns have acquired motor-driven mills.

The "industrial" plants, all very simple, function merely to serve local needs. However, they do not supply the requirements of the *concelho*. Vehicles and materials used in transport, leather goods, brandy, furniture, textiles, and other products necessary to the villagers are largely supplied by the commercial towns at the foot of the mountain area in the Lower Algarve.

Towns and trade

The sparse population of the Caldeirão is almost entirely concentrated in a few compact villages, making a very different scene from that of the dispersed farmsteads of the Lower Algarve. Since the periods of planting, care, and harvest of grains are short, and the small canyon gardens are mostly adjacent to the villages, life is largely passed along

---

[19] *Inquérito às condições de habitação da família*, p. 270.
[20] *Inquérito industrial, Distrito de Faro*, 1957, pp. 18–22.
[21] *Inquérito às condiçēs de habitação da família*, pp. 268–269.

Mértola on the Guadiana River.

the somewhat irregular streets of the settlements. Although the streets are not completely straight, at some time there has been an attempt to establish a grid pattern—perhaps at the time of founding. The church, and the plaza if there is one, are usually eccentric, often near the edge of the town. The villages are places of residence, not, fundamentally, centers of commerce; stores are few and small. Supplies—especially dry goods and notions—are purveyed largely by itinerant venders, travelling and hauling their wares on pack animals, bicycles, or small trucks; sale and purchase of animals is usually accomplished at one of the fairs which are regularly held in each of the more important villages on a specified day of the week and week of the month.[22] Services and buildings for them, that we associate in our minds with urban living, are lacking.

[22] For example, the fair in Cachopo is on the second Thursday of each month. That of S. Bartolomeu de Messines, which serves many mountain people, is held on the fourth Monday of each month.

216

Men and women go to the small towns at the base of the mountains on market day to buy items that are not brought to them by itinerant venders and, perhaps more importantly, to enjoy the pleasure of taking an occasional trip to break the routine of village living.

HOUSES

Houses in the *concelho* of Alcoutim are commonly made of the country rock, grey schist with streaks of brown. When such houses are unadorned they make a sombre scene, but not all houses are made of schist; some are made of tamped earth. As those of tamped earth are usually calcimined, they have a more pleasing appearance. In some cases, houses of schist are also plastered and calcimined, but in the smaller villages such treatment is given only to the houses of a few prosperous owners. In the large villages, such as Martim Longo and Cachopo, most houses—whatever the material—are calcimined. Furthermore, the appearance of the houses is improved by the addition of chimneys, ordinarily patterned after the decorative chimneys of the Lower Algarve. In the small villages a chimney is a relatively rare thing, and the smoke finds its way out between the interstices of the tiles above the kitchen. From the typical house of the poor, a low-walled rectangular structure with a one-slope roof, one or two rooms, and a lean-to kitchen, there are many variations and differences in quality up to the houses of the most prosperous owners, which have several rooms and subsidiary structures as well.

The poorest house has for light and ventilation but a small door, daylight reaching only the front room; any other rooms are like caves. All rooms are for multiple uses, for work as well as sleeping, but despite the poverty of their owners, the inner wall facings are nearly always neatly calcimined. In a two-room house, the parents and the youngest of the children occupy one of the rooms for sleeping, while the older children sleep in the second room.[23] The kitchen is usually dark, except for the glow of a little fire during the day, of gum cistus branches laid directly on the earthen floor. The smoke seeping through the interstices of the roof tiles leaves a cover of soot on the upper parts of the walls, the ceil-

[23] M. F. de Estanco Louro, *O Livro de Alportel*, p. 386.

217

ing rafters, and the under side of the tiles. Braided ropes of garlic, onions, and blackened sausages commonly hang above the fire. Floors are nearly always of packed earth. A slightly better house will have a window or two closed with wooden shutters, and perhaps a third room to be used exclusively as a bedroom. As the quality of house improves, the number of windows, and sometimes of doors, increases. Only houses of the most prosperous people have glazed windows and multiple rooms, each used just for a single function, such as sleeping, cooking, or reception.

According to the economic status of the owner, there are various appended structures, a pigpen, a pen for storage of tools, or for grain. There may be a separate shed to be used as a summer kitchen, having one or possibly both ends open and containing an oven. A detached, outside, round oven made of stone, somewhat removed from the house, is not uncommon.

House equipment and diet

Equipment within the house is meagre: a bed for the parents and mats to put on the floor for the other members of the family, a wooden table, simple, angular, wooden chairs of the size used for small children in the United States, a large wooden chest for storage of winter clothing and of blankets woven on hand looms by the mountain folk from the coarse carpet wool of the long-haired sheep. The Neolithic quern—handmill for grinding grains—is still a standard piece of equipment. The earthen floors of modest houses are beaten so hard that they can be kept clean. Even with chickens and other animals wandering in and out at will, they are usually immaculate. Hanging from the rafters by esparto ropes is a mat where cheeses made of goats' milk are put to ripen, away from the rats.

For the average person, the diet is meagre. Maize is greatly esteemed, but even though it is the most important crop of the market gardens, the supply is limited. It is eaten in the form of *polenta*, a gruel. Wheat is standard for the excellent, heavy white bread made once a week, although barley bread of an ancient type is still made in some of the vil-

A demonstration of the use of the quern.

lages.[24] Breakfast often consists of bread alone. For dinner in the middle of the day in winter, the main dish is usually stew, of boiled potatoes or broad beans, cooked with a few greens and cabbage and flavored with a bit of garlic, pork fat, or olive oil. It is usually poured over bread. At the end of the day, any remnants of the stew are eaten. In summer, tomatoes, cucumbers, pimentos, and other vegetables give more variety to the diet, and sometimes, with luck in hunting, a partridge or a rabbit is added to the stew. The poorest people may have only bread, dipped in water and moistened additionally with a little oil and vinegar, as the basis of their main meal. In addition, they may have a few olives, figs, and a bit of garlic. Sweetening is mostly of honey.

Such are some of the aspects of life in the Caldeirão. For the simple people, either owners or workers of small plots, it is a frugal existence limited to the immediate area. Many of the inhabitants of the mountains,

[24] Mariano Feio, *Le Bas Alentejo et L'Argarve,* p. 101.

living according to modes and values quite strange to the more sophisticated coastal Algarvians, have never been more than a few miles from their dwellings. Now, as a result of highways, contact between most mountain settlements and the Lower Algarve is a matter, at most, of an hour by car. With the introduction of machinery for plowing, threshing, milling, and increasingly for other needs, the simple self-sufficient life cannot continue to exist in its present forms. Within another generation or two the changes will be radical. Yet these mountain people have not been entirely without contacts with the coast, and through the coast with the world at large. In view of such contacts—limited though they were—one might have expected greater changes than have taken place up until now. It will be interesting to see the selection or rejection of the different ways of life that will be offered to them. Will all of the ancient aspects of life—some harking back to the Neolithic—be effaced, or will these conservative people cautiously accept only a few new ideas and material items and fit them into their accustomed mode of life?

6. Monchique

▪▪

Wᴇsᴛ ᴏꜰ ᴄᴇɴᴛᴇʀ in the Algarve, the Caldeirão Mountains slope downward to the low pass of the São Marcos da Serra. Beyond that lowland to the west, a sharp front of schists, the same rock as that of the Caldeirão, rises in a fault scarp to form the edge of a western mountain area. Within these western mountains appears a surprising enclave of granitelike rock, syenite, which stores water in a way that has permitted an agricultural development strikingly different from anything else in the province; this is Monchique, another region of distinction, Algarvian, but obviously different from other subareas.

Tʜᴇ sᴄʜɪsᴛ ᴀʀᴇᴀ

The schists surrounding the syenite core of Monchique offer the same opportunities for agriculture and settlement as do those of the

221

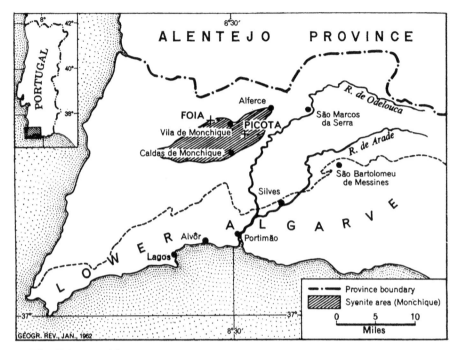

The Western Algarve

Caldeirão. This situation is reflected in the general economy; most of the natural vegetation has been eliminated in order to plant grains—and with the same melancholy result as in the Caldeirão. The long slopes (especially on the north), in fallow most of the time, yield pitiful returns for labor expended. The grain, planted in small areas cleared of the spontaneous growth, is so thin in the fields that one wonders if it could possibly pay the planter for his time.

In widely separated locations, areas with available water support small clusters of population. In a few deep canyons just north of the crest, which are protected against the north wind and where springs yield water, agricultural terraces have been built. Lower down, gardens similar to those of the Caldeirão are found in the narrow valley bottoms, where the *nora* and the sweep bring up water from shallow wells to irrigate maize, fruit trees, and vegetable gardens.

In general, dwellings here have a dejected appearance and give one more the impression of the houses of Giões, rather than those of Martim

222

Terraces on the syenite, with schist mountains in the background.

Longo; commonly they are made of tamped earth, and a large proportion of them are not calcimined. Earth floors are standard; few houses
have chimneys; and cooking is done, when weather permits, in beehive
ovens standing by themselves in the yards. Gathering and simple crafts
are essentially those of the Caldeirão.

The syenite area

But what gives character to Monchique is an oasis that appears
islandlike, high above the drab encircling hills of schist. As a beneficent
consequence of erosion, its granitelike syenite, first intruded and bulged
between layers of schists, has been exposed. The relatively impermeable
schists are reduced each year by sheet wash, but the surface of the syenite is little affected as rainwater percolates along jointing surfaces. On
the slopes below, this water reappears from dozens of perennial springs,
which make possible a thriving agriculture, contrasting sharply with that
on the penurious schists all around. An early nineteenth-century travel-

223

ler, coming to Monchique, spoke of the "desert" through which he had passed before reaching an enchanting vista of chestnuts, oranges, and lemons, in irrigated areas.[1]

The "desert" referred to was that of the schists; the "enchanting vista" was that of syenite Monchique, which differs from the encircling schist lands along sharp boundaries where contrasts in present economy are clearly influenced by the physical environment. Its economy seems to be so neatly and efficiently adjusted to the physical base that, at first glance, a strong case is offered for environmental determinism. Yet this is an area that has had a checkered career of exploitation (or lack of it) and its present pattern of life is a matter of no great antiquity. In fact, its excellent opportunities may not have been recognized by local people, but rather by immigrants possessing techniques perfected elsewhere and brought by them into the area.

It is the rainiest area of southern Portugal. The peak of Foia, standing nearly three thousand feet above the level of the sea, is known inelegantly to the inhabitants of the region as the "chamber pot of heaven," but the rainfall average cannot be accurately given, as the record there has been started only recently. However, the record kept at the Vila de Monchique (about 1,500 feet elevation), below the peak, shows an average of about fifty inches of precipitation per year,[2] most of which becomes available for irrigation. In addition to this advantage, Monchique has enough warmth in summer to make crops grow lustily with the copious supply of water from the springs. Although Caldas de Monchique (666 feet elevation) records considerable range of temperature (22° F.) between the mean for the warmest and that for the coldest month, this situation is due to the warmth of summer days, for the area has neither the winter cold of some of the lowland stations nor the warmth of the

[1] H. F. Link, *Voyage en Portugal,* II, 121–122.

[2] Actually the record shows forty-nine inches average precipitation for the years 1932–1950 and nearly fifty-three inches average for the years 1951–1958 inclusive. These statistics are taken from *O Clima de Portugal,* Part VII, "*Baixo Alentejo e Algarve,*" 1952, Map. 24 for the period 1932–1950; for the years 1951–1958 data are taken from the yearly publication *Anuário Climatológico de Portugal,* Part I, Vols. III–XII inclusive.

summer nights of others. The number of summer days with maximum temperatures above 77° F. (135) is greater than that of any other Algarvian station.

With such contrasts in rock and climate, it is not surprising that the natural vegetation of the syenite area is sharply different from that of the schist. In the remnants of the former great chestnut copses are peony (*Paeonia mascula*), spurge (*Euphorbia amygdaloides*), king fern (*Osmunda regalis*), and the pontic rhododendron (*Rhododendron ponticum*). On the slopes around them are maritime pine (*Pinus maritima*), mimosa (*Acacia cynophylla*, Ldey.), and strawberry tree (*Arbutus unedo*). On the upper levels of Foia, because of greater coolness, the essentially Mediterranean type of vegetation is mixed with members of north Portuguese or mid-European vegetation, made up of brooms (*Ulex epistolepis*, Webb), *Erica* species of cistus, grasses, ferns, asphodel, scilla, and others.[3] Its variety and luxuriance are an augury of the fertility that has been demonstrated by its cultivators.

SETTLEMENT OF THE AREA

Nearly four thousand years ago farmers established themselves on lands at the contact of the schists and the syenite, where Caldas de Monchique is situated. Remains from the period of transition from the Neolithic to the early Bronze Age, testifying to such settlement, have been found in several Megalithic burials.[4] Since then settlement in the area has probably been continuous. The Romans "took the cure" at its hot mineral springs,[5] but seemingly paid little attention to the forested mountain slopes above; at least no record has been found of such interest. That the successors to the Romans, the Visigoths, knew the area is not to be doubted, because evidence of their presence has been found; but such traces are so few that Visigothic interest in the area was obvi-

---

[3] Lautensach, Hermann, "Portugal: Auf Grund eigener Reisen und der Literatur": I. "Die portugiesichen Landschaften," *Petermann's Mitteilungen*, No. 230 (Gotha) 1937, p. 119.

[4] Abel Viana, Octávio de Veiga Ferreira, and José Formosinho, *Necropolis de las Caldas de Monchique*, pp. 9–22.

[5] José Formosinho. "Vestígios dos Romanos, nas Caldas de Monchique," reprint from *I Congresso Luso-Espanhol de hidrologia*, 1948, pp. 5–12.

ously minor.[6] This fact is not surprising, in view of Visigothic society and its interests. More surprising is the fact that their successors, the Moslems, should have evinced no more concern with an area that is today profitably exploited according to techniques that were known to Moslem farmers and were, to a considerable extent, the product of Moslem skills.

In 1189, when the Christians captured and temporarily held Silves, the Moslem capital of the Algarve, they also captured several castles that apparently served as lookouts and forward posts in the defense of the capital. Two such outposts were probably located on the slopes of Foia and Picota. The first was called Munchite in a document of the period; it was probably located on or near the site of the present Vila de Monchique. However, the document states that all of the people from Munchite and from seven other castles as well had left to take refuge in the city of Silves.[7] Such a report does not suggest that there were settlements at these outlying places, but that they were merely garrisons in fortified lookouts. Nevertheless, Herculano may have been correct in his contention that Monchique, at that time, was an established settlement.[8] The second outpost was called Montagut. This may well have been the castle whose remnants are still extant on the hill called "the mountain of the castle of the Arabs," which rises above the little town of Alferce.[9]

Herculano's statement regarding Monchique lacks evidence, but it is

[6] Abel Viana, José Formosinho, and Octávio da Veiga Ferreira, "O Conjunto visigótico de Alcaria (Caldas de Monchique)," reprints of Nos. 33–34 (1949) of *Revista do sindicato nacional dos engenheiros auxiliares, agentes técnicos de engenharia e condutores*, p. 2.

[7] João Baptista da Silva Lopes (ed. and commentator), *Relação da derrota naval, façanhas, e successos dos Cruzados que parti rão do Escalda para a Terra Santa no anno de 1189*, p. 42.

[8] A. Herculano, *História de Portugal*, 7th ed., Tomo III, Livro III, 168.

[9] José António Guerreiro Gascon, *Subsídios para a monografia de Monchique*, pp. 61, 291. This volume was written by the last of a long line of local historians belonging to one family in the Vila de Monchique. The author's great-grandfather wrote an informative account of the Vila in the early nineteenth century and his grandfather contributed another in the mid-nineteenth century. The author of the above volume gathered more material and wrote an interesting and valuable account of the settlement, using the reports of his ancestors. Unfortunately, he did not live to see it published.

not unreasonable. The fact may be that although the Romans, the Visigoths, and the Arabs showed no interest in the use of the syenite mountain slopes (except for lookouts and forward posts for Moslem contingents), there may have been families living there according to prehistoric modes established centuries earlier. This sort of continuance of age-old ways of life in isolated areas is not strange in Portuguese history, nor, indeed, today,[10] and it is difficult to believe that the prehistoric farming people who knew the area would give up the use of luxuriant chestnut and oak forests, wonderful sources of mast for their pigs and food for themselves. It is easier to believe that the organized, urbanized Romans would lack interest, as might also the Visigoths, with their predilection for the low, open plains, and the Arabs, who consistently evinced almost a revulsion to living in wet, green, heavily forested zones.

Any mystery regarding the presence or absence of settled people on the syenite was ended by a report in 1495, when García de Resende described the journey taken in that year by King João II of Portugal to the baths of Caldas de Monchique, in a vain effort to be rid of the malady that killed him shortly after his arrival in the Algarve. The King left Alcáçovas, near Evora, and, striking diagonally across the Alentejo, arrived at Monchique, where he stayed two days before descending to Caldas de Monchique for treatment at the baths.[11] The settlement of Monchique was of sufficient importance at that date to be at least mentioned and to be the stopping place of the King. By the latter part of the next century another king (Sebastian, in 1573) visited Monchique and was so taken with the aspect, and, presumably, the importance of the place that he decided to grant it privileges as a *vila* (a decision that was not carried out because of pressure from the members of the council at Silves).[12]

Through the centuries the forested slopes were exploited for mast and for chestnut wood to be exported to other parts of Portugal. The canyon and valley bottoms were increasingly used with irrigation, until

[10] Dan Stanislawski, *The Individuality of Portugal,* pp. 108–109, 120.
[11] García de Resende, *Chronica de El-Rei D. João II,* III, 66.
[12] José António Guerreiro Gascon, *Subsídios para a monografia de Monchique,* p. 145, citing a document in the archive of the Torre de Tombo.

by the end of the eighteenth century a thriving agriculture and a lumbering industry supported a specialized economy, importing grain and exporting chestnut wood from the forests and fruits and vegetables from the orchards and gardens. It seems probable that wine was another item of their specialization, for vineyards are frequently mentioned and a series of laws had come into being to protect them against damage.[13]

The forests on the upper slopes of Foia, essentially unchanged in several thousand years of existence, were doomed when rights to the land were granted by the King to the inhabitants of the Vila de Monchique in 1824.[14] The rights to the land meant the rights to remove the trees and burn the slopes for planting, which was promptly done. However, the change was not an unmixed evil, for it brought additional land under cultivation. By the middle of the century Monchique was the service center of an important agricultural region that exported its fruits, vegetables, and wood to the ports of Lagos, Portimão, and Silves for local consumption or for trans-shipment to other parts of Portugal.[15]

Comparing the area today with the description of it as given in the cited report of 1860, one notes immediately that at least two obvious changes have taken place during the century. First, the luxuriant vineyards are no longer present, having been largely eliminated by a fungus blight,[16] and later by phylloxera. Second, terraces are not mentioned as being used by the cultivators of a century ago, nor are they mentioned in the cited reports of the early nineteenth century. In fact, these reports lead one to believe that cultivation was limited to the canyon and valley

[13] An interesting document in the local archive is cited and partially quoted in José António Guerreiro Gascon, Subsídios para a monografia de Monchique, pp. 180–193, relating to the ordinances existing in the Vila de Monchique in 1793. By its phrasing it is obvious that these ordinances had come down through long generations of use.

[14] Monchique had been made a vila in 1773 (J. Fernandes Mascarenhas, O que os documentos nós dizem sobre alguns aspectos da vida económica do Algarve no século XVIII, Ref. #1).

[15] José António Guerreiro Gascon, Subsídios para a monografia de Monchique, pp. 88 et seq., quoting from the report of his grandfather in 1860. His grandfather was living in Monchique at the time of the grant, and observed the changes wrought on the hillsides.

[16] José António Guerreiro Gascon, Subsídios para a monografia de Monchique, p. 129.

bottoms. However, in one place in the document of 1793 there is a clue to the possible existence of terraces. Relating to the matter of prohibitions and penalties, the population is enjoined not to remove stones from *muros e vellados*. Clearly a *vellado* is something other than an ordinary wall (*muro*). As the word *valado* is used in Monchique and other parts of the Algarve today to identify the supporting wall of a terrace, this almost buried reference makes it seem probable that agricultural terraces existed in Monchique, even though they could not have been as numerous and important as they are now. The circumstance that gave impetus to their extension arose in the twentieth century when a blight ruined a large part of the chestnut forests, which had been exploited up until then for export of wood,[17] as well as for mast and food. Professor Jorge Dias, the Portuguese ethnographer, told me of masons in the Algarve who had mentioned to him that they or their parents had come from the Minho of northern Portugal, where terrace-building techniques are probably immemorially old. They may have been imported for such work after the forests of Monchique were reduced by the blight and the landowners sought other ways of exploiting their properties, ways that were old in the area, but of little extension.

TERRACES

The syenite slopes, wherever water is available from springs or the streams derived from them, now have been converted into a spectacular landscape with flat-floored terraces, supported by high, carefully made walls of dry-stone masonry. Not uncommonly one may see a wall of ten feet or more in height supporting a terrace floor that may be less than ten feet in width; walls considerably higher than ten feet above the surface are not uncommon. Such construction is the work of specialized masons, who ordinarily earn 40 escudos ($1.40 U.S.) for an eight-hour day, a relatively high wage for Portuguese labor. Usually two or three helpers, each earning about 18 escudos ($.63 U.S.) a day, assist the maestro. Such a group of men will ordinarily take half a day to make one square yard of wall, as the work is done slowly and carefully, fitting each stone into the general outline of the adjacent stones.

---

[17] *Ibid.*, pp. 88–90.

Monchique terraces.

Although expertly done, terrace-making in Portugal is accomplished without modern equipment. It is the achievement of men who seem to decide and act intuitively; but intuition in their case—if the word should be used at all—is the result of generations of trial and error. The first step in the process is a decision as to the proper width of the terrace floor, made by sighting the chosen slope. With the determined width in mind (from a few feet up to several yards) a stone wall is built at the lower edge, high enough to sustain a level planting surface. Then with simple equipment—shovels and baskets—material removed from the upper slope is dumped below until the top of the wall is reached and the floor is essentially level. Rocks and poor soils have been put at the bottom and a thick layer of good soil spread over the top.

Each case, to some extent, is special in its requirements. Commonly, excavation at the site of the wall is made at least three feet deep, so that the base will have solid foundation. At times, because of the special height of the walls or unusual local conditions, greater excavation may be made, and the thickness of the wall at the base depends upon the intended height. For example, a terrace wall of three yards in height would require a base of at least one yard in thickness and, if the slope were especially steep, possibly a yard and a half. A wall of four yards in height on a steep slope would probably have a thickness of two yards at the base. The top of such walls would ordinarily be eighteen inches thick. No mortar is ever used nor is it needed. The large stones of the wall are roughly fitted into those adjacent and any small interstices are plugged with small stones.

In building a terrace wall a mason must know his business. To decide upon the amount of excavation necessary for the base, he must take into account both slope and the quality and amount of soil. Slope also indicates the height of the proposed wall. Not only the height, but the natural foundation (type of rock and soil) as well, should determine the width of the base. The inward inclination of the outer face of the wall is a function of height, for with unusually high walls it must be greater than it would be for low walls; in any case it will not be less than 10 per cent and may be as much as 30 per cent. The mason's conclusions are reached without the aid of instruments; he looks at the slope, feels the soil, and makes up his mind. Only simple tools are used in construction, but the product is one of obviously high skill. Given ordinary care, such a wall lasts for generations, almost indefinitely.

Water in sufficient amounts for irrigation is essential to terrace cultivation, but not every owner controls a spring; with such deficiency, rights to a certain amount of water each week are written into the contract of purchase of the land, or if there is no written contract there will be an understanding that is founded upon such length of tenure that it has the strength of a contract. In 1959 a new set of terraces was built outside of the Vila de Monchique in territory that was made valuable by the construction of a new highway. On the land of the builder of these terraces were five springs, and three storage tanks were being built to impound the water. An informant said that probably the owner would have more water than he needed for his own use, so that part of the water could be sold if another owner built terraces below.

Construction of terraces, tanks, canals, connecting paths, and innumerable other smaller necessities of this intensive agriculture cannot be justified within conventional economics. Much of the construction is done by small owners and their families in spare time, and for this work there can be no estimate of cost. Other terrace construction can be explained only in terms of the low wages paid to the laborers and of the extreme land hunger of nearly all Portuguese. Terraces are still being built at costs as high as two thousand dollars an acre. Many men—perhaps all—who invest cash in such construction have no exact idea as to costs, nor do they have precise knowledge as to the size of their properties. The driving urge for prestige and security in the ownership of land is sufficient to make men with capital invest in terrace construction, where possible, as it is extremely difficult to find productive property for sale.[18] These owners do not intend to work upon the properties them-

[18] The real estate agent is unknown in Portugal insofar as I know. When death or other serious events cause a family to give up property, the knowledge of possible sale is known immediately and buyers are always available. The prospective buyer probably knows the property, but in the event that he does not he will look it over and subjectively reach a conclusion as to its value. He makes an offer and, after dickering, he and the owner agree upon a price. Then the village notary draws up the contract of sale.

The villa of Monchique.

selves, for they live as absentees either in the Vila de Monchique or in Lisbon, while plots of two to five acres are worked by a peasant family on shares.

CROPS

With available water and mild winters, as well as summer warmth, terraces from Caldas de Monchique to somewhat above the Vila ordinarily yield two crops each year, and with some rotations, three. Nearly every surface supports mixed plantings; tree crops are associated with a low crop, usually a grain, but sometimes legumes and vegetables. While with mixed planting each individual crop is not as large as it would be if it were planted alone, the total return is satisfactory, and mixed planting is a hedge against loss through crop failure or poor market conditions which might affect a single crop.

A wide variety of crops can be grown under the especially favorable conditions of the Monchique area. Maize is fundamental and to be seen on all sides in summer. Oranges, lemons, and tangerines yield high prof-

233

its and usually do not share the ground with another crop, although this is not invariably the case. Occasionally maize is planted under oranges; as both need irrigation, some farmers think that the combination is satisfactory. This opinion, however, is rejected by the majority of landowners, and most orange trees stand alone on the land. Somewhat the same condition exists with regard to the stone fruits, although it is a commonly expressed opinion that an undercrop is more satisfactory with them than with citrus. Three of the famous four unirrigated lower Algarvian trees are found in the area, but in a far less important position in the general economy than on the lowland. Commonest is the olive, planted in some cases at the edge of terraces, but also on unterraced slopes. Both the almond and the fig fit well into a scheme of mixed planting, but they are not common. As they do not require irrigation, it is better planning to put them on unterraced land at lower elevations. The other member of the four, the carob, is lacking in the Monchique area. Obviously, it would be a waste of terraced land for this hardy calcophile, that finds perfect conditions for growth on the raw limestone of the Lower Algarve, to occupy irrigable terraces. In addition to this fact, the vigor of the carob discourages underplanting. Scattered medlars appear, not because they are greatly prized, but because they yield fruit earlier than other trees. Grapes are usually limited to the terrace edges.

Virtually all of the vegetables and grains of the Lower Algarve are planted here and produce bountifully: peas, beans, cabbage, cauliflower, white and sweet potatoes, broad beans, chick-peas, onions, tomatoes, or squash. A common rotation includes potatoes, usually with squash, in the spring, followed by maize, commonly interplanted with beans, in the summer. The maize and beans are planted in trenches in rows dug with a broad, heavy hoe by the man of the family. The woman of the house walks behind, carrying a bag of seeds, a few of which she drops into the trenches at intervals of several inches. The seeds are covered by the earth from the excavation of the next trench. Or there may be two crops of potatoes. A choice must be made as to the variety of white potatoes grown. One type commonly grown in the Monchique area is planted in March and is ready to harvest after three months. Another variety is planted in April, but, while it produces a larger crop,

Making syenite stones for an olive press.

it takes four months to mature. In winter the terraces are often compart-
mented for various vegetables and for green fodder (oats and barley),
as well as for considerable wheat and, at the upper elevations, rye. Cab-
bages are grown somewhere on the terraces in each month of the year.
On the highest terraces, above the Vila, two crops are not possible in the
year, and fruit trees do not thrive. Commonly, a crop of maize or potatoes in summer is followed either by a forage crop or by fallow in winter.

Processing the crops

Primitive-type crushers are used for part of the olive crop. The
great crushers are chiselled by hand out of large blocks of syenite,
blasted out of the mountain side just below the Vila. The flat stones for
the base are made in the shape of quarter sections of a circle. The crush-
ing stones are truncated cones with a base diameter and height of about
four feet each. Four of such cones, each with an iron rod projecting from
the apex, are put on their sides, so that the rod of each fits into a re-
volving center shaft which turns them round in the circular trough into

which olives have been dumped. Another type of stone crusher consists of syenite wheels, each with a diameter of about four feet and a thickness of ten inches. Rolled around on their edges, they crush the olives in a narrow trough. However, the greater part of the relatively large olive production is now being handled by modern steam crushers. One such crusher is in the Vila and another in the village of Alferce, at the eastern edge of the syenite region. In all cases, no matter what the type of mill, the mill owner takes about one-half of the oil for his services. He also keeps the pressings, which he sells, mixed with grain remnants, for cattle feed.

Milling of grains is done either in a modern mill or in one of the water mills that have been common to the area for more time than is recorded. Monchique has never had the problem of the Lower Algarve, where water is available through only a part of the year and where men have turned to the windmills during the dry summer season. Streams starting from the persistent springs of the syenite slopes of Monchique make the water mill dependable throughout the year. Only with the advent of the modern motor-driven mills have they lost importance. Nevertheless, several are still in use.

LAND SYSTEMS AND LABOR

The Census of 1950 indicates that half of the inhabitants of the region of Monchique live in houses of their own,[19] but this figure cannot be used to express the relation between privately owned lands and lands worked either by share workers or by renters. Although some small owners have more land than they can work themselves and at least three owners in the parish have large holdings worked by several hundred share workers, it is probable that more proprietors have insufficient land to support their families and must work not only their own small plot, but other land that they rent or from which they receive part of the harvest. Comments that I received in the area from a variety of informants gave me the impression that more property was worked by nonowners than by the owners themselves.

Although five acres are needed to support a family in modest comfort,

[19] *Inquérito às condições de habitação da família, Anexo ao IX Recenseamento Geral da População, em 15 de Dezembro de 1950*, p. 8.

few of the share workers have this much land to cultivate. The house that is furnished them by the landowner is usually a two-room stone dwelling. The proprietor also normally furnishes a cow or an ox for plowing, a small pig or two, and half the cost of the seed and of any commercial fertilizer used. The share worker must supply the few articles of furniture for the house, the steel-tipped, single-handled, wooden plow, the broad hoe, half the seed, and half the cost of any commercial fertilizer.

Field crops are divided equally if the farmer and the owner have divided the cost of the seed and fertilizer. If, however, the owner has furnished everything but labor, he takes two parts to the farmer's one.

Tree crops are divided into three parts, one to the farmer and two to the owner, if the farmer picks the crop. If the farmer does not pick the crop and this work is done at the owner's expense, he takes three parts of four. Chickens are not part of the contract. If he wants them, the share worker buys them for himself.

In all cases, houses, sheds, terrace walls, and other such permanent fixtures are the responsibility of the owner. If the share worker has consumed any of the crop, it is deducted from his share. The offspring of the animals are owned equally and if it has been necessary to buy food for them, which is rare, as the cattle are pastured and the pigs live on garbage, the cost is divided. Milk is little prized as food outside of the larger cities; the share worker may take what he wants after the calves have been fed. All of the manure is carefully saved and spread on the terrace fields, but animals are not numerous and manure is usually insufficient, so that commercial fertilizer must be used as well.

OTHER ECONOMIC ACTIVITIES

Caldas de Monchique continues to serve, as it has for nearly four thousand years, as a mineral-water health resort. Now it is a spa with large hotels where the ailing may come for mineral baths, and its water is sold commercially in the Lower Algarve. The Vila de Monchique continues to be the center of a prosperous area based on agriculture, but it is sufficiently far from the main routes so that some traits remain of an earlier period, when crafts based on local materials were important.

Making chestnut baskets.

The memory of luxuriant chestnut groves (now in remnants) is maintained by the basketmakers, who produce the durable containers sent to Albufeira and other parts of the Algarve for the shipment of agricultural produce. The chestnut wood, cut in January or February when it is tender, is split and then soaked and heated so that it will bend easily. A man takes three hours to make one of the strong baskets that will hold forty pounds of tomatoes or fruit and last for two or three years. For this labor he earns seven cents U.S. per hour. Other articles of chestnut are: long poles for ox prods, long-handled spatulas to push the unbaked dough into the bread ovens and pull out the bread, tool handles, and beaters to knock olives from the trees. A few remaining craftsmen work as carvers of spoons and knives from chestnut and strawberry tree wood and of decorated shepherds' canes from chestnut.

Weaving is no longer a craft of importance, but some of the country women still make heavy blankets and handsome saddlebags. Rag rugs of many colors are woven on heavy, chestnut hand looms. The warp is of linen (from flax raised on the surrounding hills) and the woof from

A loom for making rag rugs.

balls of thin rag strips made of old clothing. The rugs are used as bed-covers or as sweat pads under the saddles of burros. A few linen stock-ings and socks of an open-work crocheting are still made in Monchique. Back of Casais, on the slopes of Monchique, the mountain women weave highly colored saddlebags for use by family or close friends (they are not made for sale, they insist).

Copper working, especially of stills for the manufacture of distilled brandy from the fruit of the strawberry tree, occupies the time of at least one maestro in the Vila. The stills themselves are used in the coun-try places where the strawberry trees are found.

Willows (*Salix*) are planted along the streams near Monchique and trimmed each year so that the branches can be used to make baskets. Some of the branches are also sent to Faro, where they are made not only into baskets but also into tables and chairs. Although willow peels easily and can be bent without breaking when green, the Monchique basketmakers always soak it for forty-five minutes before working with it to make it even more pliable. Cane (*Arundo donax*) is also used ex-

A saddlebag of the type still made by the women in the mountains.

tensively for basket making. The basketmakers pay the owners of the land from which the canes have been gathered eight escudos ($.28 U.S.) for each hundred canes, and then sit by the streamside to make the baskets.

At the present time the parish of Monchique is the Algarvian leader in cork production; nearly one-third of the cork oaks of the province are growing in the parish.[20] Only in occasional years does any other parish surpass its production (e.g. Loulé in 1955).[21] Even though men in the cork factories of Silves contend that Monchique cork is lower in quality than that of many regions of the Algarve, it seems that production—even though it may not be of the best quality cork—is better managed than that of other parishes. At least statistics show a steadiness of production that indicates well-managed business.

Cork production is not a new activity for this part of the country, if it

[20] *Inquérito às explorações agrícolas do continente, 1952, I, Provincias do Ribatejo, Alto Alentejo, Baixo Alentejo e Algarve,* pp. 70–73.

[21] *Estatística agrícola, 1957,* pp. 111–112.

is reasonable to attribute such exploitation to Monchique as is known to have taken place in other cork regions of Portugal. In the early fifteenth century the export of cork from Portugal to the north of Europe was "older than memory."[22] As Monchique may have been taking part in the general economy and activities of the country as a whole by this time, it is very possible that its cork forests were commercially exploited. Perhaps here, as in other parts of Portugal, the trees may have been badly cut out in the fifteenth century, as the wood was highly esteemed for ships in that century of energetic shipbuilding.[23] If such was the case, they were either replaced in subsequent centuries, or the shipbuilding industry had a less baleful effect here than in other places.

The parish of Monchique, although now the most important producer of cork in the Algarve, does not, except in small degree, make articles for sale. This activity is centered in towns of the Lower Algarve such as Silves and Faro and São Brás. In the Monchique parish there are but two plants for processing cork, with a total fixed capital of a little over $13,500 U.S. (386,000 Portuguese escudos)[24] in 1957, hiring only sixteen employees, twelve of whom were wage earners, the others, presumably, owners. The average number of working days during the year for these twelve workers was slightly over one hundred, and for their labor they received an average of $140 U.S. each for the year.[25]

Another source of income—and of personal satisfaction—is the manufacture of brandy from the fruit of the strawberry tree (*Arbutus unedo*). When the reddish-yellow fruits are ripe they are gathered and put into a vat with water, where they soak for a month or more. After this soaking they are boiled, usually over a fire of cistus or heather, which are close at hand and can be burned green.[26] Distillation is ac-

[22] J. Vieira Natividade, *Subericultura*, p. 41. See also Henrique da Gama Barros, *História da administração pública em Portugal nos seculos XII a XV*, IX, p. 115.

[23] Henrique da Gama Barros, *História da administração pública em Portugal nos seculos XII a XV*, IX, p. 43.

[24] *Inquérito Industrial, Distrito de Faro, 1957*, p. 75.

[25] In total, 48,000 Portuguese escudos was paid to the dozen men. See *Inquérito industrial . . . Faro, 1957*, pp. 72–73.

[26] Cistus is also a source of cash income to the mountain people for in the Lower Algarve it is in demand by bakers who use it for fuel, and by farmers, who use the straightest stems as supports for peas and beans.

A still for making strawberry-tree brandy.

complished by the use of one of the simple copper stills made in the Vila de Monchique. On the first run through the still the product is a clear brandy of about 13 per cent alcohol. During the second run the percentage of alcohol is raised to 20 per cent. The product is not considered fit for sale until it reaches at least this percentage. Then, at the stills, it sells for six to nine escudos per liter (approximately $.20 to $.30 U.S. per quart). A publication of 1951 estimated that production averaged 600,000 liters per year.[27] Occasionally, a liquor is distilled from figs, but this use of figs is not common in the mountains, where they are too valuable as food to be distilled into liquor.

The most important economic activities within the Monchique region have been outlined above. In the main, they seem to be well suited to the area and intelligently pursued. It is difficult to believe that in its basic production, agriculture, radical improvement can be made; if a more efficient use of hillslopes has ever been accomplished, this observer does

[27] M. Gomes Guerreiro, *Valorização da Serra Algarvia*, p. 9.

not know it. Almost surely, however, changes will be made in the community because of the new highways, already in use, which will bring about more intimate relations with the rest of Portugal. Some of the traditional customs will be eliminated; some of the frugal ways of living will be forgotten. Caldas de Monchique may be modernized. Perhaps tourism will become important to the whole area; certainly the charm of the zone recommends it.

Although in Monchique there is some of the conservatism common to all of Portugal, it is dissimilar to that of the Caldeirão Mountains, its eastern neighbor, where ancient traditions still dominate the life. Acceptance of new economic and social conditions is not hypercautious in Monchique; major changes in economic attitudes and activities have taken place more than once. The present period offers another invitation to change. One wonders if, and how, Monchique will accept it.

Some Final Words

▀▀▀

T HIS IS A BOOK of descriptive geography. No attempt has been made to be encyclopedic. The facts presented are those which seem best fitted to describe the personality of the area, an area that to some degree has found its own solutions to problems of economy and association of men with land. Perhaps more generalizations should have been made based on these facts or others that might have been used; further generalization is a tempting prospect but one that I have avoided because, in my opinion, generalizations have been reached too casually in the social sciences. More materials relative to disparate culture areas are needed before useful judgments can be made. With this idea in mind, this book has been written to sketch the important aspects of life in a little publicized part of the world. If the reader realizes something of the character of the area and some of the values inherent in its human geography, then the book has succeeded.

The Algarve made an appealing subject of study, not only because it

244

has strong color but because it is not a simple unit; each of its constituent subareas has its unique personality. Yet, with all their differences, there is always a family resemblance.

Another reason for its appeal comes from the uncertain future that it faces and the opportunity that we will have to observe its willingness to change or its capacity to resist. The Algarve has not been unwilling to accept change in the past, even though its reluctance has been profound in some places and at some times; it has always wanted (more clearly than many areas of the world) to accept change on its own terms and on the basis of its own predilections. To some extent it has been successful in this determination. Like China, it has absorbed its conquerors; at least it has always remained clearly Algarvian. Even at the times of conquest and control by Romans and Arabs the changes brought were Mediterranean and out of a common cutural background.

Now, however, the province faces pressures of another sort, those of an industrialized society that has had its success in techniques quite different from those that have proved to be useful in typical Mediterranean areas. Within the next few years we shall probably see greater impact of north European industrialized society upon this area, that heretofore has been reluctant to change according to others' designs.

If this book has given a sense of life and values in the Algarve, geographers in the future, by further observation, should know more about the processes of change in the association of men with land, and they will be able, therefore, to make better judgments as to the virtues or demerits of such changes.

BIBLIOGRAPHY

Abu Zacaria Iahia aben mohamed ben ahmed ebn el awam. *Libro de agricultura*, 2 vols. (trans. and annotated by Josef António Banqueri), Madrid, Imprenta Real, 1802.

Anuário climatológico de Portugal (annual), Lisbon, Serviço Meteorológico Nacional, Tipografia Técnico-Científica, 1951–1959.

Balbi, Adrien. *Essai statistique sur le royaume de Portugal et d'Algarve*, 2 vols., Paris, 1822.

Barros, Henrique da Gama. *História da administração pública em Portugal nos seculos XII a XV*, 2nd ed., 11 vols., Lisbon, Livraria Sá da Costa, 1950.

Bonnet, Charles. *Algarve (Portugal) Description géographique et géologique de cette province*, Lisbon, l'Académie Royale des Sciences de Lisbonne, 1850.

Brito, Raquel Soeiro de. "Um pequeno porto de pesca do Algarve: Albufeira," *Comptes Rendus du Congrès International de Géographie*, Lisbon, Centro Tipografia, 1949, Vol. III.

Clima de Portugal, O, Part VII, "Baixo Alentejo e Algarve," Serviço Meteorológico Nacional, Lisbon, 1952.

Costigan, Arthur William. *Sketches of Society and Manners in Portugal*, London, T. Vernor, 1787, Vol. I.

Dias, Jorge, and Fernando Galhano. *Aparelhos de elevar a água de rega*, Porto, Junta de Provincia do Douro-Liboral, 1953.

Eca, Vicente M. M. C. Almeida d'. "As pescas em Portugal," *Notas sobre Portugal*, 2 vols., Lisbon, Imprensa Nacional, 1908.

Edrisi, Abu-Abd-Alla-Mohamed-al. "Descripción de España," *Viajes de extranjeros por España y Portugal* (ed. J. García Mercadal), Madrid, Aguilar, S.A., 1952.

Estatística agrícola (yearly). Instituto Nacional de Estatística, Lisbon, Tipografia Portuguesa, Lda.

Estatística das pescas marítimas (yearly). Ministério da Marinha, Imprensa Nacional, Lisbon.

247

Estatística Industrial (yearly). Instituto Nacional de Estatística, Bertrand (Irmãos), Lda., Lisbon.

Evans, H. Muir. *Sting-fish and Seafarer*, London, Faber and Faber Ltd. (no date).

Feio, Mariano. *Le Bas Alentejo et l'Algarve: Livret-Guide de l'excursion E, Congrès International de Géographie*, Lisbon, Centro Tipografia Colonial, 1950.

Ferro, Gaetano. "I centri dell'Algarve occidentale," reprint from *Annali di ricerche e studi di geografia*, XI, Genoa, No. 3 (July-September, 1955).

————. *L'Algarve*, Genoa, Società d'Arte Poligrafica S.P.A., 1956.

————. "La Pesca nel mare dell'Algarve," reprint from *Annali di ricerche e studi di geografia*, Genoa, X, No. 4 (September–December, 1954).

————. "Ricerche di geografia urbana nell'Algarve (Portogallo): Faro e Vila Real de Santo António," reprint from *Annali di ricerche e studi di geografia*, Genoa, X, No. 2 (April–June, 1954).

Forbes, R. J. "Power," Chapter 17, *The Mediterranean Civilization and the Middle Ages, c. 700 B.C. to c. A.D. 1500*, Vol. II in *A History of Technology* (ed. Charles Singer, et al.). New York and London, Oxford University Press, 1956.

Formosinho, José. "Vestígios dos Romanos, nas Caldas de Monchique," *I Congresso Luso-Espanhol de hidrologia*, Lisbon, Sociedade Tipographia Lda., 1948.

Franco, Mario Lyster. "A pesca do atum na costa do Algarve," reprint from the *Correio do Sul*, Faro, 1947.

————. *O Algarve: Exposição Portuguesa em Sevilha*, Lisbon, Imprensa Nacional de Lisboa, 1929.

Fuero Juzgo, Madrid, Ibarra, La Real Academia Española, 1815.

Gado e animais de capoeira, Instituto Nacional de Estatística, Lisbon, Bertrand (Irmãos) Lda., 1955.

Galvão, António Miguel. *Um século de história de pescarias do Algarve*, 2nd ed., Faro, Tipografia Uniao, 1953.

García y Bellido, António. "Colonización Púnica," *Historia de España* (ed. R. Menéndez Pidal), Madrid, Espasa Calpe, S.A., 1952, Tomo I, Vol. II, 311–494.

————. "La Colonización Griega," *Historia de España* (ed. R. Menéndez Pidal), Madrid, Espasa Calpe, S.A., 1952, Tomo I, Vol. II, pp. 495–680.

Gascon, José António Guerreiro. *Subsídios para a monografia de Monchique*, Portimão, Portucalense Editora, 1955.

Girão, Aristides de Amorim, *Geografia de Portugal* (2nd ed.), Porto, Portucalense Editora, 1949–1951.

Girão, Aristides de Amorim, and Fernanda de Oliveira Lopes Velho. *Evolução demográfica e ocupação do solo continental (1890–1940)*, Vol. I, *Estudos da população Portuguesa*. Coimbra, Faculdade de Letras, Universidade de Coimbra, 1944.

Guerreiro, M. Gomes. *Valorização da Serra Algarvia*, Lisbon, Direcção Geral dos Serviços Florestais e Aquícolas, 1951.

Hehn, Victor. *The Wanderings of Plants and Animals from Their First Home* (James Steven Stallybrass, ed.), London, Swan Sonnenschein and Co., 1885.

Herculano, Alexandre. *História de Portugal*, 7th ed., Paris-Lisbon, Livrarias Aillaud & Bertrand, 1914–1916, III.

Herrera, Alonso de. *Agricultura general*, Madrid, Don Josef de Urrutia, 1790.

Inquérito às condições de habitação da família, anexo ao IX Recenseamento Geral da População (em 15 de Dezembro de 1950), Instituto Nacional de Estatística, Lisbon, Bertrand (Irmãos), Lda., 1952.

Inquérito às explorações agrícolas do continente, 1952, I, Províncias do Ribatejo, Alto Alentejo, Baixo Alentejo e Algarve, Instituto Nacional de Estatística, Lisbon, Bertrand (Irmãos), Lda., 1953.

Inquérito industrial das pescas, 1890. Document of the Office of Fisheries in Lisbon—probably unpublished. Prefatory statement credits José Bento Ferreira de Almeida and Victorio Miguel Maria das Chagas Roquette with authorship.

Inquérito industrial, Distrito de Faro, 1957. Instituto Nacional de Estatística, Lisbon, Bertrand (Irmãos), Lda., 1959.

Jornal do Pescador (monthly publication). Casa dos Pescadores, Lisbon.

Köppen, W. "Das geographische System der Klimate," *Allgemeine Klimalehre*, Band I in *Handbuch der Klimatologie* (W. Köppen and R. Geiger, eds.), Berlin, Verlag von Gebrüder Borntraeger, 1936.

Lautensach, Hermann. "Portugal: Auf Grund eigener Reisen und der Literatur": I. "Die portugiesichen Landschaften," *Petermann's Mitteilungen*, No. 230 (Gotha), 1937.

Lévi-Provençal, E. *Histoire de l'Espagne Musulmane: Le Siècle du Califat de Cordoue*, Vol. III, Paris-Leiden, 1953.

Link, H. F. *Voyage en Portugal*, 3 vols., Paris, 1803–1805.

Livermore, H. V. *A History of Portugal*, Cambridge, Cambridge University Press, 1947.

Lobo, A. de Sousa Silva Costa. *História da sociedade em Portugal no seculo XV*, Lisbon, Imprensa Nacional, 1904.

Lobo, Constantino Botelho de Lacerda. "Memoria sobre a decadencia das pescarias de Portugal," *Memorias económicas da academia real das scien-*

249

cias de Lisboa, Tomo IV, Lisbon, na typografia da mesma academia, 1812.

———. "Memoria sobre o estado das pescarias da costa do Algarve no anno de 1790," *Memorias económicas da Academia Real das Sciencias de Lisboa,* Tomo V, Lisbon, no officina da mesma academia, 1815.

Lopes, João Baptista da Silva. *"Corografia" ou memória económica, estadística e topográfica do Reino do Algarve,* Lisbon, [n. p.], 1841.

———. *Memorias para a história ecclesiastica do Bispado do Algarve,* Lisbon, typografia da mesma academia, 1848.

———. *Relação da derrota naval, façanhas, e successos dos cruzados que parti rão do Escalda para a Terra Santa no anno de 1189,* Lisbon, Academia Real das Sciencias de Lisboa, 1844.

Louro, M. F. de Estanco. *O Livro de Alportel,* Lisbon, Direcção Geral de Ensino e Fomento, 1928.

Madeira, José António. *Características meteorológicas do Algarve no quadro geral da climatologia Portuguesa,* Vol. II, Lisbon, Congresso Regional Algarvio (1951), 1952.

Mascarenhas, J. Fernandes. *O que os documentos nós dizem sobre alguns aspectos da vida económica do Algarve no século XVIII,* Coimbra, Coimbra editora, 1942.

Natividade, J. Vieira. *Subericultura,* Ministério da Economia, Direcção Geral dos Serviços Florestais e Aquícolas, Porto, Tipografia da Oficinas de Fotogravura de Marques Abreu, 1950.

Oliveira, Francisco Xavier d'Athaide. *A monografia de Alvôr,* Porto, Tipografia Universal, 1907.

———. *Monografia do concelho de Villa Real de Santo António,* Porto, Livraria Figueirinhas, 1908.

Oppian. *Oppian Colluthus Tryphiodorus* (English translation by A. W. Main), London, Heinemann, 1928, and New York, G. P. Putnam's Sons, 1928.

Popielovo, Nicolas de. "Viaje de Nicolas de Popielovo," *Viajes de Extranjeros por España y Portugal en los siglos XV, XVI, XVII Colección de Javier Liske,* Madrid, Casa editorial de Media, 1878.

Portvgaliae monvmenta historica a saecvlo octavo post Christvm vsqve ad qvintvmdecimvm ivssv Academiae scientiarvm olisiponensis edita. Volvmen I, *Inqvisitiones,* Olisipone, Typis academicis (Academia das Sciencias de Lisbon), 1888–1917.

Ptolemy, Claudius. *Geography of Claudius Ptolemy* (trans. by Edward Luther Stevenson), New York, New York Public Library, 1932.

Recenseamento Geral da População, IX, 15 de Dezembro de 1950, Lisbon, Tipografia Portuguesa, Lda., 1952.

Resende, Garcia de. *Chronica de El-Rei D. João II*, Lisbon, Escriptorio, 1902.

Ribeiro, Orlando. "Cultura do milho, economia agrária e povoamento," *Biblos* XVII, Tomo II, Coimbra, 1941, pp. 645–663.

————. *Portugal: Geografía de España y Portugal* (ed. Manuel de Teran), Barcelona, Montaner y Simón, S.A., 1955. Vol. V.

————. "Cultura do Milho, economia agrária e povoamento," *Biblos* XVII, Tomo II, Coimbra, 1941.

Schott, Gerhard. *Geographie des Atlantischen Ozeans*, Hamburg, C. Boysen, 1944.

Silva, A. A. Baldaque da. *Estado actual das pescas em Portugal*, Lisbon, Imprensa nacional, 1891.

Southey, Robert. *Journals of a residence in Portugal, 1800–1801, and a visit to France*, Oxford, Clarendon Press, 1960.

Stanislawski, Dan. *The Individuality of Portugal*, Austin, University of Texas Press, 1959.

————. "The Monchique of Southern Portugal," *The Geographical Review*, LII, No. 1 (January, 1962), 37–55.

————. "The Livelihood of the Ordinary People of the Portuguese Algarve," *Culture in History*, essays in honor of Paul Radin (Stanley Diamond, ed.), Columbia University Press, New York, 1960.

Storr-Best, Lloyd. *M. T. Varro on Farming*, London, 1912.

Stevens, John. *The Ancient and Present State of Portugal*, London, 1706.

Strabo. *The Geography of Strabo* (trans. by Horace Leonard Jones), New York, G. P. Putnam, 1932.

Vasconcellos, J. Leite de. *Etnografia Portuguesa*, 3 vols., Lisbon, Imprensa Nacional de Lisboa, 1933–1941.

Vasconcelos, Damião Augusto de Brito, *Notícias históricas de Tavira, 1242–1840*, Lisbon, Livraria Lusitana, 1947.

Veiga, S. P. M. Estacio da. *Povos Balsenses*, Lisbon, 1866.

Viana, Abel. "Ossónoba, o problema da sua localização," reprint from *Revista de Guimarães*, Guimarães, Sociedade Martins Sarmento, 1952, LXII.

Viana, Abel, José Formosinho and Octávio da Veiga Ferreira. "O conjunto visigótico de Alcaria (Caldas de Monchique)," *Revista do sindicato nacional dos engenheiros auxiliares, agentes técnicos de engenharia e condutores*, Nos. 33–34 (1949), Lisbon.

Viana, Abel, Octávio de Veiga Ferreira, and José Formosinho. *Necropolis de las Caldas de Monchique*, Madrid, 1950.

Wailes, Rex. "A Note on Windmills," *The Mediterranean Civilizations and the Middle Ages, c. 700 B.C. to c. A.D. 1500*, Vol. II in *A History of Tech-*

nology, (ed. Charles Singer, *et al.*). Oxford University Press, New York and London, 1956.

Willkomm, M. *Grundzüge der Pflanzenverbreitung auf der Iberischen Halbinsel (Die Vegetation der Erde,* ed. A. Engler and O. Drude), Leipzig, O. Spamer, 1896. Trans. for the *Boletim da Sociedade Broteriana* of Coimbra as "As Regiões botánicas de Portugal," Vol. 17 (1900), pp. 89–154.

World Atlas of Sea Surface Temperatures. H.O. No. 255, Washington, Hydrographic Office of the United States Navy, 1944.

INDEX

variety in, 55; as fishing center, 88; complexity of, 244–245; future of, 245; and change, 245; and industrialization, 245

—, the eastern: map of, 197

—, the Lower: as subarea, 55; as farming area, 56

—, the western: map of, 222

Algarvians; personality of, 11, 206; costume of, 12; economic status of, 14; and love of land, 18, 77, 168, 232; attitude of, toward change, 166; and cleanliness, 172. SEE ALSO tradition in Algarvian life

Algibre River: 182

Aljezur: as subarea, 55 n. 20

Aljezur graben: extension of, at Alfambra, 86

Aljustrel: 190

alluvium: in physical regions, 15 (map)

Almadena: 79

Almodôvar: 190

almonds: in landscape, 16, 68 (ill.); in share farming, 21; distribution of, 23; of Coastal Plain, 24 (ill.); in candy making, 42; in Sotavento, 67; planting of, 70; pruning of, 70; in Guadiana River Valley, 73; in Western Transition Area, 74; in Barlavento, 77–78; in Cape area, 80, 81; at Tavira, 137; in Limestone Zone, 171, 175, 180; history of, 180; growth conditions for, 180; in S. Bartolomeu, 191; in Caldeirão Mountains, 204; in Monchique, 234

Alportel: 167, 171, 181

Alte: 171, 181, 188, 193

Alvôr: history of, 157–158; importance of, 157–158; atmosphere of, 158–159; netmaking at, 158 (ill.); fishing at, 158, 159; fish trap at, 159 (ill.)

Americans: 199

Andalusia: 9

Andalusians: at Monte Gordo, 163

anchovies: as export, 11 n. 9; in the catch, 55; at Vila Real, 97–98, 98 n.

17; at Faro, 112; at Olhão, 115, 122; at Lagos, 129

animals: for farming, 48, 208; for transportation, 49–50; for packing, 53, 192, 202; in the economy, 71; in Limestone Zone, 180–181; of Caldeirão, 208–210. SEE ALSO cattle; chickens; cows; donkeys; goats; mules; oxen; pigs; sheep

apples: in Limestone Zone, 171

apricots: in the Sotavento, 60; pruning of, 70; in Barlavento, 78; in Limestone Zone, 171

Arabs: gardens of, 77; in Faro, 108–109; in eastern Algarve, 161; and carobs, 178; at Silves, 183; at São Brás, 190; mentioned, 184, 245. SEE ALSO Moslems

Arade River: dam on, 77; with cork barge, 186 (ill.); as cork route, 187; mentioned, 183

Arade-Odelouca waterway: 99

Armação de Pera: as fishing base, 140; coast at, 148 (map); tourist industry in, 149; mentioned, 73, 145

Artemidorus: 157

Arzila: conquered by Affonso V, 10–11 n. 7

asneiro. SEE mules

asphodel: in Limestone Zone, 168; in Monchique, 225

Ator: 182

Ayamonte: 94

Baesuris: 161

Baetica: 9

Baleeira, Bay of: crayfish at, 151–152; fishing fleet at, 152 (ill.); fish auction at, 154 (ill.); mentioned, 151, 155

Balsa: 133

Barlavento, the: and farm ownership, 58; sheep in, 71; as agricultural area, 74–79; topography of, 74; soils of, 74–75; geology of, 74–75; sheltered position of, 75; climate of, 75–76; rainfall of, 75–76; figs in, 81 (ill.);

254

and the Cape area, 87; urban balance in, 129; and "diverse" fish, 129; minor fishing centers in, 155–160; mentioned, 102, 125, 140

barley: as medicine, 24; in crop rotation, 70; as sheep food, 71; in Western Transition Area, 74; in Caldeirão, 201; as human food, 218–219; for fodder, 235

barqueira, the: variant of, 118 (ill.); described, 119

barqueta: 117

basketry: cane in, 37, 37 (ill.); willow in, 38 (ill.); in Salir, 193; in Monchique, 238, 238 (ill.)

bass: as catch, 121

beans: as new product, 57; in Sotavento, 60; rotation of, 67; at Tavira, 137; in canyon gardens, 203–204; in Monchique, 234

—, broad: in Sotavento, 60; in crop rotation, 67, 70; in underplanting, 68; as fodder, 68; as human food, 68; planting of, 70; as sheep food, 71; threshing of, 173; in Limestone Zone, 175; in Caldeirão Mountains, 204; in Monchique, 234

—-, horse: as fodder, 24; as medicine, 24; as human food, 24

—, lima: in Limestone Zone, 174

—, string: in rotation, 62; in Limestone Zone, 174

beehives: in Caldeirão Mountains, 213 (ill.); from cork, 213–214; transport of, 214 (ill.)

Benagil: fishing at, 160

Bensafrim: 167, 181

boats, fishing: fishermen's, 112 (ill.); in Faro, 113; at Olhão, 115–116, 116, 122; at Fuzeta, 123, 124; at Tavira, 137; at Quarteira, 142; at Baleeira, 152 (ill.)

Boaz, Franz: on culture groups, 6; bogue: at Quarteira, 143–144

Boliqueime: 171, 182

Bordeira: as isolated village, 86; intensive farming at, 86

brandy making: from gathered material, 40; in Monchique, 239, 241–242; process of, 241–242

bream, sea: at Faro, 113; as catch, 117, 119; at Quarteira, 143; and *toneira*, 144

broom: in grey schists, 16

broom making: oleander in, 37; in Portimão, 42; factories for, 43 (ill.); at Loulé, 189

Bruges: 134

Budens: 81, 167, 181

British fleet: bombardment by (1596), 110

Burgau: fishing at, 156

Byzantium: emperors of, 9

Cabanas: as fishing center, 160–161

cabbage: in Sotavento, 60; availability of, 61; importance of, 61; in rotation, 62; in Limestone Zone, 174; in canyon gardens, 203; in Monchique, 234, 235

caçada: 117

caçanal: at Quarteira, 142

Cacela: importance of, 161; as fishing center, 164–165; history of, 164–165; mentioned, 93

Cachopo: fairs in, 216 n. 22; mentioned, 204, 217

Cadiz: 137

Caldas de Monchique: and water carts, 53; as source of water, 76; temperature of, 224–225; as health resort, 237; mentioned, 225, 227

Caldeirão Mountains, the: 196–220; schists in, 15 n. 12; windmills in, 30; as subarea, 55; as protection to Sotavento, 58; land ownership in, 175; as culture area, 196; resistance to change in, 196–199; map of, 197; grain harvest in, 198 (ill.); deforested slopes of, 199 (ill.); agricultural conditions in, 199; weather in, 201; crops of, 201; cistus in, 204 (ill.); gardens in, 205 (ill.); people of, 206–208; animals of,

208–210; beehives in, 213 (ill.); towns of, 215–217; diet in, 218–219; and changes, 219–220; conservatism of, 243; mentioned, 168, 170, 195, 221

Caliphate of Córdoba: and Tavira, 133

Camões: and Sagres, 81

candy making: in Faro, 36; almonds for, 180

cane: in crafts, 37, 37 (ill.), 239–240

cangalhas: 202, 202 (ill.)

Cape area: as agricultural district, 79–87; unique in Algarve, 79–80; climate in, 84; geology of, 84–85; vegetation of, 84–85; three isolated settlements in, 85–86; fogs in, 85; winds in, 85, 86, 149; history of, 86–87; economic decline of, 87; poverty of, 87; minor fishing centers in, 149–155; as fishing point, 149

Cape Santa Maria: salt pans at, 39; religious aspects of fishing at, 89 n. 2; tuna net at, 90; as tuna fishing center, 111; and Faro, 111, 112

Cape S. Vicente: temperature of, 18; day labor on farms near, 20; and figs, 23; and carobs, 23; temperature of, 75; wheat and figs in, 82 (ill.); dolomites at, 83; rainfall in, 84; trees near, 85 (ill.); and tuna nets, 89; myths concerning, 151; mentioned, 75, 79, 90, 116, 117, 150, 167, 179

caprification: of figs, 176

capsicum: as new product, 57; in Sotavento, 60

Carboniferous formations: in physical regions, 15 (map)

carinha. SEE carts, carinha

carobs: under Moslems, 9; as export, 11 n. 9; in landscape, 16, 67; in share farming, 21; distribution of, 23; and interplanting, 23–24; in Sotavento, 67; beauty of, 67; planting of, 70; as sheep food, 71; in Western Transition Area, 74; in Barlavento, 77; in Cape area, 79–80, 80; and fog, 80; at Tavira, 137; in Limestone Zone, 168, 171, 172, 175, 178–179, 179 (ill.); "spontaneity" of, 178; names for, 178;

as food, 178–179, 206; soil for, 178; as construction wood, 179; value of, 179; uses for, 179; processed in S. Bartolomeu, 191; as fodder, 191; absence of, in Monchique, 234

Carrapateira: as isolated village, 86; agriculture in, 86; as fishing town, 150

carro. SEE carts, carro

carro canudo: 53

carroço. SEE carts, carroço

cart making: tradition in, 41

carts: decoration of, 12–13, 53, 189; in transportation, 22, 35 (ill.), 50; kinds of, 52–53; two-wheeled, 53 (ill.); in Limestone Zone, 182; in transport of grain, 200

—, carinha: description of, 52–53; illustrated, 53

—, carro: with upper framework, 12 (ill.); a typical, 13 (ill.)

—, carro canudo: 53

—, carroço: described, 53

—, water: in the landscape, 53; in transportation, 54 (ill.); in Barlavento, 76

Carvoeiro: fishing at, 160

Carthaginians: and the nora, 59; and fishing industry, 88, 89, 108; at Lagos, 125; in Cape area, 151; at Alvôr, 157; mentioned, 9

Casa dos Pescadores: 97

Casais: 239

Castile: 134

Castro Marim: salt pans near, 39, 163; importance of, 161–163; history of, 161–163; as fortress, 161, 163; and Vila Real, 163; mentioned, 93, 165

Catalans: at Monte Gordo, 163

cattail: commercial use of, 38

cattle: sea grazing of, 37; in S. Marcos Depression, 194

cauliflower: in Monchique, 234

cegonha. SEE noras

Celts: 9, 125

cerco: in purse-seining, 102–103; elimination of, 103

channel nets. SEE fishing nets, channel

charcoal: from heather, 35–36; wood for, 210 (ill.)

charcoal making: for supplementary income, 211; mound for, 211 (ill.); process of, 211–213

cherries: in Limestone Zone, 171

chestnuts: in Monchique, 224, 225, 238; as food, 227; as material for baskets, 238 (ill.); wood of, in crafts, 238

chickens: in Limestone Zone, 181; in Caldeirão Mountains, 210

chick-peas: distribution of, 24; with figs, 67; in crop rotation, 70; in Limestone Zone, 175; in canyon gardens, 203–204; mentioned, 234

chimneys, Algarvian. SEE houses, chimneys of

chinchorro: distribution of, 142

Christianity: accepted by Moslems, 10

Christians: rule of, and economy of Algarve, 10; in Faro, 108; at Tavira, 133; as farmers, 134; at Alvôr, 157; in eastern Algarve, 161; in Limestone Zone, 170, 171; at Silves, 184; in Monchique, 226; mentioned, 177, 184, 190

cisterns: in Limestone Zone, 173

cistus: in grey-schist area, 16; as food for goats, 52; in Limestone Zone, 168; in Caldeirão Mountains, 199, 204 (ill.); burning of, 201, 203; in Monchique, 225; as fuel, 241, 241 n. 26

——, gum: as fuel, 34; for training stalks, 36; as food for goats, 209–210; mentioned, 81. SEE ALSO cistus

citrus fruits: harvest of, 57; in Guadiana River Valley, 73; in Western Transition Area, 74; in Barlavento, 78; in S. Marcos Depression, 194

clams: at Faro, 113; as bait, 116; at Olhão, 122; catch of, value of, 122; at Fuzeta, 125; at Alvôr, 159; at Cacela, 165

climate: and landscape, 13; mildness of, 16; and rainfall, 16, 18; and temperature, 16, 16–18; of Sotavento, 58–59;

protection of plants from, 72 (ill.); and agriculture, 72, 72 (ill.), 73, 84, 174, 233; of Western Transition Area, 73; of Barlavento, 75–76; of Cape area, 80–82; of Limestone Zone, 169–170; and figs, 175; and almonds, 180; at Silves, 183

climatic stations: in Limestone Zone, 169–170

clover: as fertilizer, 61

Coastal Plain, the: farm renting on, 20; as agricultural area, 23, 25, 56, 71–72; terracing in, 39–40; intensive farming in, 25; as subarea, 55; economic subgroups of, 55; land ownership in, 58, 175; climate of, 58–59, 75; rainfall of, 75; mentioned, 73, 108, 167, 168, 173, 174, 182, 188, 189, 194

cockles: at Faro, 113; at Alvôr, 159

cod: at Fuzeta, 124; at Lagos, 128; at Lisbon, 160

Coimbra, Duke of: 145

construction, general: in Faro, 114

copper working: at Alte, 188; at Loulé, 188–189; in Monchique, 239

Coriolis force: effect of, in Cape area, 84

cork: as export, 11 n. 9; in Alentejo, 11; for charcoal, 36; in tanning, 42; at Faro, 110; at Silves, 185, 186–187; transportation of, 186 (ill.); in S. Marcos Depression, 194; in Caldeirão, 204; for supplementary income, 213; uses of, 213–214, 241; in shipbuilding, 241; mentioned, 200. SEE ALSO cork industry

cork industry: importance of, 41; in Faro, 113; methods of processing in, 186–187, 241; at São Brás, 190; tradition in, 190; trimming in, 212 (ill.), 213; in Monchique, 240–241; history of, 241–242

Cortes, the: 134

cotton: and Moslems, 9

cows: as plow animals, 49, 181, 208; in the economy, 71

crabs, spider: at Carrapateira, 150; at Alvôr, 159

crafts: gathering for, 40; dwarf palm in, 40; esparto grass in, 40; at Loulé, 188–189; materials used in, 189 (ill.); tradition in, 189; in villages, 193; in Monchique, 223, 238–240. SEE ALSO basketry; broom making; brandy making; candy making; copper working; crocheting; stone working; terracing; weaving

crayfish: at Quarteira, 142; in Cape area, 149–150; at Baleeira, 151–152

crops: most important, 22; processing of, in Monchique, 235. SEE ALSO agriculture; agricultural calendar; almonds; apricots; apples; barley; beans; cabbage; carobs; cauliflower; chick-peas; citrus fruits; clover; cork; cotton; cucumbers; flax; fruits; grains; grapes; legumes; lemons; maize; oats; olives; onions; oranges; peaches; peanuts; pears; peas; plums; pomegranates; potatoes; quinces; rice; roughpeas; rye; squash; tangerines; tomatoes; vetch; wheat

croakers: as catch, 119; at Lagos, 126; and *toneira*, 144; at Quarteira, 144; at Albufeira, 148; at Salema, 155

crocheting: in Monchique, 239

crustaceans: in the catch, 55, 121

cucumbers: in Sotavento, 60

cultures, individual: understanding of, 3–4; American culture in relation to, 3–6; in relation to the land, 3–6; and economic factors, 4; in Portugal, 11; generalizations in describing, 244

cuttle-fish: as bait, 117, 119; at Quarteira, 144; at Armaçao, 149; mentioned, 124

Cynetes: in the Algarve, 9

dams: in use of land, 77

deforestation: at Silves, 184–185; in Caldeirão, 199 (ill.), 199–200, 200–201

Dias, Jorge: on terraces, 229

Diniz, King: taxes grains, 109

distilling: in Monchique, 242 (ill.)

dogfish: at Vila Real, 98; as catch, 117; at Fuzeta, 124

dolomites: in physical regions, 15 (map); at Point Sagres, 83

donkeys: as mounts for women, 14, 181; in transportation, 49 (ill.), 49–50, 214 (ill.); in plowing, 49; in landscape, 49–50; in the economy, 71; in Cape area, 80; in Limestone Zone, 181; versatility of, 181; in Caldeirão Mountains, 208

earthquake of 1755, the: and Lagos, 128; and Tavira, 136; at Albufeira, 145; at Alvôr, 158; at Cacela, 165; effect of, on Algarvian coast, 165 n. 132; at Silves, 185; mentioned, 110, 141–142

Edrisi (historian): on Silves, 10, 183, 183 n. 19; on Lagos, 126; on figs, 176; on olive oil, 178; and Loulé, 188; mentioned, 77

eels, conger: as catch, 117; at Lagoa, 130 (ill.)

England: as purchaser of peas and tomatoes, 74

Ephorus (historian): 151

equariço. SEE mules

erosion: in Caldeirão Mountains, 199, 200, 202; in Monchique, 222, 223

esparto grass: commercial use of, 38; in crafts, 40

Estoi: 182

eucalyptus: in Caldeirão Mountains, 200

Europe: windmills introduced into, 27; waters of, 53; mentioned, 83, 90

Europe, Western: water mills in, 34

Europeans: 199

Evans, H. Muir: on scabbard fish, 156

Evora: 227

exports: agricultural, 74, 137–138, 180; of fish, 95, 137; to Italy, 95, 96; from Limestone Zone, 175; from Monchique, 227, 228; mentioned, 11, 11 n. 9

fishermen: among the dolomites, 83–84; attitude of, toward fishing, 88; economic status of, 88, 96, 96–97, 97, 105, 164, 166; and taxes, 94, 97; at Vila Real, 94; boats of, at Faro, 112 (ill.); at Olhão, 114, 122; way of life of, 88, 124, 166; near shore, 124–125; at Lagos, 126, 160; at Tavira, 135; and tradition, 140, 142, 166; and agriculture, 140; at Quarteira, 142; at Alvôr, 158; character of, 160; of Ferragudo, 160; conservatism of, 142, 166; houses of, 48, 113, 113 (ill.), 163, 164 n. 129. SEE ALSO Algarvians; labor, fishing; tradition in Algarvian life

fishing: bases for, established, 9; long history of, 11; methods of, 55, 98 n. 17, 112–113, 113; as a way of life, 88, 124, 166; diversification in, 98 n. 20; with sacada, 119–120; at Olhão, 119–121; at Ferragudo, 160. SEE ALSO boats, fishing; fish; fishermen; fishing gear; fishing industry; fishing lines; fishing nets

fishing boats. SEE boats, fishing

fishing companies: at Vila Real, 94

fishing craft. SEE boats, fishing

fishing gear: fixed tuna net as, 89; at Olhão, 115, 116; qualities of, at Olhão, 116; description of, 116; at Lagos, 129; at Tavira, 139; at Quarteira, 142, 142–144; at Albufeira, 146; at Armação, 149; at Salema, 155; at Alvôr, 159; at Monte Gordo, 164; at Cacela, 165. SEE ALSO fishing lines; fishing nets

fishing industry: packing in, and salt evaporation, 39; importance of, 41; antiquity of, 55, 88; tuna, 90–92; establishment of, by Pombal, 94; reference works for, 98–99 n. 20; in Vila Real, 97–98; unloading of boats in, 105; at Portimão, 106, 106–107; in Faro, 111, 112; in Olhão, 115–123; seasons for, 116; in Lagos and Tavira, 125; at Lagos, 125, 128, 129, 131; at Tavira, 125, 135, 137, 138–139; exports of, 138; at Albufeira, 145–146;

minor centers in, 149–166; auctions in, 154; at Ferragudo, 160; in Sotavento, 160–166; at Monte Gordo, 164

fishing lines: at Faro, 113; at Olhão, 115–119; laying of, 116–117; and trotlines, varieties of, 117–119; at Ferragudo, 160; at Monte Gordo, 164

fishing nets: tuna, 89, 89–90, 90–92, 91 (ill.), 111, 128; sardine, 113; channel, 113, 121–122, 144; stick dip, 113, 119, 119–120; shore seines as, 113, 121; at Olhão, 119–121; trammel, 120–121; at Lagos, 126; traps as, 159 (ill.); at Ferragudo, 160; at Monte Gordo, 164

fish meal: as export, 11 n. 9; as fertilizer, 61

fish spears: 112

fish traps. SEE fishing nets

fish truckers: from Olhão, 98 n. 17

flax: in underplanting, 68; in mountain areas, 68; at Tavira, 137

fodder: source of, 24; gathering of, 34, 36–37; kinds of, 36–37; broad beans as, 68; figs as, 177; in Limestone Zone, 180; in Monchique, 235

fogs: in Cape area, 84, 85, 149

Foia (mtn.): and rainfall, 224; mentioned, 225, 226, 228

forkbeard: as catch, 119

France: and tidal mills, 34

French, the: and Lagos, 127

frogfish: as catch, 117

fruit fly: damage by, 67

fruits: of Barlavento, 78; in Carrapateira, 86; in Tavira, 134, 135; as food, 219; in Monchique, 228. SEE ALSO apples; apricots; carobs; cherries; citrus fruits; figs; grapes; lemons; olives; oranges; peaches; pears; plums; pomegranates; quinces; tangerines

fruits, dried: as export, 11 n. 9

fuel: olive tree as, 34, 35; fig tree as, 35, 177; bush oak as, 35; gathered, 35 (ill.); heather as, 35; transportation of, 35 (ill.); preferences in, 36; pine as, 36; lavender as, 36; strawberry tree as, 36; gum cistus as, 34; roots as, 34

furniture making: willow in, 37–38

Fuzeta: 123–125; as wine center, 69, 79; compared to Olhão, 123; history of, 123; coast at, 123 (map); prosperity of, 123; fishing techniques at, 123–124; mentioned, 137

galiao, the: in purse-seining, 102

Garcia de Resende: as historian, 227

gardens, canyon: in Caldeirão, 78 (ill.), 203–204, 205 (ill.), 215; in Monchique, 222, 228–229

gathering: for fabrication, 37–38; for crafts, 40; for honey, 40; for brandy making, 40; of dwarf palm, 40; purposes in, 34; for fuel, 34, 35 (ill.); in Caldeirão, 211–215; in Monchique, 223. SEE ALSO basketry; cart making; fodder; fuel; furniture making; pottery; salt industry; stone working

Genovese: as fishermen, 89

geology: rocks in, 14–15; and schists of the Carboniferous, 15 n. 12; physical regions in, 15 (map); and sandstones, 15–16; and conglomerates, 15–16; and dolomites, 16; and limestones, 16; related to economy, 73; of Western Transition Area, 73; of Barlavento, 74–75; of Cape area, 80, 83–84; of Limestone Zone, 167–181; and distribution of population, 181–182; of Monchique, 221–224

Gibraltar: 137

Gilão River: silting of, 137, 138

gilthead: 117, 119, 121, 149

Giões: 202

goats: skins of, for tanning, 42; distribution of, 52; herding of, 52; in the economy, 71; in Barlavento, 76; in Limestone Zone, 180–181; products from, 181; in Caldeirão, 209–210

goose barnacle: in Cape area, 149

gorse: in grey schists, 16; in Caldeirão, 199

Goths. SEE Visigoths

grains: in landscape, 16; as secondary crop, 22; interplanting of, with trees, 23–24, 67; small, 70; in Cape area, 81; at Carrapateira, 86; at Tavira, 135–136, 137, 138; in Limestone Zone, 175; at Silves, 185; in S. Marcos Depression, 194; in Caldeirão, 198, 198 (ill.), 201–202, 202 (ill.), 207; in Monchique, 222, 234–235, 236. SEE ALSO agriculture; agricultural calendar; barley; maize; oats; rice; rye; vetch

grapes: in Huelva, 11; for wine, 78–79; natural enemies of, 79; at Sagres, 82; in Limestone Zone, 171, 173; in Caldeirão, 204; in Monchique, 234. SEE ALSO wine; wine industry

grass, esparto: in crafts, 193

grazing: in Barlavento and Sotavento, 76; rights, 77. SEE ALSO herding

Greeks: and windmills, 27; and figs, 175; and olives, 177; mentioned, 9

Guadalquivir Valley: 9

Guadiana River: and figs, 23; and almonds, 23; agricultural area of, 73; and tuna nets, 89; as site for Vila Real, 93; and Mértola, 216 (ill.); mentioned, 11, 18, 30, 51, 52, 71, 79, 95, 161, 164, 200

gum cistus. SEE cistus, gum

hake: 124

Halc-ac-Zâwia: 126

harvesting: of fruits and vegetables, 70; of wheat, 86 (ill.); in Caldeirão, 198 (ill.)

heather: in grey schists, 16; as fuel, 35, 241; as food for goats, 52, 209–210; in Caldeirão, 199

Hehn, Victor: on figs, 175

henequin: 13

Henry the Navigator, Prince: and Sagres, 81; and Cape area, 86; and tuna fishing rights, 89; taxes Faro, 109; and Lagos, 126; and Monte Gordo, 163; mentioned, 132, 135, 151

Herculano: 226, 226–227

Hercules: temple to, 151; in olive legend, 177

herding: of sheep, 50; financial terms in, 50; products from, 50; of goats, 52; tool used in, 52; in Limestone Zone, 180–181

Hesiod: on the olive, 177

High Plain, the: as grain area, 201–202; mentioned, 199, 202, 204

homes. SEE houses

honey: from gathered material, 40; in Caldeirão, 213–215

horses as work animals: in Limestone Zone, 181; in Caldeirão, 208

houses: colors in, 13, 44; cleanliness of, 13, 43–44; chimneys of, 13, 43, 46 (ill.), 47, 172, 194, 195 (ill.), 217; calcimining of, 13–14, 44; distinction of, 14, 42–43, 43; roofs of, 43, 139 (ill.), 172; typical, 43–44, 44; round, 44 (ill.); African influence on, 44; shape of, 44; tamped-earth, 44–45, 45 (ill.), 217, 223; ventilation of, 47, 217, 218; floors of, 47, 83, 217, 218; equipment of, 47, 47–48, 48 (ill.), 218; of fishermen, 48, 113 (ill.), 141; repair of, 71; of Olhão, 114, 114–115, 115 n. 52; at Fuzeta, 123; of Limestone Zone, 170; of São Brás, 172–173; plan of, 172; garden areas of, 172–173; appearance of, 194, 217; ownership of, 207; rock, 217; of Caldeirão, 217–218; of Monchique, 222–223, 237; as neighbor, 11–12, 14

Iberia: and windmills, 27; and water mills, 34; tamped-earth houses in, 44; cold winds from, 58; and noras, 80 n. 9; figs in, 175–176; olives in, 177; mentioned, 9, 10, 168, 193. SEE ALSO Portugal; Spain

Ibne Harune: and Faro, 109

industries: reference works for, 98–99 n. 20. SEE ALSO basketry; brandy mak-

ing; broom making; candy making; copper working; cork industry; crafts; fishing industry; furniture making; lumbering; milling; netmaking; olive oil industry; pastry making; pottery making; rug making; shipbuilding; shipping industry; stone working; tanneries; tile making; weaving; wine industry

insurance: medical, 97; disaster, 97

irrigation: and Romans, 9; under Moslems, 9, 10; in Coastal Plain, 20; in share farming, 22; and intensive farming, 25; and the nora, 59; in Sotavento, 60; and women workers, 62, 79; in Western Transition Area, 74; in Barlavento, 77; and modern engineering, 77; for rice, 80; in Cape area, 80; at Carrapateira, 86; in Bordeira, 86; in Alfambra, 86; at Tavira, 133; in Limestone Zone, 171, 173, 182–183; at Silves, 183, 187–188; in S. Marcos Depression, 194; in Monchique, 222, 224, 227; in terrace cultivation, 232. SEE ALSO windmills

Italians: interest of, in Algarvian tuna, 95, 95 n. 14

Italy: as export market, 96

João II, King: 157, 227

João III, King: 127

John Dory (fish): as catch, 117

Jurassic formations: in physical regions, 15 (map), 167. SEE ALSO geology

Kew Gardens: and orange development, 174

"Kings of Portugal and the Algarves": 10

Kingdom of the Algarve, the: unique culture of, 14–15

Köppen, W.: and climatic stations, 18

Knights of Santiago: 133, 134, 164–165

labor, agricultural: staggering of, 14; classes of, 19; supplementary activities of, 19; income of, 19, 20, 211; arrangements for securing, 19–20; Algarvian farmer in, 21 (ill.); in rotation system, 57, 65; in Sotavento, 62; seasonal variations in, 70–71, 71; demand for, in Coastal Plain, 73; in Barlavento, 79; in Sagres area, 82; and fishing, 140; for figs, 176; in Caldeirão, 207; as share croppers, 232–233; in Monchique, 234. SEE ALSO farmers; share farming; women

—, cork working: 241

—, craft: 188, 189

—, fishing: in purse-seining, 106; at Faro, 111–112; income of, 117, 120, 121, 124, 143, 144, 155, 161; at Olhão, 122; in cod industry, 124; in clam industry, 125; as purse-seiners, 129, 131; and dislike of agriculture, 140; at Quarteira, 142; at Albufeira, 148; at Monte Gordo, 164 n. 129, 163–164. SEE ALSO fishermen

—, herding: wages for, 50; in Limestone Zone, 180; in Caldeirão, 209, 210

—, industrial: in Faro, 113; in Portimão, 113; in Caldeirão, 215

—, stone-working: in terraces, 229, 232

Lacobriga: 125

Lacobrigans: 131

Lagoa: pottery in, 39; wine making in, 79; conger eels at, 130 (ill.); taxes at, 160

Lagos: 125–132; and almonds, 23; and millstones, 40; temperature of, 75; and Portimão, 100, 101–102, 129, 131; decline of, 101–102, 131–132; coast of, 103 (map); and Tavira, 125; history of, 125–128; and Silves, 127; strategic position of, 127; view of, 127 (ill.); importance of, 128; trade of, 127, 128; economy of, 128; development of, 128–129; river at, 131 (ill.); atmosphere of, 132; future of, 132; as port for Prince Henry, 151; and scabbard fish, 155; mentioned, 78, 79, 101, 108, 109, 116, 132, 135, 145, 156, 157, 185, 191, 228

land: ownership of, 18, 77, 79, 82, 175, 204, 207, 210, 232–233, 236; family relations to, 57; care of, in winter, 70;

use of, 77, 194; Algarvian desire for, 77, 232; man association with, 175, 206–208, 244; systems of working, 207, 236–237; fractionalization of, 204, 207–208; rights to, and deforestation, 228; water rights in, 232; sale of, 232 n. 18. SEE ALSO farms

landowners: conservatism of, 68–69. SEE ALSO farmers

landscape: color in, 12–13, 14–15, 16; houses in, 13; walls in, 13, 175, 229, 229–232; and climate, 13; variety of planting in, 14; small plots in, 14; harvesting in, 22; oleander in, 37; gatherers in, 34; fences and walls in, 48; carts and pack animals in, 53–54; in Sotavento, 58, 60; carob trees in, 67; almonds in, 68 (ill.); west of Lagos, 79–80; at Tavira, 137, 138; of Limestone Zone, 168–170; of S. Marcos Depression, 194; of Caldeirão, 200; terraces in, 229

lavender: as fuel, 36; in Limestone Zone, 168

legumes: as medicine, 24; in crop rotation, 70; as fertilizers, 70; as fodder, 70

Leite de Vasconcellos: as historian of Algarve, 82

lemons: introduced by Moslems, 9; in Sotavento, 60; in Monchique, 224, 233–234

levante, the: 58. SEE ALSO winds

limestone: in physical regions, 15 (map)

Limestone Zone, the: 167–195; vegetation in, 16, 168–169; and almonds, 23; and chick-peas, 24; fuel in, 36; terracing in, 40; house chimneys in, 47, 169 (ill.); sheep in, 50; goats in, 52; as subarea, 55; and farm ownership, 58; unirrigated trees in, 67; as purchaser of vegetables, 74; geology of, 167–168, 181; size and shape of, 167; culture of, 168; landscape of, 168–170; climate of, 169–170; agriculture in, 168–169, 171, 173–181; soil of, 168–169; and schist mountains, 170 (ill.); rainfall of, 170; population of, 170–171, 171–172, 172 n. 6, 181–183; history of, 170–

mimosas: in Monchique, 225

Minho, the: terraces in, 228

molluscs: in the catch, 55

Moncarapacho: pottery in, 39; and wine industry, 69

Monchique: 221–243; schists in, 15 n. 12; and basketry, 37, 37–38, 238 (ill.); stone working in, 39; terracing in, 39, 230 (ill.); olives in, 23; tamped-earth houses in, 44–46; water of, 53; as subarea, 55; and olive oil, 67, 235 (ill.); settlement of, 225–229; geology of, 221–224; agriculture of, 221–222, 233–236; economy of, 221–222, 224, 227–228, 242–243; "desert of": 223–224; "enchanting vista" of, 224; climate of, 224–225; vegetation of, 225; history of, 225–229; rug making in, 239 (ill.); weaving in, 240 (ill.); distilling in, 242 (ill.); charm of, 243; conservatism of, 243; mentioned, 55 n. 20, 75

Montagut: 226

Monte Gordo: and Vila Real, 94; importance of, 161; as fishing center, 163–164; history of, 163–164; site of, 164; mentioned, 93

Moors. SEE Arabs; Moslems

Moslems: as rulers of the Algarve, 9–10; and windmills, 27; and fences, 48; and the nora, 59; and tuna net, 89; and Lagos, 126, 127; and Silves, 132; as farmers, 133, 134; as traders, 134; at Albufeira, 140; at Alvôr, 157; at Cacela, 164–165; in Limestone Zone, 171, 172 n. 6; and Loulé, 188; and Monchique, 226, 227; mentioned, 77, 80, 191

morays: as catch, 117; at Salema, 155

Morocco: 193

mullet: at Vila Real, 98; as catch, 121, 122; at Fuzeta, 124; at Quarteira, 143, 144; at Armação, 149; at Monte Gordo, 164

mules: in transportation, 13, 14, 22, 49–50, 182, 195, 203; as work animals, 49, 173, 181, 194, 208; breeding of,

49; in the economy, 71; in Cape area, 80

Munchite: 226

Munich: 189

Mussiene (castle): capture of, 190–191

Near East, the: 193

netmaking: at Alvôr, 158 (ill.)

nets. SEE fishing nets

New York: 114

nora, the: in action, 59 (ill.); use of, 59; history of, 59, 80 n. 9; repair of, 60 (ill.); modern, 61 (ill.); description of, 80 n. 9; in Carrapateira, 86; in Alfambra, 86; and irrigation, 133; carob wood in, 179; in S. Marcos Depression, 194; mentioned, 222

North Africa, Spanish: 38, 127

nuts. SEE almonds; chestnuts

oaks: in Caldeirão, 199; as food, 227

—, bush: as fuel, 35

—, holm, in Limestone Zone, 168; in Caldeirão, 200, 204

—, scrub: in Limestone Zone, 168

—, cork. SEE cork

oats: as medicine, 24; in crop rotation, 70; as sheep food, 71; in Caldeirão, 201; for fodder, 235

octopus: at Fuzeta, 125; at Quarteira, 142; at Armação, 149; at Burgau, 156; at Luz, 156; at Santa Luzia, 160, 161; catch of, 162 (ill.)

Odeleite: and basketry, 37

Odelouca River: 183, 194

Odiáxere River: 77

oleander: in landscape, 37; in crafts, 37, 189; in Caldeirão, 200

Old Testament: and figs, 175

Olhão: 114–120; and wine industry, 69; fishing industry at, 98 n. 17, 115–123; truckers from, 98 n. 17; coast at, 111 (map); description of, 114; houses, of, 114, 114–115; history of, 114–115; inhabitants of, 114, 122; character of,

115; industries of, 115; boats at, 115–116; and Fuzeta, 123; mentioned, 121, 124, 138

olive oil industry: in Tavira, 67, 135; in Monchique, 67; seasonal activities in, 70; in Seville, 178; quality of oil in, 178; in S. Bartolomeu, 191; stones for presses in, 235 (ill.); presses for, 235 (ill.); in Monchique, 235–236; income from, 236

olives: under Moslems, 9; in landscape, 16; in share farming, 21–22; distribution of, 23; and interplanting, 23; in Sotavento, 67; planting of, 70; pruning of, 70; in Guadiana River Valley, 73; in Western Transition Area, 74; in Barlavento, 77; in Cape area, 79–80, 80; at Tavira, 137; in Limestone Zone, 175, 177–178; history of, 177–178; importance of, 177, 178; in S. Marcos Depression, 194; in Caldeirão, 204; in Monchique, 234; illustrated, 24. SEE ALSO olive oil industry; olives, wild; olives, wood of

—, wild: in Limestone Zone, 168

—, wood of: in water mills, 33; as fuel, 34, 35

onions: in Caldeirão, 204; in Monchique, 234

Oppian (Greek poet): describes tuna nets, 89 n. 2

oranges: harvest of, 57; in Sotavento, 60; planting of, 70; in Faro, 110; in Limestone Zone, 174; in canyon gardens, 203–204; in Monchique, 224, 233–234

—, bitter: introduced by Moslems, 9

—, sweet: and Moslems, 9

Orwell, George: 74

Ossónoba: under Visigoths, 108; and Faro, 108

oxen: as plow animals, 49, 83 (ill.); in the economy, 71; in Cape area, 80; in transportation, 86 (ill.); in fishing, 121; in Limestone Zone, 181

oysters: packed at Olhão, 122

Paderne: and millstones, 40; as fort, 171; mentioned, 182

palm: commercial use of, 38; in crafts, 40, 188, 189 (ill.), 193; in Limestone Zone, 168

pargo: at Quarteira, 144

partridges: 182

peaches: in Sotavento, 60; pruning of, 70; in Western Transition Area, 74; in Limestone Zone, 171

peanuts: as new product, 57: in Sotavento, 60

pears: in Sotavento, 60; in Western Transition Area, 74; in Barlavento, 78

peas: training stalks for, 36; in Sotavento, 60; with figs, 67; planting of, 70; in Limestone Zone, 74; raised for England, 74; in Monchique, 234. SEE ALSO chick-peas

peonies: in Monchique, 225

Pereiro: 182, 199

Persia: windmills in, 27

pests: and fruit trees, 67; sprayed against, 70

Phoenicians: in Cape area, 86, 150, 151; establish fishing and salt evaporation, 88; sacrifice tuna, 89 n. 2; and figs, 175–176; mentioned, 9, 193

phylloxera: as grape disease, 171

picôta: illustrated, 78. SEE ALSO noras

Picota (mtn.): 226

pigs: in Alentejo, 11; for garbage disposal, 50; for food, 50; in the economy, 71; in Limestone Zone, 181; in Caldeirão, 210

Pindar: on olives, 177

pines: as fuel, 36; as protection to Coastal Plain, 71; in Caldeirão, 200; in Monchique, 225

pipers: at Olhão, 122

plaice: as catch, 122

Pliocene formations: in Western Transition Area, 73

plow: illustrated, 21

plums: in Sotavento, 60; pruning of, 70; in Limestone Zone, 171

Point Sagres: dolomites at, 83

Pombal, Marquis of: and Vila Real, 93, 94, 164; mentioned, 93 n. 8, 95

pomegranates: in Sotavento, 60; in Western Transition Area, 74; in Barlavento, 78; at Tavira, 137

Portimão: 99–107; advantages of, 99; history of, 99–102; and shipbuilding, 41–42; tannery in, 42; broom factory in, 42; textile factory in, 42; candy making in, 42; pastry making in, 42; and water carts, 53; cliff coast of, 75 (ill.); temperature of, 75; as rival of Silves, 100; disorders in, 100; economy of, 100, 102; and agriculture, 100, 100–101, 101; and commerce, 100, 101; as seat for bishop, 100; as port, 100, 101, 129; as fishing center, 100–101 n. 24, 101, 102, 107, 160; transformation in, 101; and Lagos, 101–102, 128–129, 131, 132; atmosphere of, 102, 132; coast at, 103 (map); sardine fleet of, 104 (ill.); fish auctions in, 105; unloading of sardines at, 106 (ill.); packing of sardines at, 107 (ill.); industrial labor in, 113; and Olhão, 122; mentioned, 74, 76, 77, 78, 80 n. 9, 108, 115, 125, 142, 160, 187, 228

Portugal: southern area of, 5 (map); and the Algarve, 7; kings of, 89, 157, 163; oysters from, 122; monarchy of, 126; olives in, 177; mentioned, 9, 10, 55, 86, 88, 89, 94, 96, 106, 164, 187, 191, 206, 241, 243

Portus Annibalis: 157

potatoes: planting of, 70; at Sagres, 81; in Monchique, 235

—, sweet: as new product, 57; in Sotavento, 60; in Limestone Zone, 174; in canyon gardens, 203–204; in Monchique, 234

—, white: as new product, 10 n. 5, 57; in Sotavento, 60; in rotation, 62; in Monchique, 234, 234–235

pottery industry: in Loulé, 36, 189; centers for, 39

Praia da Rocha: rainfall of, 75–76; as home of millionaires, 101

purse-seiners: in Vila Real, 98 n. 17; schedule of trips of, 104; at Faro, 112; at Olhão, 115; at Lagos, 129, 130. SEE ALSO purse-seining

purse-seining: at Portimão, 102, 102–104; for sardines, 102; varieties of catch in, 105–106; at Salema, 155

pyrites: as export, 11 n. 9; at Sto. Domingos, 93, 95

Quarteira: 141–144; as fishing base, 140; history of, 141; coast at, 141 (map); fishing gear at, 142; beach of, 143 (ill.); mentioned, 145, 149, 206

Quaternary formations: in physical regions, 15 (map); and vegetation, 16. SEE ALSO geology

Querença: 181

querns: making of, 40; as tradition, 40; mentioned, 218, 219 (ill.)

quinces: in Western Transition Area, 74; in Barlavento, 78: in Limestone Zone, 171

rabadela: 117–118

rainfall: records of, at climatic stations, 17; in Western Transition Area, 74; in Barlavento, 75–76, 76; of Sotavento, 76; catchment floors for, 83; in Cape area, 84; at Tavira, 133; of Limestone Zone, 170; in Caldeirão, 201; in Monchique, 224

Raposeira: 81

rays: at Vila Real, 98

razor shell fish: at Alvôr, 159

renting. SEE land, ownership of

rhododendron, pontic: in Monchique, 225

rice: and Moslems, 9; in Cape area, 80

Rigueira: 81

"road to Portugal": and disparate cultures, 11

rockfish: as catch, 121

Romans: introduce innovations, 9; and windmills, 27; and water mills, 34; and *noras*, 59, 80 n. 9; at Lagos, 125; at Tavira, 133; at Alvôr, 157; at Silves, 183; at São Brás, 190; in Monchique, 225, 227; mentioned, 245

rotation of crops. SEE agriculture, rotation of crops in

rough-pea: as fertilizer, 61

rug making: in Monchique, 239 (ill.)

rye: in Caldeirão, 201; in Monchique, 235

sacadas: fishing with, 119–120, 122, 144; at Fuzeta, 125; at Lagos, 129; at Tavira, 139; at Quarteira, 142

saddlebag: from Monchique, 240 (ill.)

Sagres: and long-haired sheep, 51; description of, 81–82; poverty of, 82; earlier productivity of, 82; rainfall in, 84; wheat near, 86 (ill.); coast at, 150 (map); influenced by Phoenicians, 151; as crayfish center, 152; auctions at, 154; variety of catch at, 154–155; mentioned, 74, 79, 85, 126, 151, 155, 182

Sagres, Bay of: 83 (ill.), 151

Salema: 155, 156

Salir: as basketry center, 193; mentioned, 167, 171, 181

salt industry: established in Algarve, 9; exports in 11 n. 9; salt pans for, 38–39, 39 (ill.); and fish packing, 38–39; antiquity of, 88; at Vila Real, 94; at Lagos, 123; monopoly of, 135; at Alvôr, 157

Sancho I: conquers Silves, 10 n. 7

sand smelt: at Quarteira, 144

sandstone: in physical regions, 15 (map)

Santa Luzia: as fishing center, 160–161

Santa Maria de Harun: as name of Faro, 109

Santo António de Arenilha: importance of, 161; history of, 165

São Brás de Alportel: rainfall of, 170;

progress in, 171–172; advantageous position of, 182; as cork center, 241; mentioned, 30, 171, 190, 191

São Marcos da Serra (pass): 221

São Marcos Depression: 74, 191, 193–195

São Romão: 182

sardine industry: as export, 11 n. 9; profit from, 77; in Portimão, 107. SEE ALSO sardines

sardines: as catch, 55, 121; in Vila Real, 97, 98 n. 17, 98; millionaires from, 101; at Portimão, 102; methods of catching, 102; and Portimão fleet, 104 (ill.); unloading of, 106 (ill.); packing of, at Portimão, 107 (ill.); at Olhão, 115, 122; as bait, 116, 117, 120, 124; at Lagos, 126, 128, 128–129, 129; at Tavira, 137, 139; at Quarteira, 143; at Albufeira, 146, 148; at Armação, 149; at Salema, 155; at Ferragudo, 160. SEE ALSO sardine industry

sardinhais: at Tavira, 139

sardinheira: at Quarteira, 142

Sardinia: 59

sargo: catch of, 117, 119

S. Bartolomeu de Messines: as distributing center, 191–192; fairs in, 216 n. 22; mentioned, 167, 181

scabbard fish: at Fuzeta, 124; at Salema, 155–156; season of, 155–156; methods of catching, 156; description of, 155, 156; H. M. Evans on, 156

schist mountains: terracing in, 39–40; and figs, 23; houses of, 47–48; goats in, 52; and farm ownership, 58; and Western Transition Area, 73; mentioned, 72, 167, 168, 170 (ill.), 175, 181, 183–184, 192, 199–201, 221. SEE ALSO Caldeirão Mountains; Monchique; schists, grey

schists, grey: in Algarvian mountains, 15; in physical regions, 15 (map); and vegetation, 16; in Cape area, 84. SEE ALSO Caldeirão Mountains; geology; Monchique; schist mountains

Toledo, Spain: 108

tomatoes: as new product, 57; in Sotavento, 60; grown for export, 74; in canyon gardens, 203; in Monchique, 234

toneira: 144, 155

tools: in share farming, 20; in herding, 52; in terrace building, 231, 231–232; in Monchique, 234, 235, 237

Torre d'Aspa: 149

tourism: in Lagos, 132; in Monchique, 243

tradition in Algarvian life: querns in, 40; and factories, 41; in cartmaking, 41; persistence of, 22; and windmills, 30; in shoe making, 41; in candy and pastry making, 42; fences in, 48; in fishing methods, 55, 88, 89 n. 2, 129, 140, 146, 149, 160; and salt evaporation, 88; among fishermen, 142; at Monte Gordo, 164; at Cacela, 165; in relation to economy, 166; in crafts, 189; in São Brás, 190; in villages, 192–193; in Caldeirão, 196–199; in religion, 206; in Monchique, 227, 237, 243; in terrace building, 229, 231

traineiras: in purse-seining, 103–104, 105

trammels: as fishing device, 112; operation of, 120; description of, 120–121; at Fuzeta, 125; at Tavira, 139; at Quarteira, 142; at Albufeira, 146; at Monte Gordo, 164

transportation: by carts, 12, 14, 35 (ill.), 50; donkeys in, 14, 49–50, 54, 181; mules in, 14, 50; of crops, 22; packing as means of, 52, 53, 181, 182, 192; of water, 53–54, 54 (ill.), 76, 76 (ill.); by wheelbarrow, 53–54; by bicycle, 54; by back-carrying, 54; by head-carrying, 54; of vegetables, 71; and agriculture, 73; of grain, 86 (ill.), 202 (ill.); and Vila Real, 93; steamships in, 93, 95; in fish industry, 98 n. 17, 106, 107; and population, 182, 183, 183–184, 190, 191, 194–195; in Limestone Zone, 182; of cork, 186

(ill.); by truck, 98 n. 17, 190, 192; by buses, 192; effects of, on culture, 220; and progress, 237, 243. SEE ALSO animals; boats; carts; donkeys; mules; oxen

trees: care of, in winter, 70; affected by winds, 85, 85 (ill.). SEE ALSO almonds; apples; carobs; cherries; chestnuts; cork; deforestation; eucalyptus; fig trees; fruits; fuel; lemons; mimosas; oaks; olives; oranges; peaches; pears; pines; plums; pomegranates; quinces; strawberry trees; willows

—, irrigated: harvest from, 57; planting of, 70

—, unirrigated: kinds of, 22–23; harvest from, 57; in Sotavento, 67; planting of, 70; in Barlavento, 77–78; in Cape area, 80; in Limestone Zone, 174–180, 180; in Monchique, 234

Triassic formations: in physical regions, 15 (map); mentioned, 80, 81, 167. SEE ALSO geology

trilho: in threshing, 173, 173 (ill.). SEE ALSO agriculture, implements in

trotlines: at Quarteira, 142. SEE ALSO fishing gear; fishing lines; fishing nets

tuna fish: as export, 11 n. 9; migration habits of, 55, 89, 90; in the catch, 55; in religious rites, 89 n. 2. SEE ALSO tuna fishing; tuna industry

tuna fishing: use of nets in, 89–90; methods of, 90, 90–92; nets for, 90–92; migrations in, 90; catch in, value of, 90. SEE ALSO fishing nets; tuna fish; tuna industry

tuna industry: in Vila Real, 95, 95–96, 96–97, 97–98, 98, 98 n. 18; at Lagos, 126, 128, 129; at Tavira, 137, 138, 139; at Albufeira, 145, 148; at Santa Luzia, 161. SEE ALSO tuna fish; tuna fishing

tunny: at Quarteira, 144

urban life: introduced by Romans, 9

United States: as cork market, 187

Val do Boi: 80, 81
varestilha: 117
valenciana: at Albufeira, 146
Varro (agricultural authority): 213, 214
valado: 229
vegetables: in rotation, 62–66; harvesting of, 71; marketing of, 71, 72–73, 93; protection of, from cold, 72; prices of, 72–73; in Carrapateira, 86; in Lisbon market, 93; at Albufeira, 148; in Limestone Zone, 171; in S. Marcos Depression, 194; in Caldeirão, 203–204; as food, 219; in Monchique, 228, 234–235. SEE ALSO agricultural calendar; beans; cabbage; cauliflower; chick-peas; cucumbers; legumes; maize; onions; peanuts; peas; potatoes; rice; rough-pea; squash; tomatoes
vegetation: in grey schists, 16; in the littoral, 16; in Tertiary and Quaternary, 16; related to climate and geology, 84–85; effect of winds on, 84, 84–85; resinous leaves of, 84–85; in Cape area, 84–85; of Caldeirão, 199–200
venders: in S. Bartolomeu, 191–192; itinerant, 192 (ill.); in Caldeirão, 216
vetch: as fertilizer, 61, 67
Vila de Monchique: and King João II, 157; as climatic station, 224; olive press at, 236; mentioned, 226, 228, 232, 233, 233 (ill.), 235, 237, 239, 242
Vila do Bispo: importance of, 81; maize near, 83; rainfall in, 84; mentioned, 74, 85, 167
Vila Real de Santo António: 92–96; climate of, 18, 72 n. 7; day labor at, 20; and shipbuilding, 42; rotation near, 62; fishing industry at, 67, 95, 95–96, 97–98; as market for tomatoes, 74; history of, 92–96; coast of, 93 (map); economy of, 94–95; catastrophes in, 95; high specialization of, 97–98; and Olhão, 122; and Castro Marim, 163; establishment of, 164; mentioned, 90, 94, 108, 115, 125, 138
villages: functions of, 192–193

vineyards: increase in, 69; care of, in winter, 70; in Guadiana River Valley, 73; areas of, 79; in Monchique, 228; pest enemies of, 228. SEE ALSO grapes; wine; wine industry
vines. SEE grapes; vineyards; wine; wine industry
Visigoths: in Ossónoba and Toledo, 108; at Lagos, 125–126; at Alvôr, 157; and olives, 177; in Monchique, 225–226, 227; mentioned, 9

walls: in landscape, 13, 175, 229; in Cape area, 80; and figs, 175; in terracing, 229, 229–230
water: sources of, 25, 222; vending of, 53–54, 54 (ill.), 76 (ill.); in Sotavento, 58–59; procurement of, 59; as agricultural factor, 65; in Barlavento, 76; lifting of, with sweep, 78 (ill.); in homes, 173, 192; resources in, at Loulé, 188; and population, 188; in terracing, 232; mineral, in Monchique, 236. SEE ALSO *nora*, the; wells; windmills
watermelon: in Sotavento, 60
weather. SEE climate; rainfall; temperature; winds
weaving: in Monchique, 238–239, 240 (ill.)
weels: as bait, 160
West, the: in Cape area, 87
Western Europe: 178
Western Transition Area, the: as agricultural area, 73–74
whales: 126
whaling: at Tavira, 135
wheelbarrows: as means of transportation, 53–54, 76
wheat: in Alentejo, 11; in Huelva, 11; in binding, 36; of Coastal Plain, 24 (ill.); and milling season, 27; in rotation, 62, 66, 70; importance of, 66; in underplanting, 68; in Sotavento, 69 (ill.); in Western Transition Area, 74; in Cape area, 80; at Sagres, 81, 86; and fertilizers, 82; near Cape S. Vi-

cente, 82 (ill.), 83; at Tavira, 135; in Limestone Zone, 174, 175; in S. Marcos Depression, 194; in Caldeirão, 200, 201; as food, 218; in Monchique, 235

willows: in basketry, 37–38; in furniture making, 37–38; in crafts, 239–240

windbreaks: at Sagres, 82; at Carrapateira, 86

windmills: for grinding grain, 12; description of, 25, 27; of Caldeirão, 25 (ill.), 202, 215; history of, 27; mechanism of, 28 (ill.); grindstone of, 29 (ill.); sails of, 29; arm pots of, 30; abandonment of, 30; seasonal use of, 31; replaced by motor-driven mills, 193; in Lower Algarve, 236. SEE ALSO milling; millstones; stone working

winds: in Sotavento, 58; in Iberian Peninsula, 58; of Cape area, 80, 84, 84 n. 11, 85, 149, 151; and vegetation, 84–85, 85–86; in Carrapateira, 86

wine: from Fuzeta, 69; Algarvian, reputation of, 78–79; from Lagoa, 79; from Sagres, 82; in Faro, 110; in Tavira, 135; at Silves, 185; in Monchique, 228. SEE ALSO grapes; vineyards; wine industry

wine industry: re-establishment of, 69–70; in Sotavento, 69–70; seasonal activities in, 70, 70–71; in Barlavento, 78–79; in Lagoa, 79. SEE ALSO grapes; vineyards; wine

women: and love of homes and gardens, 13–14, 172; and use of donkeys, 14, 49, 181; and marketing, 49; as means of transport, 54; as farm laborers, 62, 79, 234; as fish buyers, 106; in fishing industry, 121, 122, 131, 139; as seasonal widows, 124; as craft workers, 188, 192

wrasse: as catch, 121

Xerxes: 193

Yemen: and irrigation, 10
Yemenites: at Silves, 183

www.ingramcontent.com/pod-product-compliance
Ingram Content Group UK Ltd.
Pitfield, Milton Keynes, MK11 3LW, UK
UKHW041651130325
456188UK00011B/37